# X-MEN
## GOLGOTHA

writer
**PETER MILLIGAN**

penciler
**SALVADOR LARROCA**

inker
**DANNY MIKI**
WITH **ALLEN MARTINEZ**

colors
**LIQUID! GRAPHICS**

letters
**CHRIS ELIOPOULOS**
VIRTUAL CALLIGRAPHY'S **CORY PETIT**

assistant editors
**SEAN RYAN**
**& STEPHANIE MOORE**

associate editor
**NICK LOWE**

editor
**MIKE MARTS**

collection editor
**JENNIFER GRÜNWALD**

senior editor, special projects
**JEFF YOUNGQUIST**

director of sales
**DAVID GABRIEL**

production
**JERRY KALINOWSKI**

book designer
**CARRIE BEADLE**

creative director
**TOM MARVELLI**

editor in chief
**JOE QUESADA**

publisher
**DAN BUCKLEY**

166

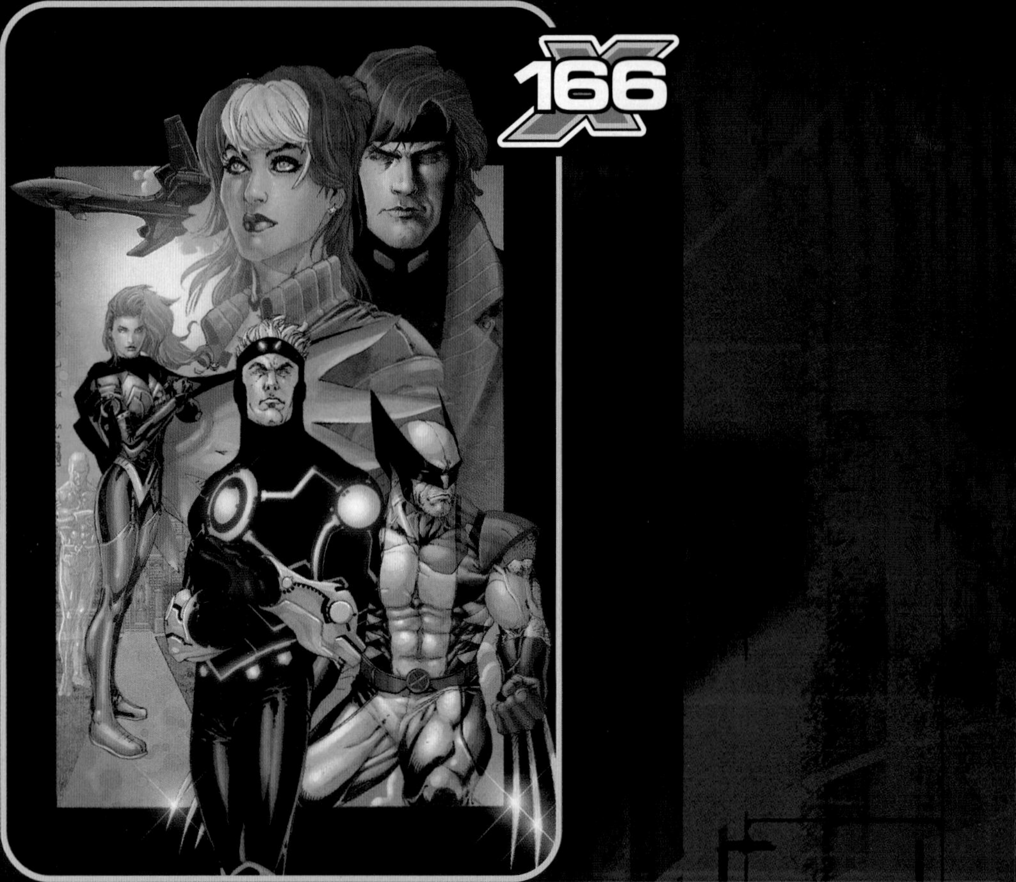

167

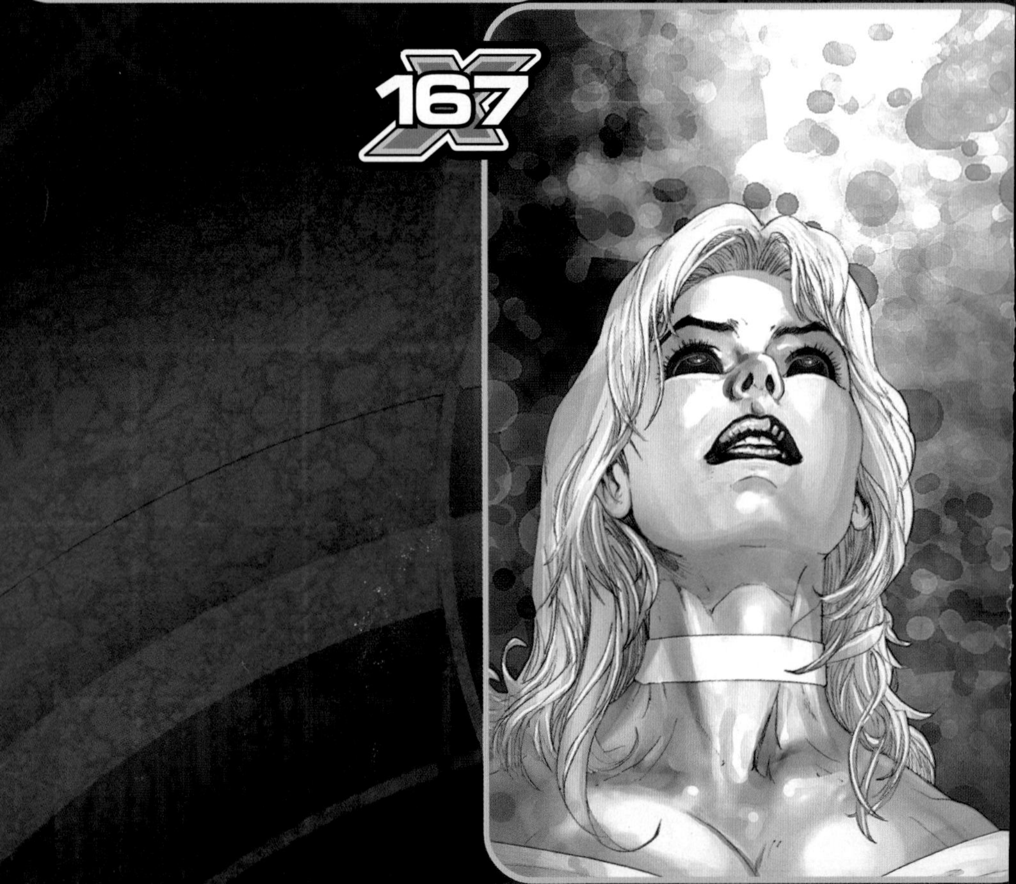

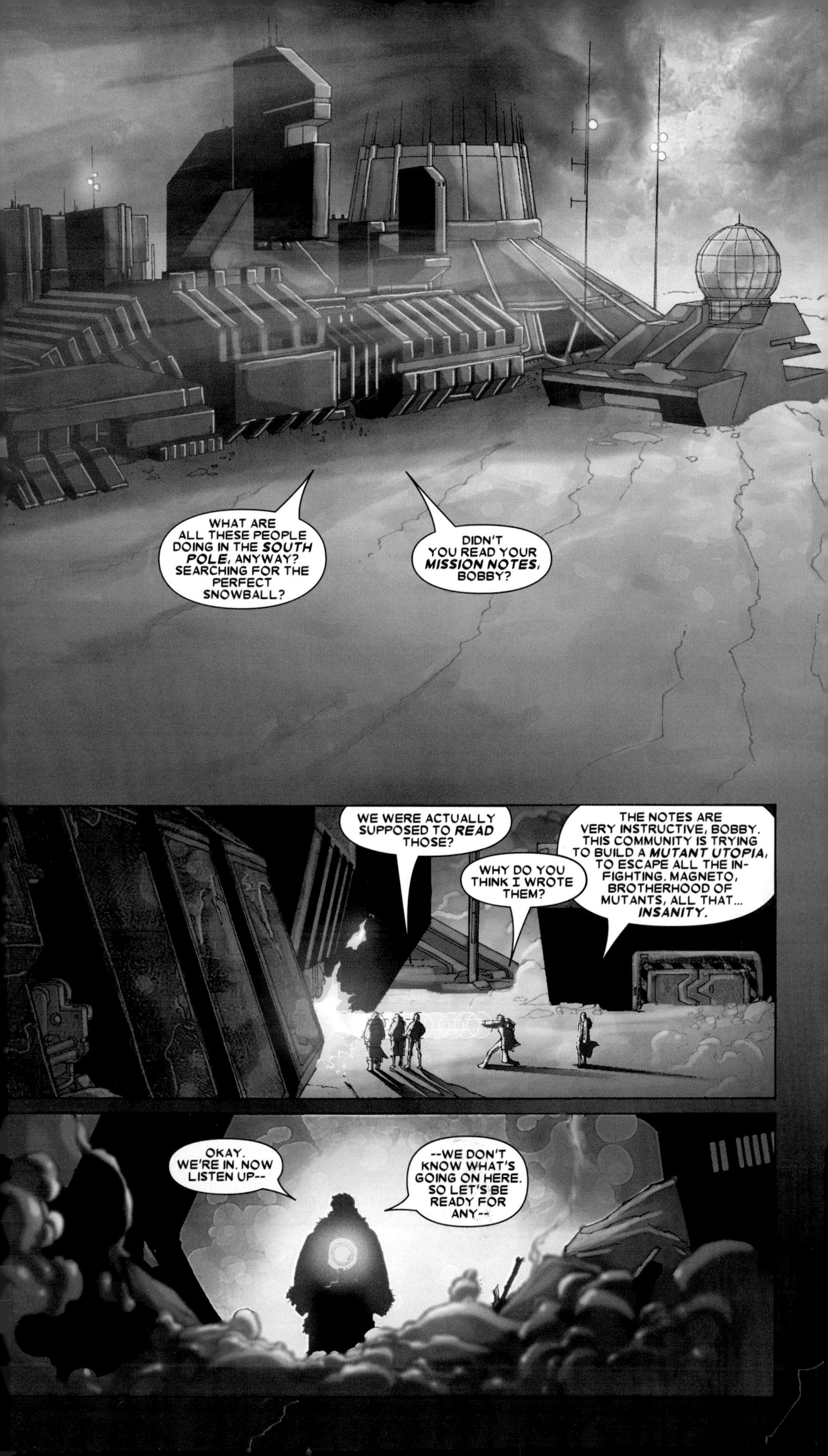
WHAT ARE ALL THESE PEOPLE DOING IN THE SOUTH POLE, ANYWAY? SEARCHING FOR THE PERFECT SNOWBALL?
DIDN'T YOU READ YOUR MISSION NOTES, BOBBY?
WE WERE ACTUALLY SUPPOSED TO READ THOSE?
WHY DO YOU THINK I WROTE THEM?
THE NOTES ARE VERY INSTRUCTIVE, BOBBY. THIS COMMUNITY IS TRYING TO BUILD A MUTANT UTOPIA, TO ESCAPE ALL THE IN-FIGHTING. MAGNETO, BROTHERHOOD OF MUTANTS, ALL THAT... INSANITY.
OKAY. WE'RE IN. NOW LISTEN UP--
--WE DON'T KNOW WHAT'S GOING ON HERE. SO LET'S BE READY FOR ANY--

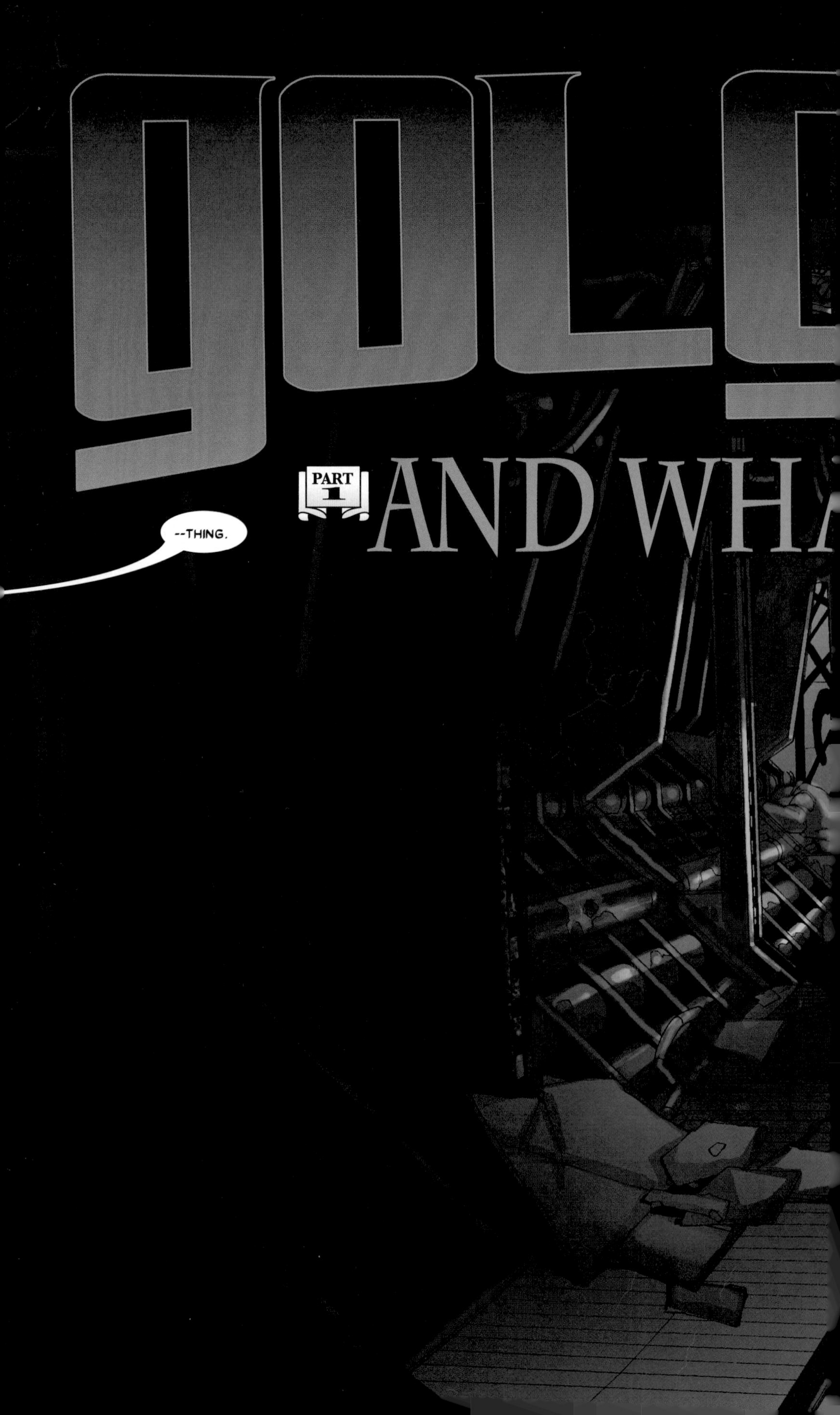
GOL
PART 1 AND WHA
--THING.

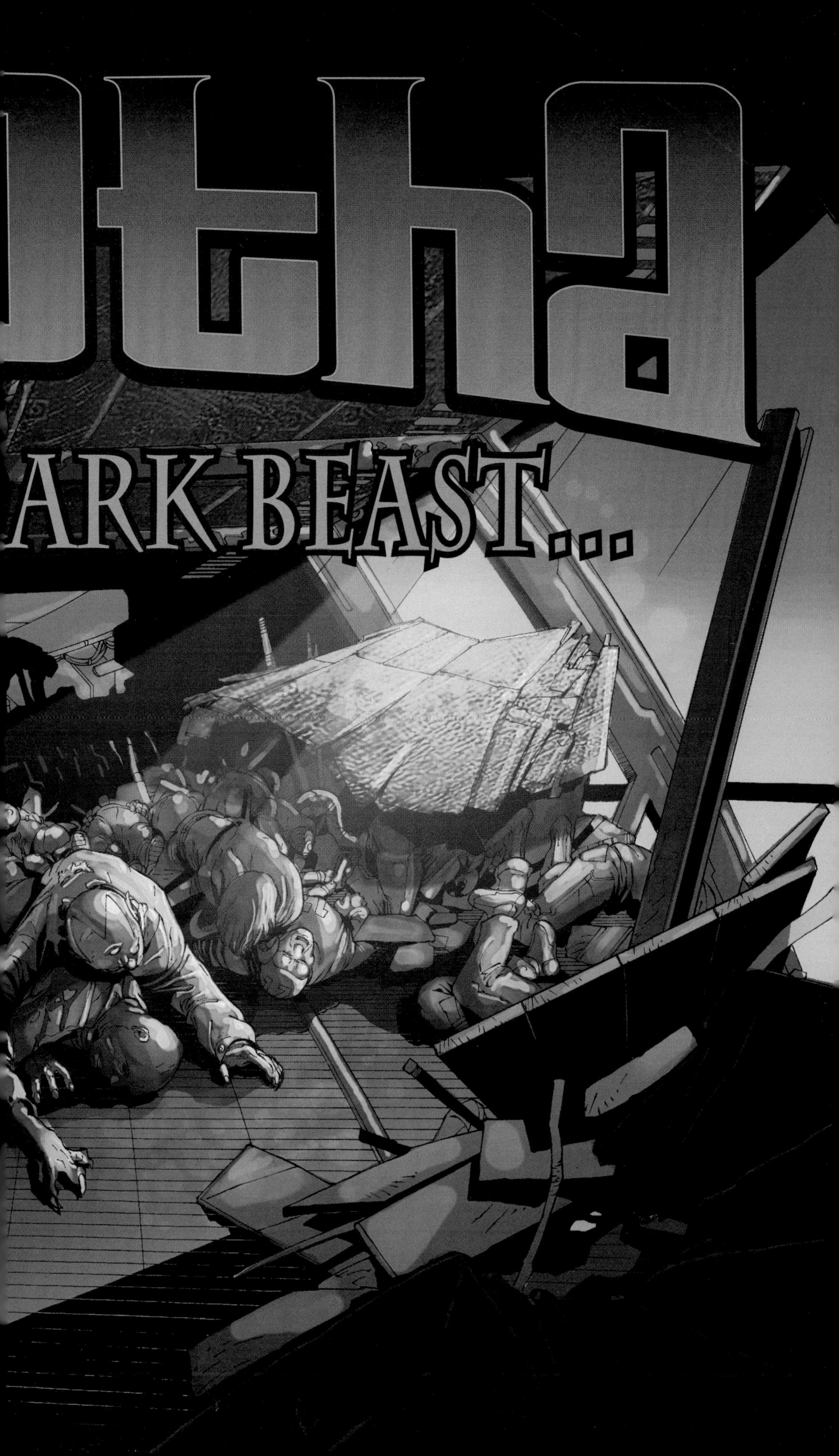
ARK BEAST...

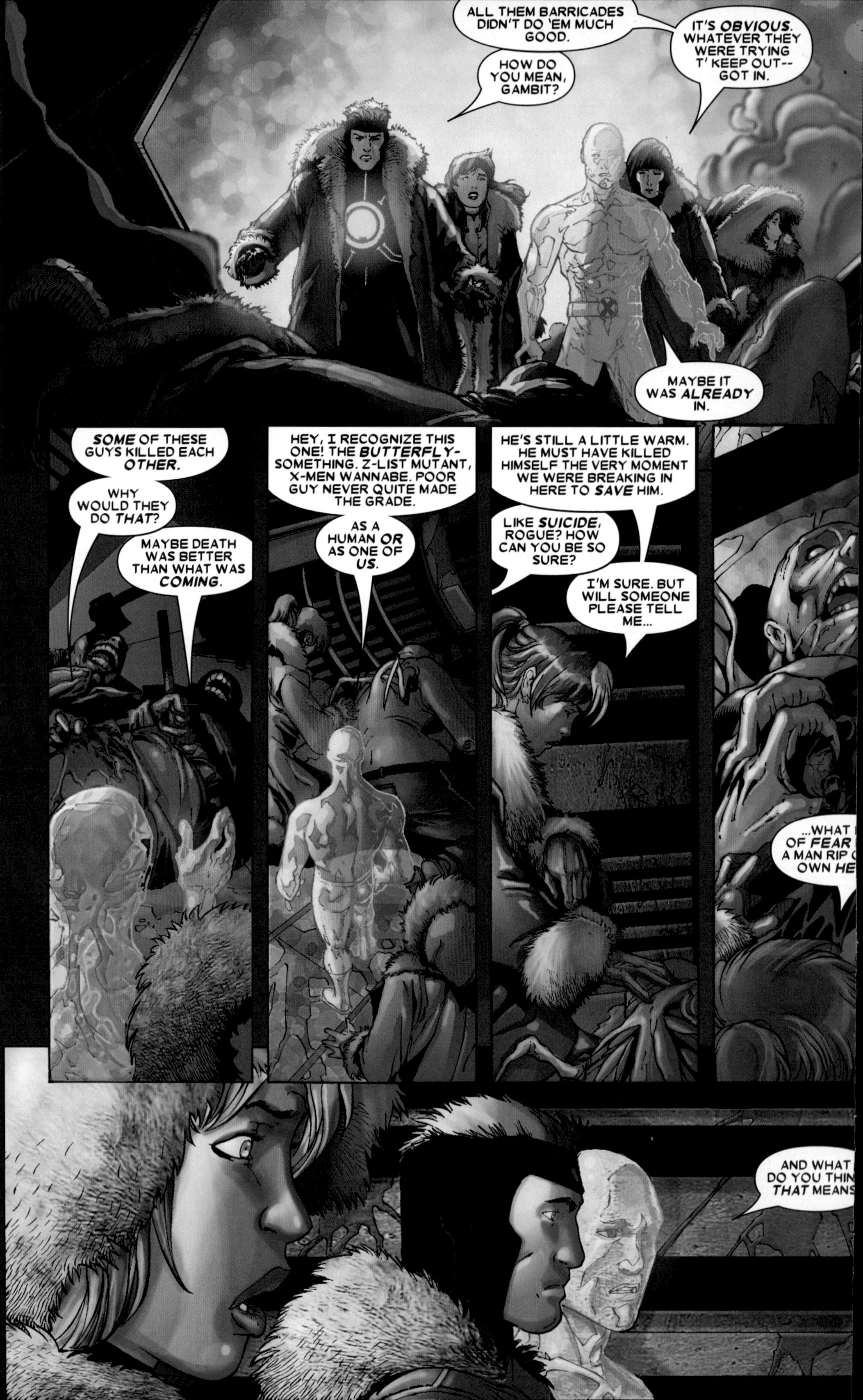
ALL THEM BARRICADES DIDN'T DO 'EM MUCH GOOD.
HOW DO YOU MEAN, GAMBIT?
IT'S OBVIOUS. WHATEVER THEY WERE TRYING T' KEEP OUT-- GOT IN.
MAYBE IT WAS ALREADY IN.
SOME OF THESE GUYS KILLED EACH OTHER.
WHY WOULD THEY DO THAT?
MAYBE DEATH WAS BETTER THAN WHAT WAS COMING.
HEY, I RECOGNIZE THIS ONE! THE BUTTERFLY-SOMETHING. Z-LIST MUTANT, X-MEN WANNABE. POOR GUY NEVER QUITE MADE THE GRADE.
AS A HUMAN OR AS ONE OF US.
HE'S STILL A LITTLE WARM. HE MUST HAVE KILLED HIMSELF THE VERY MOMENT WE WERE BREAKING IN HERE TO SAVE HIM.
LIKE SUICIDE, ROGUE? HOW CAN YOU BE SO SURE?
I'M SURE. BUT WILL SOMEONE PLEASE TELL ME...
...WHAT OF FEAR A MAN RIP OWN
AND WHAT DO YOU THIN THAT MEANS

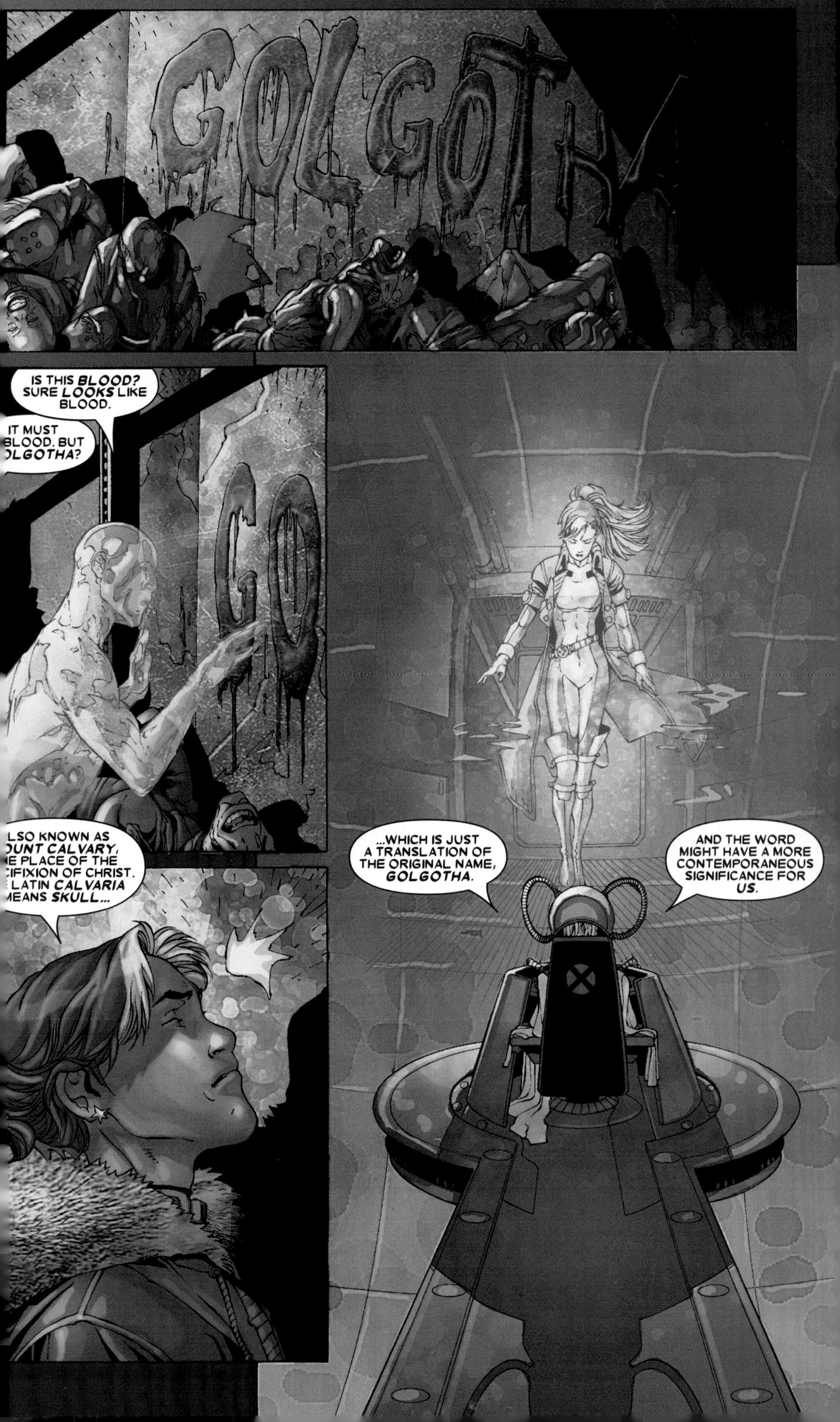
GOLGOTH
IS THIS BLOOD? SURE LOOKS LIKE BLOOD.
IT MUST BLOOD. BUT OLGOTHA?
LSO KNOWN AS OUNT CALVARY, E PLACE OF THE CIFIXION OF CHRIST. LATIN CALVARIA MEANS SKULL...
...WHICH IS JUST A TRANSLATION OF THE ORIGINAL NAME, GOLGOTHA.
AND THE WORD MIGHT HAVE A MORE CONTEMPORANEOUS SIGNIFICANCE FOR US.

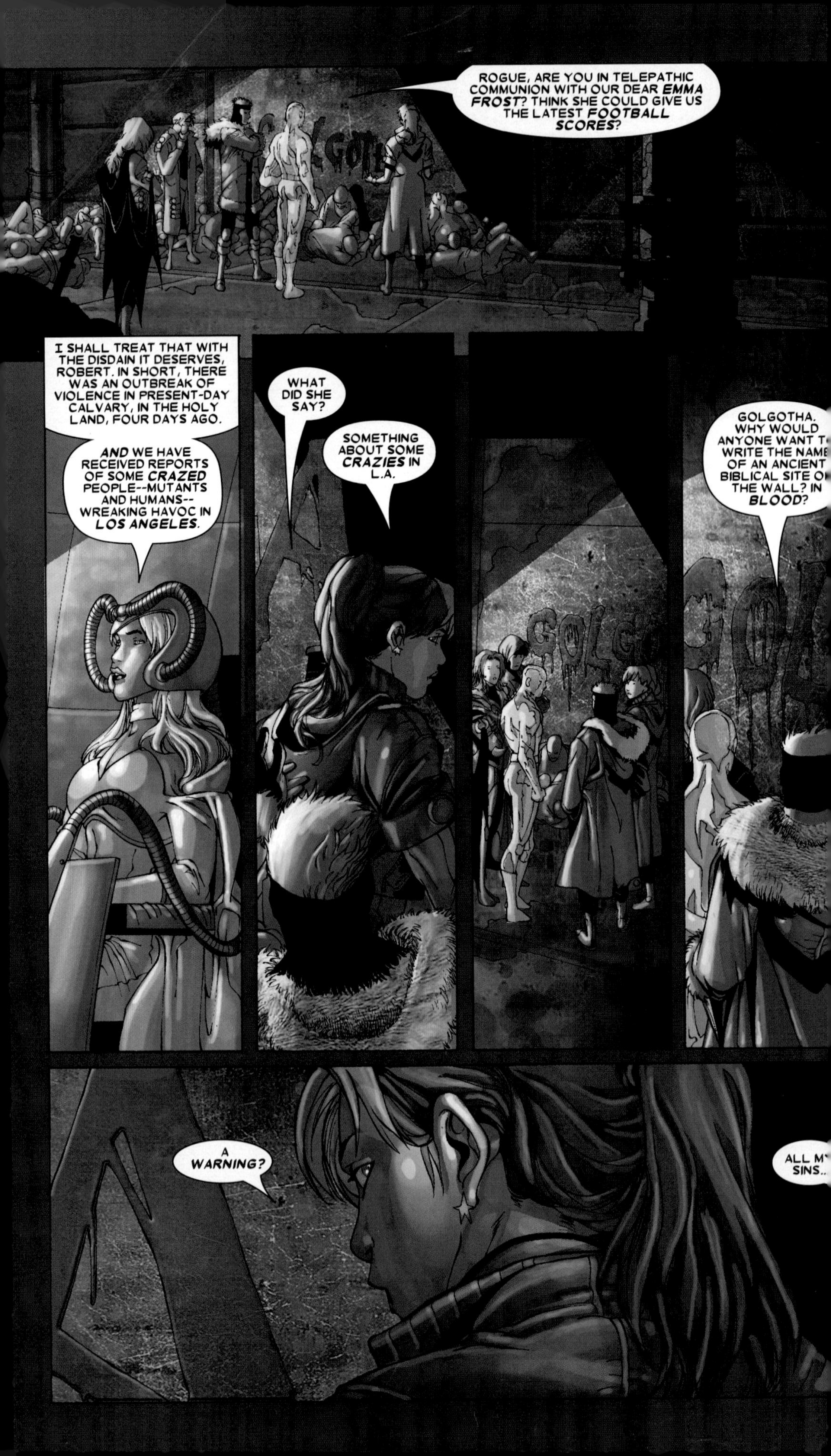
ROGUE, ARE YOU IN TELEPATHIC COMMUNION WITH OUR DEAR EMMA FROST? THINK SHE COULD GIVE US THE LATEST FOOTBALL SCORES?
I SHALL TREAT THAT WITH THE DISDAIN IT DESERVES, ROBERT. IN SHORT, THERE WAS AN OUTBREAK OF VIOLENCE IN PRESENT-DAY CALVARY, IN THE HOLY LAND, FOUR DAYS AGO.
AND WE HAVE RECEIVED REPORTS OF SOME CRAZED PEOPLE--MUTANTS AND HUMANS--WREAKING HAVOC IN LOS ANGELES.
WHAT DID SHE SAY?
SOMETHING ABOUT SOME CRAZIES IN L.A.
GOLGOTHA. WHY WOULD ANYONE WANT T WRITE THE NAME OF AN ANCIENT BIBLICAL SITE O THE WALL? IN BLOOD?
A WARNING?
ALL M SINS..

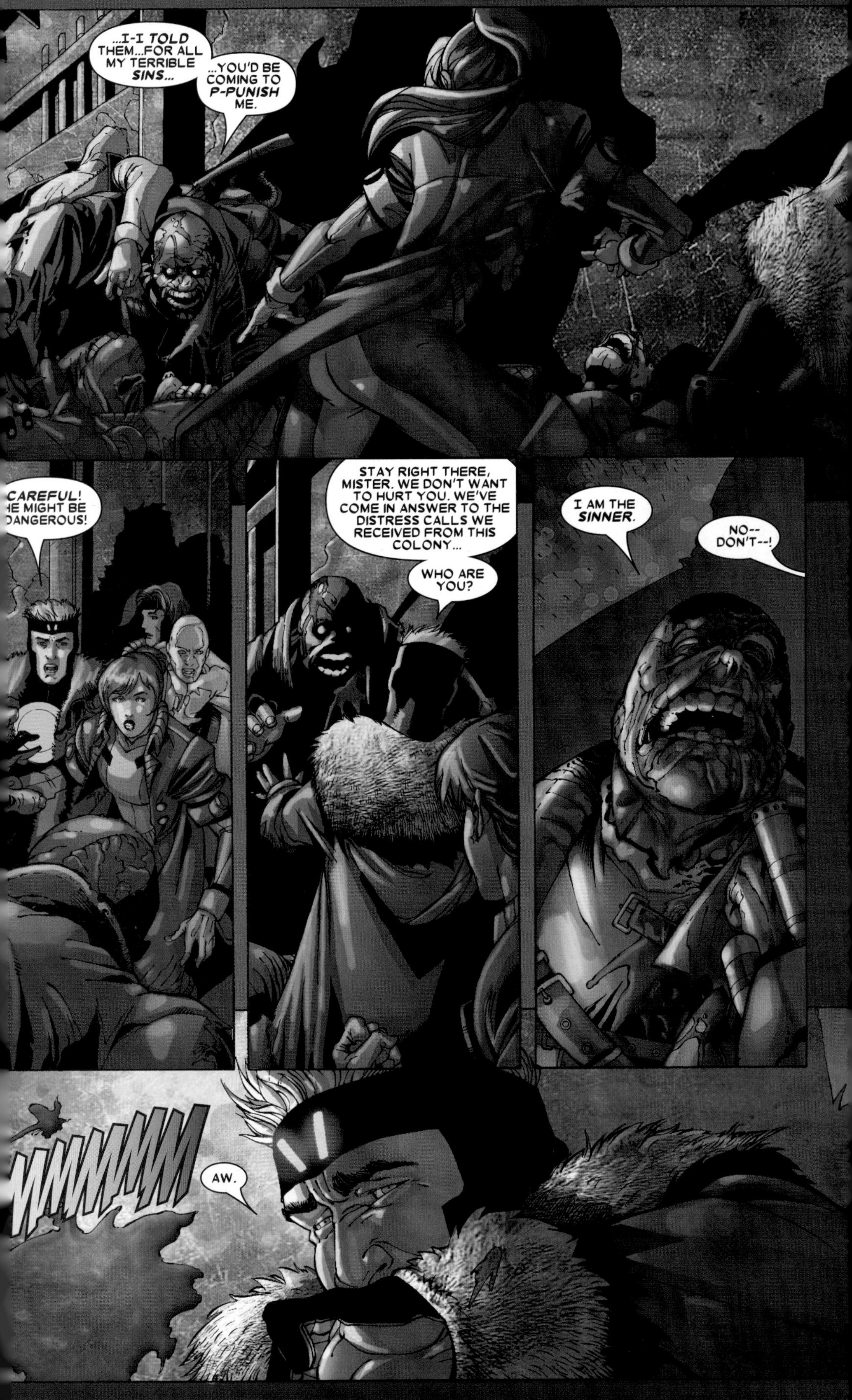
...I-I TOLD THEM...FOR ALL MY TERRIBLE SINS...
...YOU'D BE COMING TO P-PUNISH ME.
CAREFUL! HE MIGHT BE DANGEROUS!
STAY RIGHT THERE, MISTER. WE DON'T WANT TO HURT YOU. WE'VE COME IN ANSWER TO THE DISTRESS CALLS WE RECEIVED FROM THIS COLONY...
WHO ARE YOU?
I AM THE SINNER.
NO-- DON'T--!
AW.

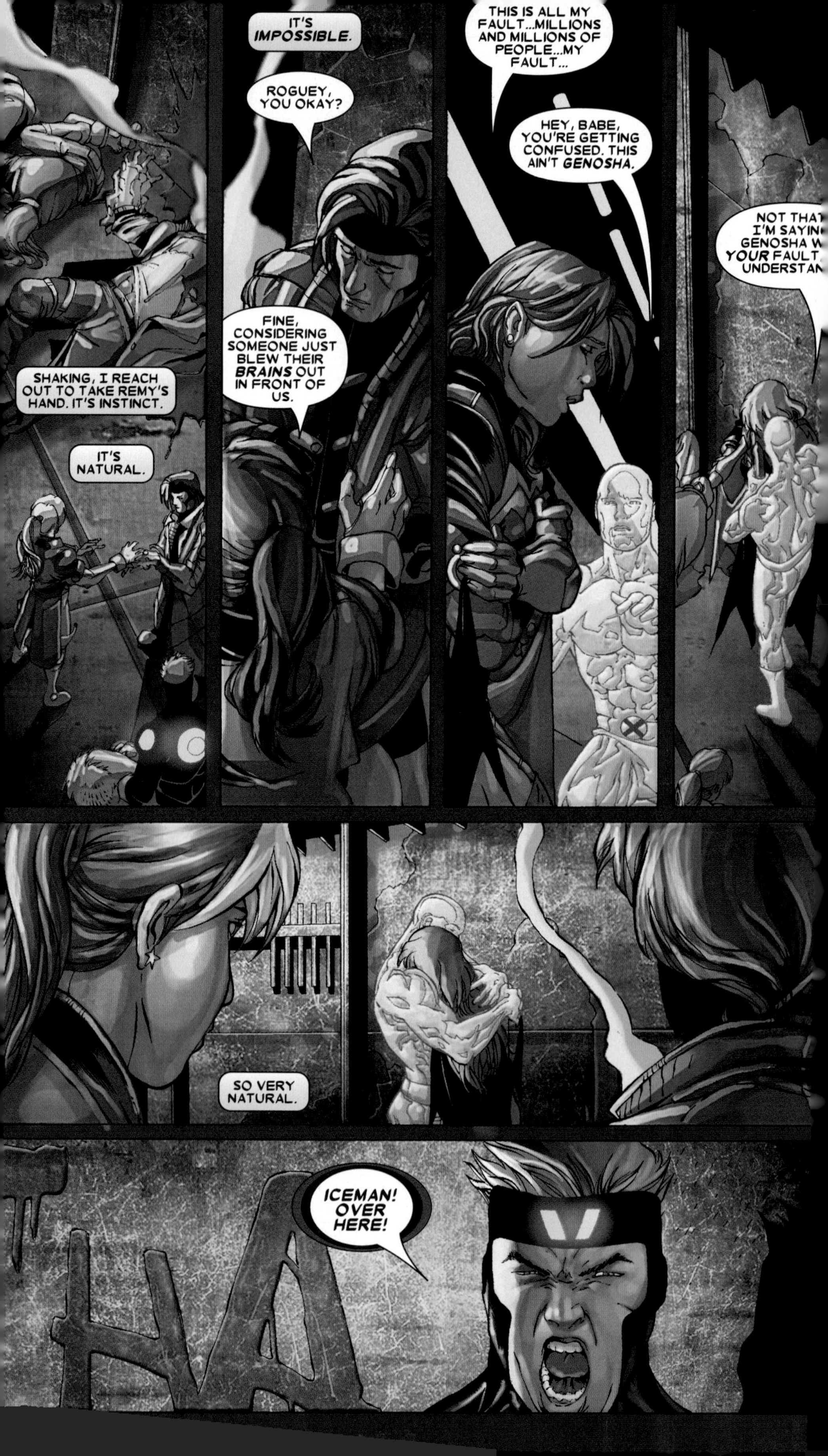
SHAKING, I REACH OUT TO TAKE REMY'S HAND. IT'S INSTINCT.
IT'S NATURAL.
IT'S *IMPOSSIBLE.*
ROGUEY, YOU OKAY?
FINE, CONSIDERING SOMEONE JUST BLEW THEIR *BRAINS* OUT IN FRONT OF US.
THIS IS ALL MY FAULT...MILLIONS AND MILLIONS OF PEOPLE...MY FAULT...
HEY, BABE, YOU'RE GETTING CONFUSED. THIS AIN'T *GENOSHA.*
SO VERY NATURAL.
*ICEMAN! OVER HERE!*

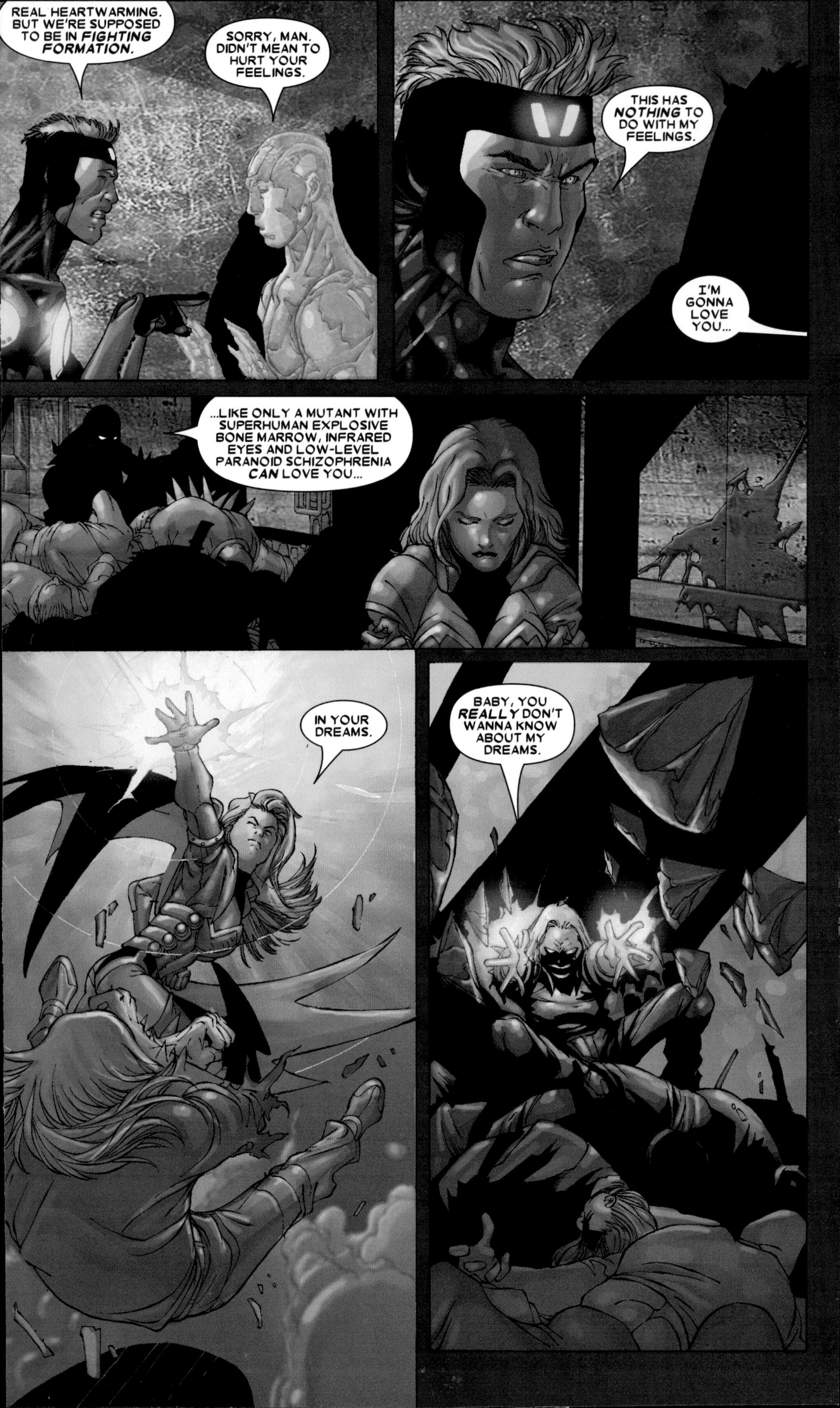
REAL HEARTWARMING. BUT WE'RE SUPPOSED TO BE IN FIGHTING FORMATION.
SORRY, MAN. DIDN'T MEAN TO HURT YOUR FEELINGS.
THIS HAS NOTHING TO DO WITH MY FEELINGS.
I'M GONNA LOVE YOU...
...LIKE ONLY A MUTANT WITH SUPERHUMAN EXPLOSIVE BONE MARROW, INFRARED EYES AND LOW-LEVEL PARANOID SCHIZOPHRENIA CAN LOVE YOU...
IN YOUR DREAMS.
BABY, YOU REALLY DON'T WANNA KNOW ABOUT MY DREAMS.

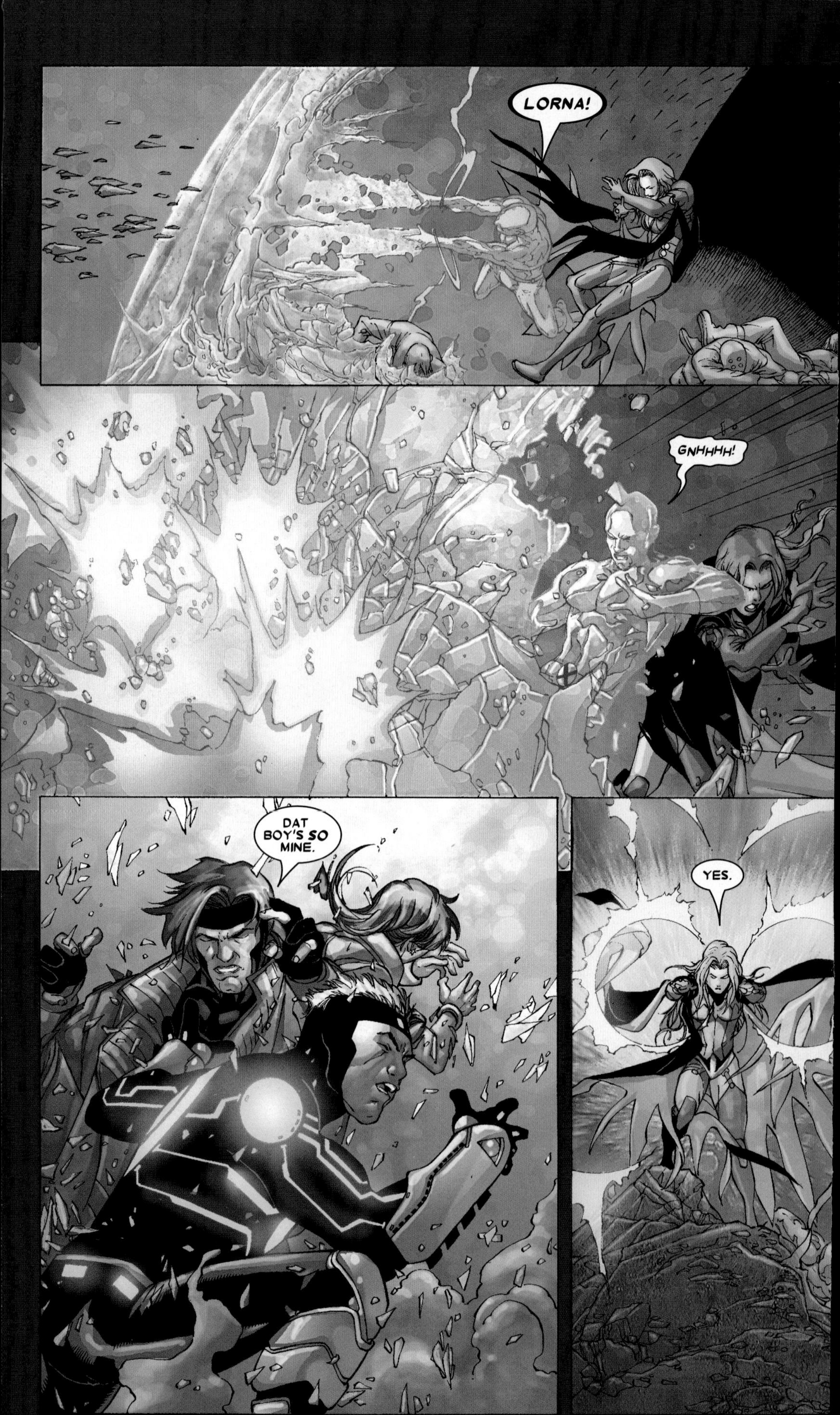
LORNA!
GNHHHH!
DAT BOY'S SO MINE.
YES.

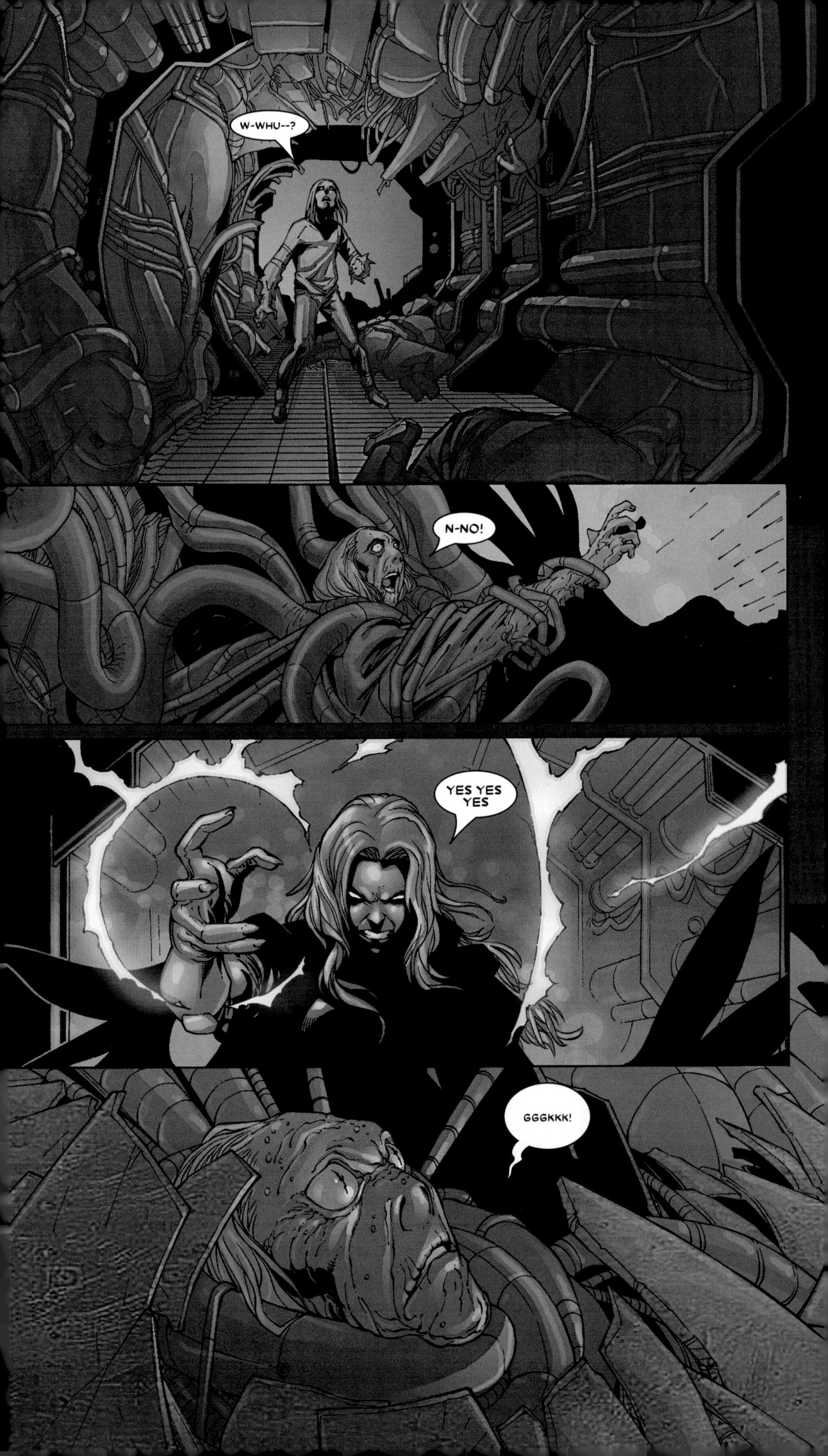
W-WHU--?
N-NO!
YES YES YES
GGGKKK!

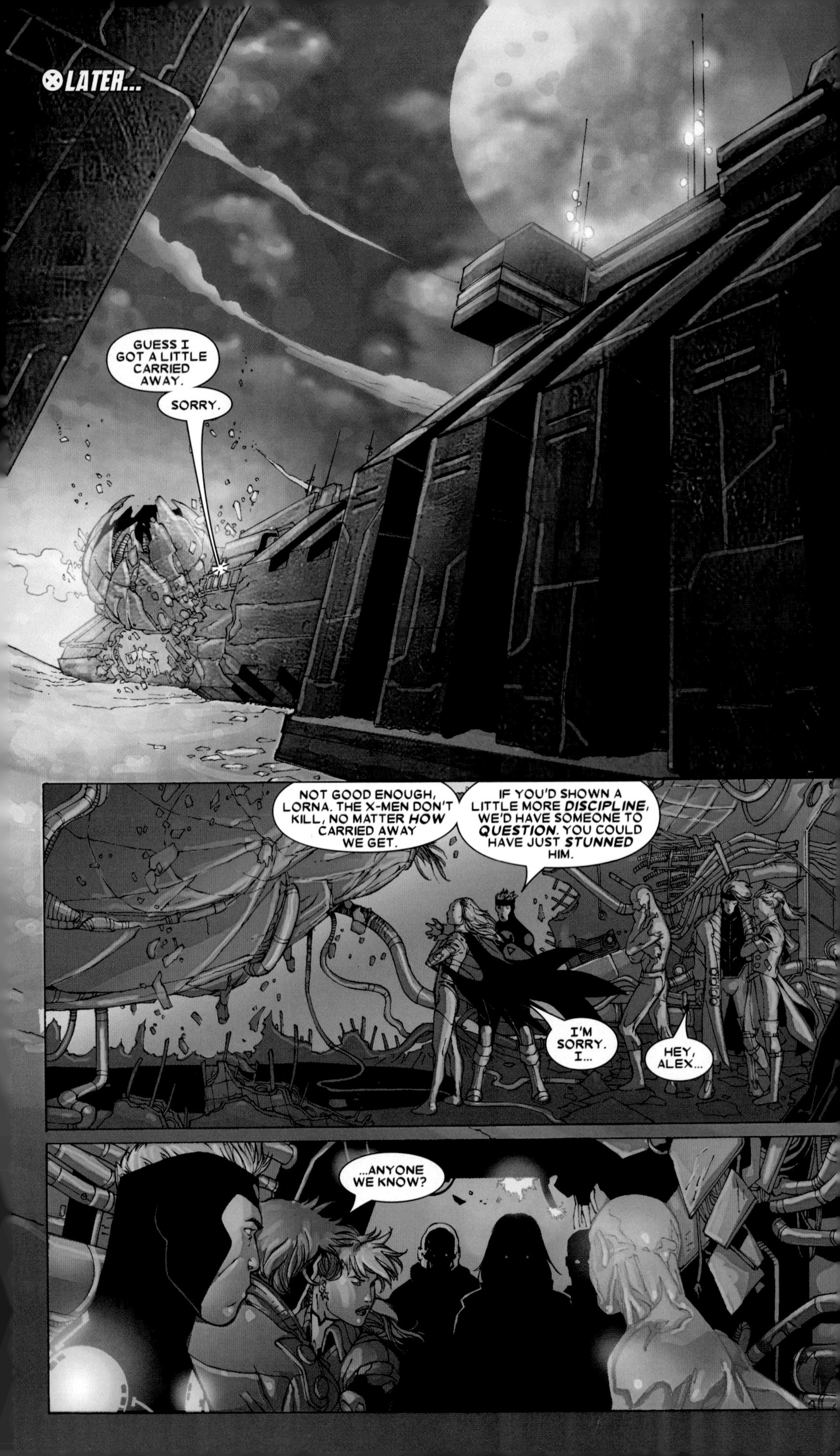
LATER...
GUESS I GOT A LITTLE CARRIED AWAY.
SORRY.
NOT GOOD ENOUGH, LORNA. THE X-MEN DON'T KILL, NO MATTER HOW CARRIED AWAY WE GET.
IF YOU'D SHOWN A LITTLE MORE DISCIPLINE, WE'D HAVE SOMEONE TO QUESTION. YOU COULD HAVE JUST STUNNED HIM.
I'M SORRY. I...
HEY, ALEX...
...ANYONE WE KNOW?

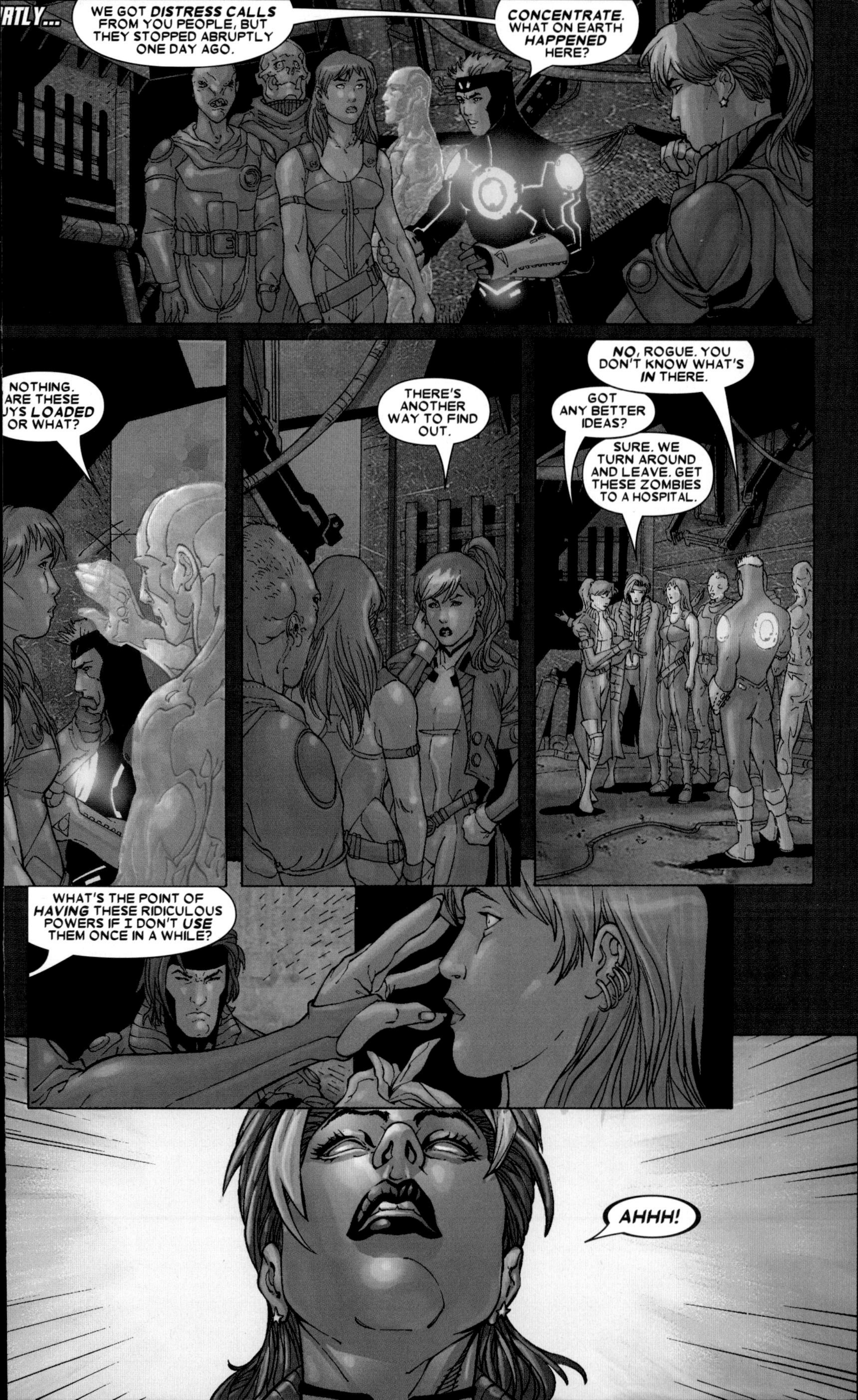

RTLY...
WE GOT DISTRESS CALLS FROM YOU PEOPLE, BUT THEY STOPPED ABRUPTLY ONE DAY AGO.
CONCENTRATE. WHAT ON EARTH HAPPENED HERE?
NOTHING. ARE THESE UYS LOADED OR WHAT?
THERE'S ANOTHER WAY TO FIND OUT.
NO, ROGUE. YOU DON'T KNOW WHAT'S IN THERE.
GOT ANY BETTER IDEAS?
SURE. WE TURN AROUND AND LEAVE. GET THESE ZOMBIES TO A HOSPITAL.
WHAT'S THE POINT OF HAVING THESE RIDICULOUS POWERS IF I DON'T USE THEM ONCE IN A WHILE?
AHHH!

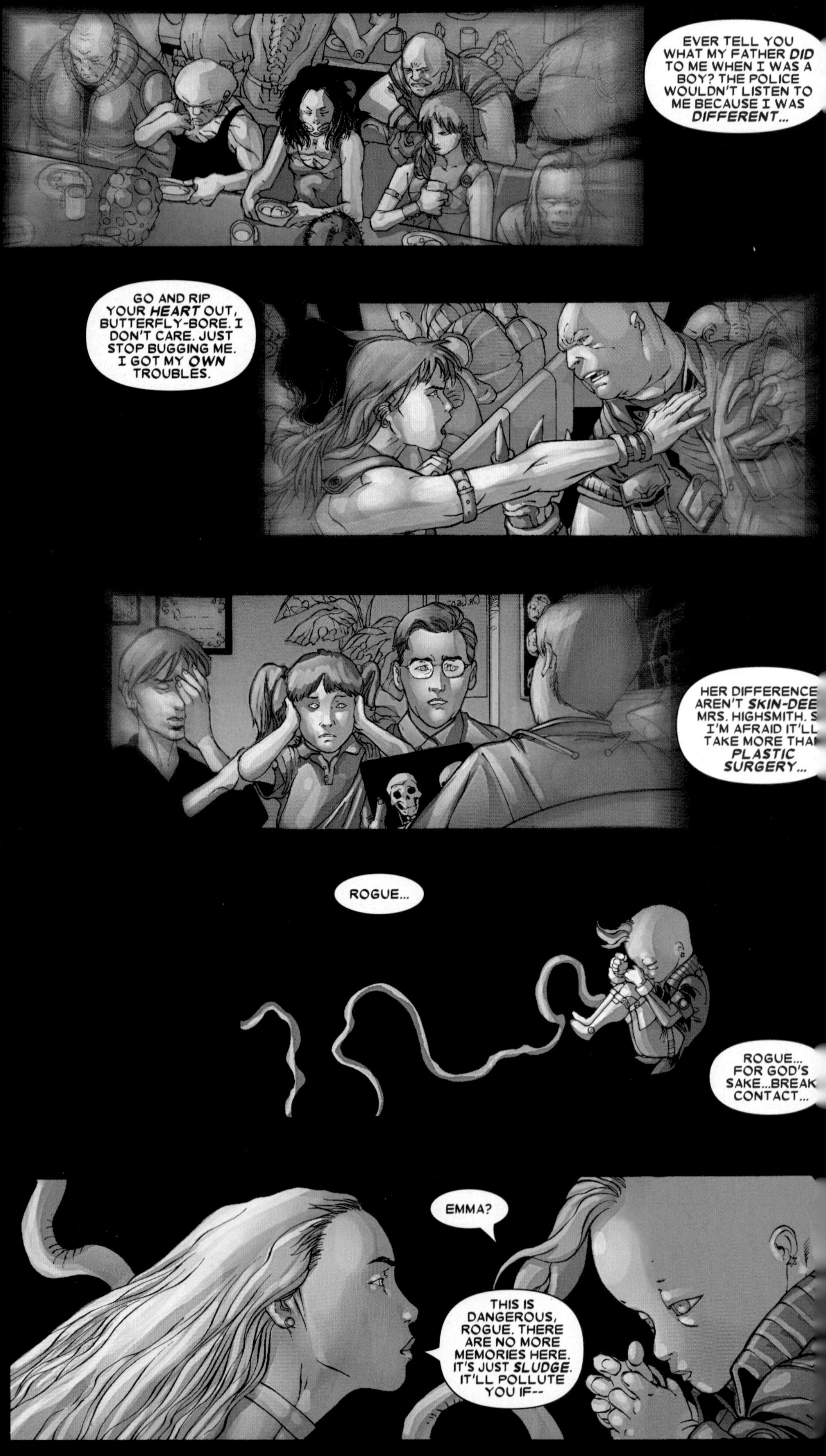
EVER TELL YOU WHAT MY FATHER *DID* TO ME WHEN I WAS A BOY? THE POLICE WOULDN'T LISTEN TO ME BECAUSE I WAS *DIFFERENT*...
GO AND RIP YOUR *HEART* OUT, BUTTERFLY-BORE. I DON'T CARE. JUST STOP BUGGING ME. I GOT MY *OWN* TROUBLES.
HER DIFFERENCE AREN'T *SKIN-DEE* MRS. HIGHSMITH. S I'M AFRAID IT'LL TAKE MORE THA *PLASTIC SURGERY*...
ROGUE...
ROGUE... FOR GOD'S SAKE...BREAK CONTACT...
EMMA?
THIS IS DANGEROUS, ROGUE. THERE ARE NO MORE MEMORIES HERE. IT'S JUST *SLUDGE*. IT'LL POLLUTE YOU IF--

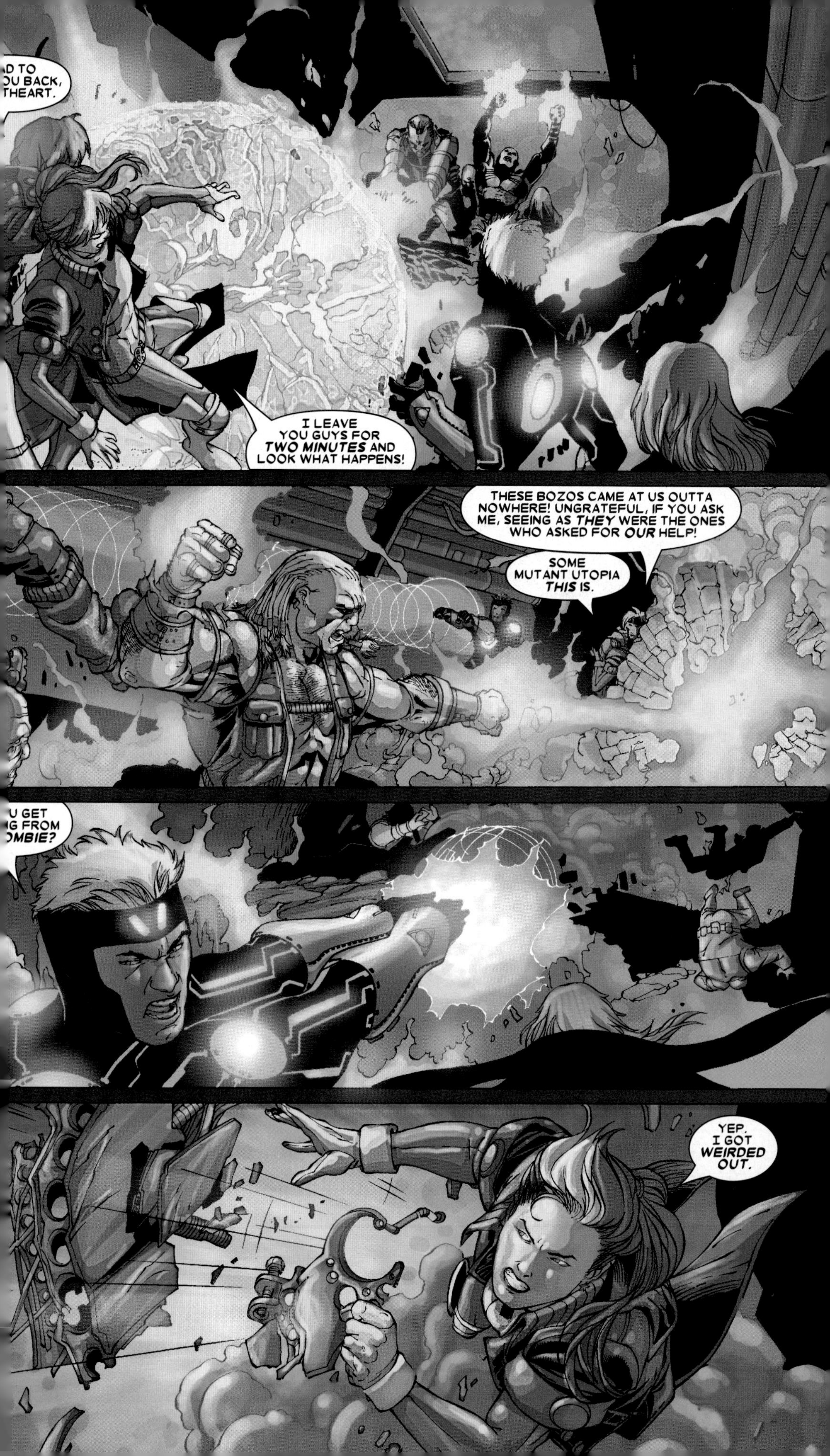

D TO OU BACK, THEART.
I LEAVE YOU GUYS FOR *TWO MINUTES* AND LOOK WHAT HAPPENS!
THESE BOZOS CAME AT US OUTTA NOWHERE! UNGRATEFUL, IF YOU ASK ME, SEEING AS *THEY* WERE THE ONES WHO ASKED FOR *OUR* HELP!
SOME MUTANT UTOPIA *THIS* IS.
U GET G FROM OMBIE?
YEP. I GOT *WEIRDED* OUT.

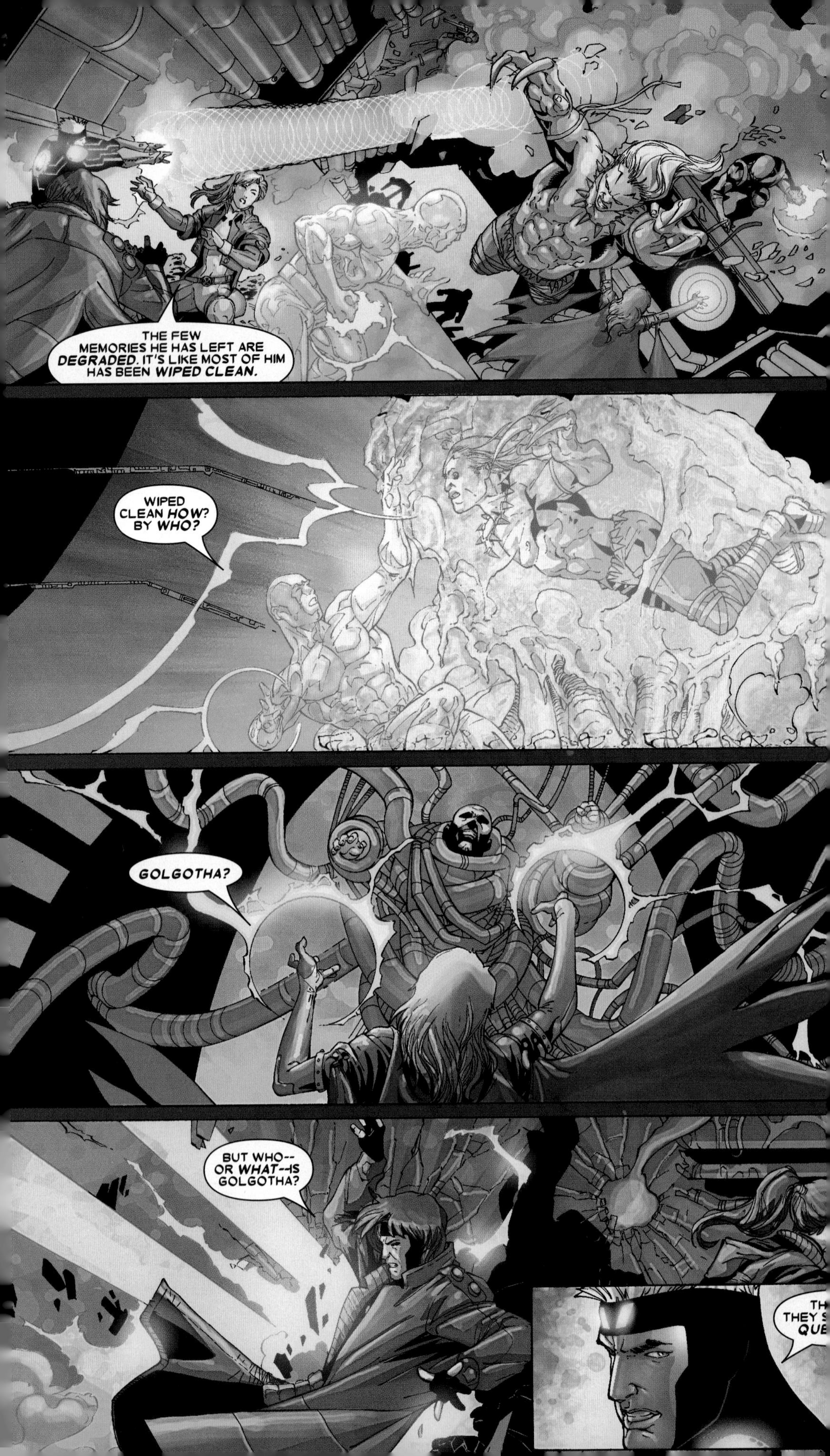
THE FEW MEMORIES HE HAS LEFT ARE DEGRADED. IT'S LIKE MOST OF HIM HAS BEEN WIPED CLEAN.
WIPED CLEAN HOW? BY WHO?
GOLGOTHA?
BUT WHO-- OR WHAT--IS GOLGOTHA?

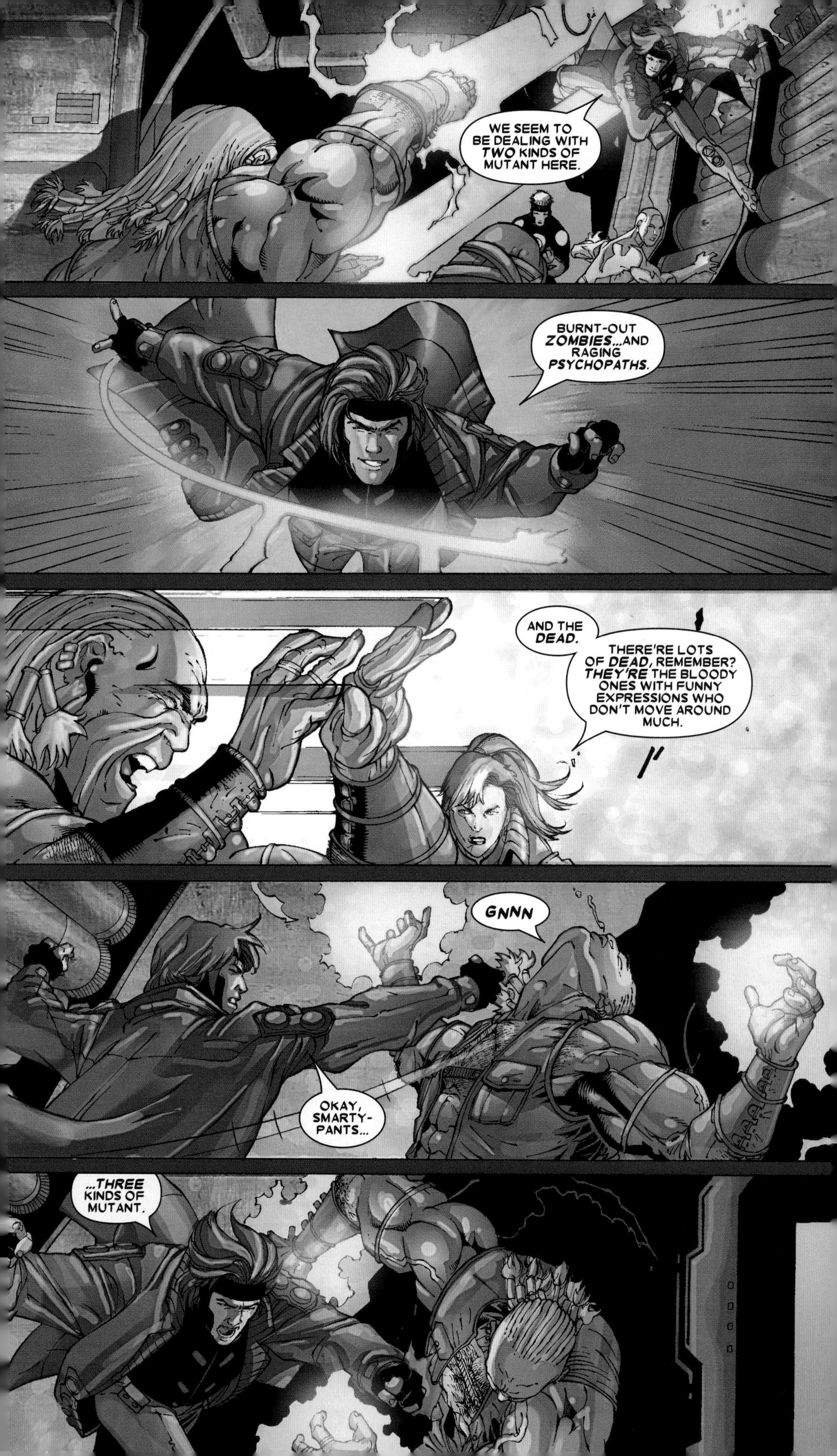
WE SEEM TO BE DEALING WITH TWO KINDS OF MUTANT HERE.
BURNT-OUT ZOMBIES...AND RAGING PSYCHOPATHS.
AND THE DEAD.
THERE'RE LOTS OF DEAD, REMEMBER? THEY'RE THE BLOODY ONES WITH FUNNY EXPRESSIONS WHO DON'T MOVE AROUND MUCH.
GNNN
OKAY, SMARTY-PANTS...
...THREE KINDS OF MUTANT.

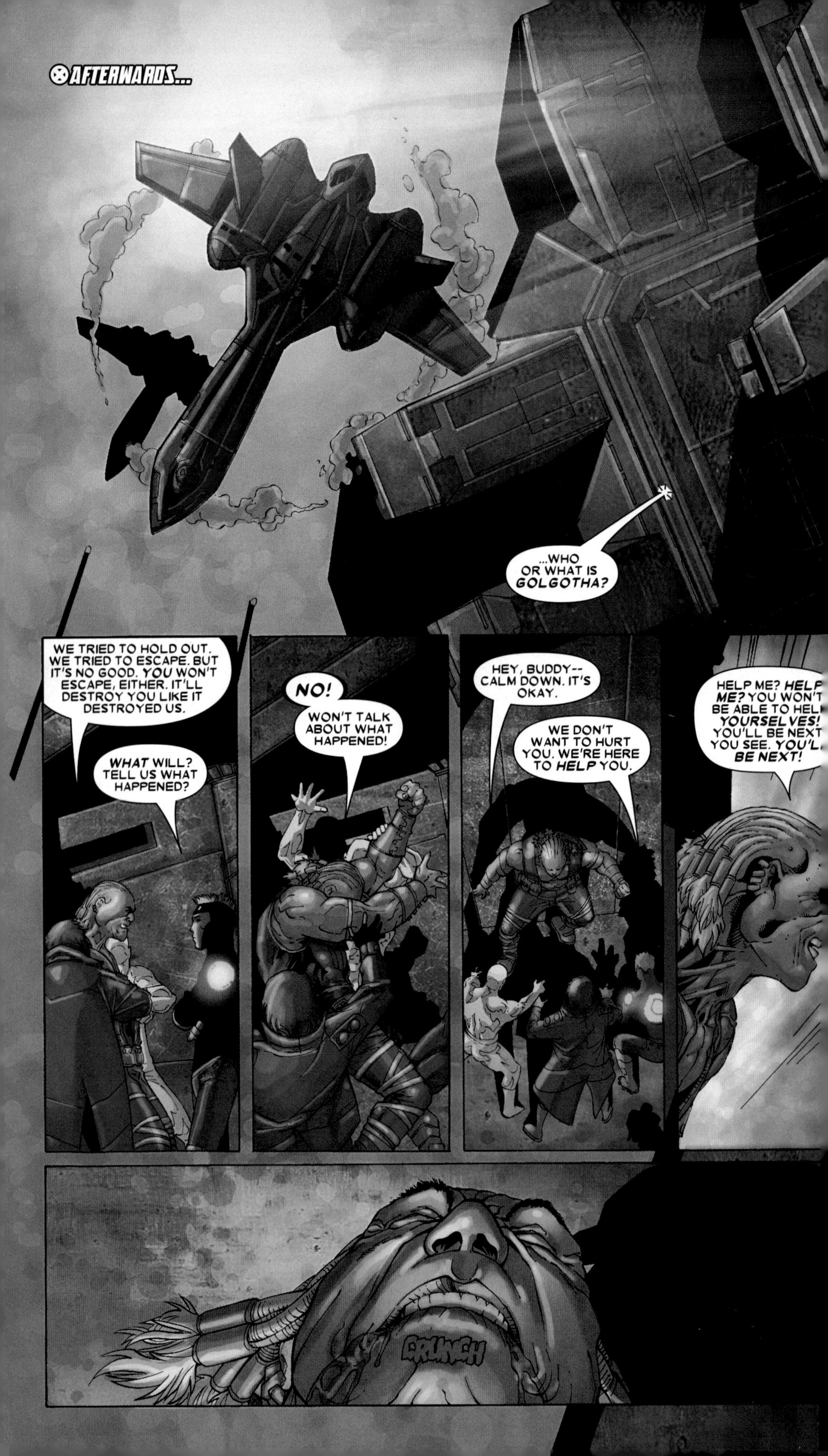
AFTERWARDS...
...WHO OR WHAT IS GOLGOTHA?
WE TRIED TO HOLD OUT. WE TRIED TO ESCAPE. BUT IT'S NO GOOD. YOU WON'T ESCAPE, EITHER. IT'LL DESTROY YOU LIKE IT DESTROYED US.
WHAT WILL? TELL US WHAT HAPPENED?
NO!
WON'T TALK ABOUT WHAT HAPPENED!
HEY, BUDDY-- CALM DOWN. IT'S OKAY.
WE DON'T WANT TO HURT YOU. WE'RE HERE TO HELP YOU.
HELP ME? HELP ME? YOU WON'T BE ABLE TO HEL YOURSELVES! YOU'LL BE NEXT YOU SEE. YOU'L BE NEXT!
CRUNCH

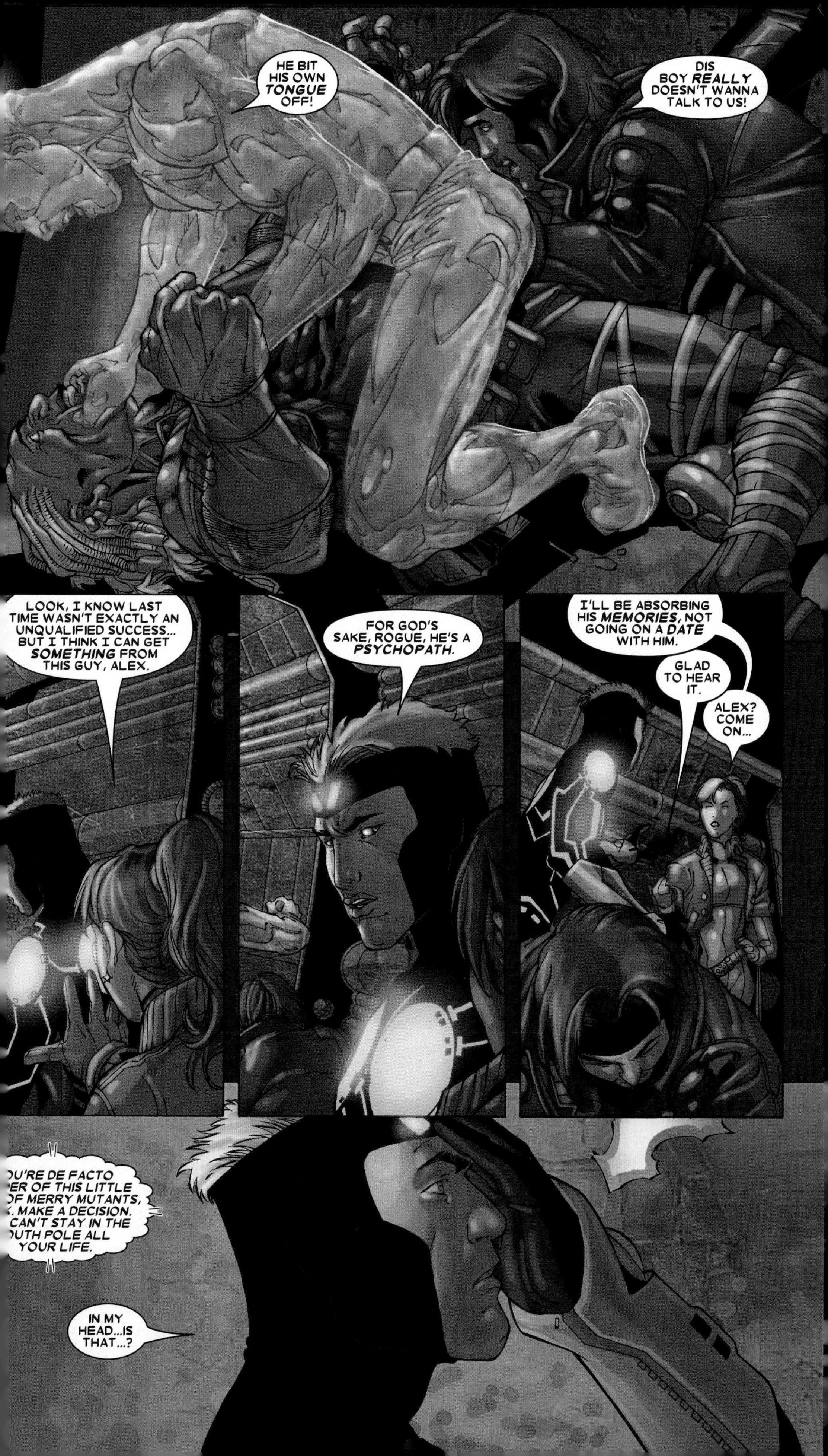
HE BIT HIS OWN *TONGUE* OFF!
DIS BOY *REALLY* DOESN'T WANNA TALK TO US!
LOOK, I KNOW LAST TIME WASN'T EXACTLY AN UNQUALIFIED SUCCESS... BUT I THINK I CAN GET *SOMETHING* FROM THIS GUY, ALEX.
FOR GOD'S SAKE, ROGUE, HE'S A *PSYCHOPATH*.
I'LL BE ABSORBING HIS *MEMORIES*, NOT GOING ON A *DATE* WITH HIM.
GLAD TO HEAR IT.
ALEX? COME ON...
OU'RE DE FACTO
PER OF THIS LITTLE
OF MERRY MUTANTS,
MAKE A DECISION.
CAN'T STAY IN THE
UTH POLE ALL
YOUR LIFE.
IN MY HEAD...IS THAT...?

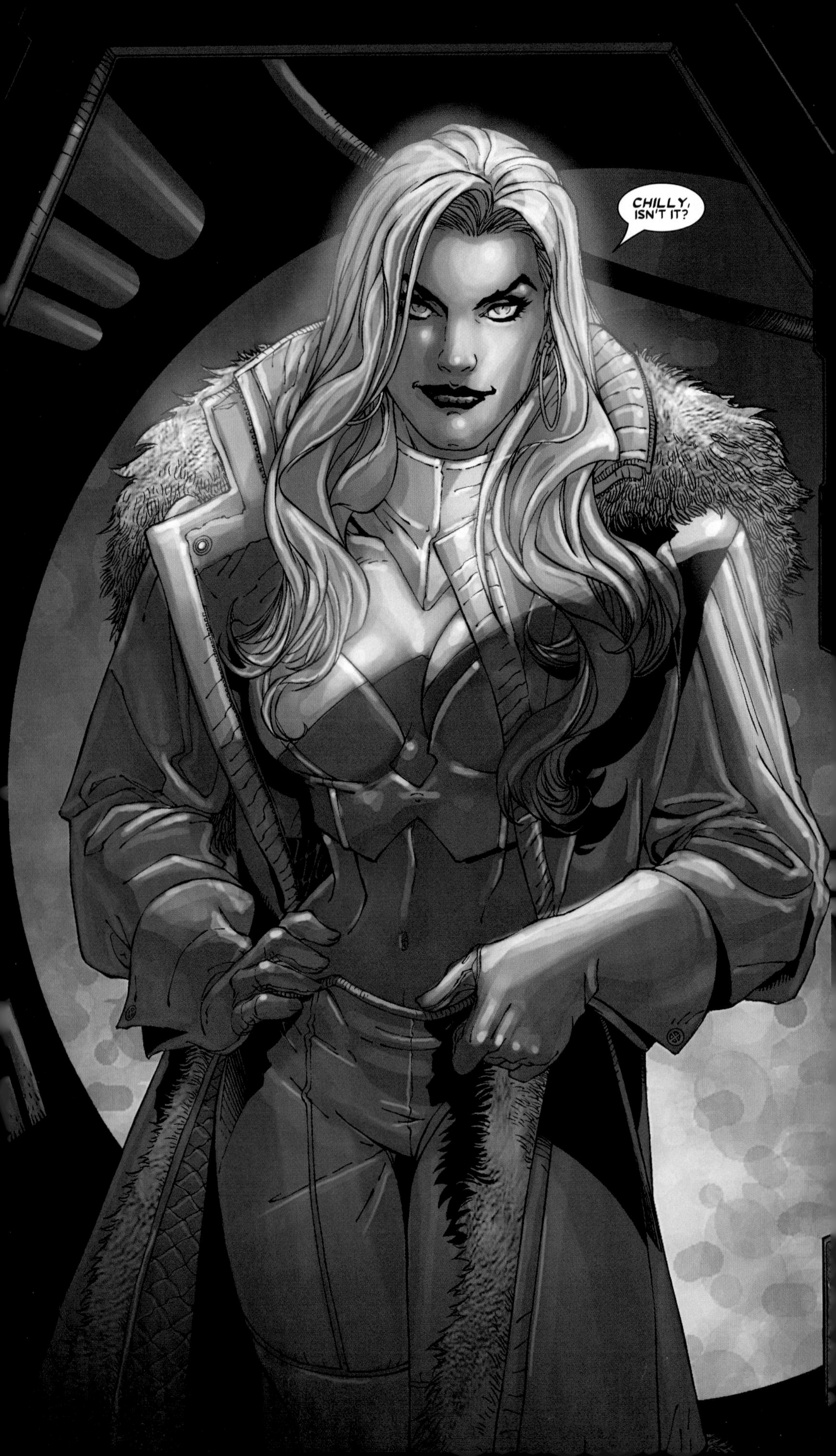
CHILLY, ISN'T IT?

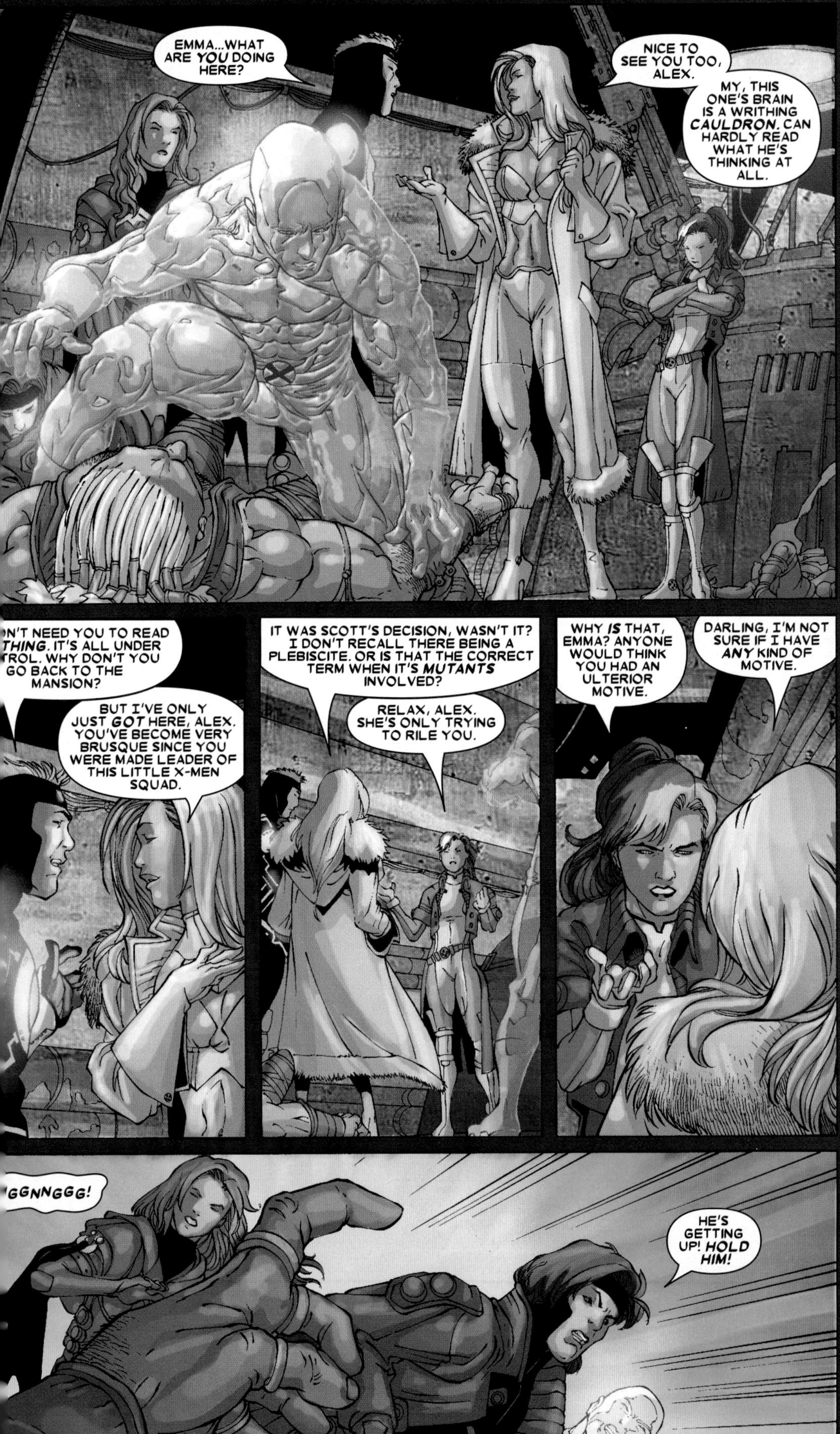
EMMA...WHAT ARE YOU DOING HERE?
NICE TO SEE YOU TOO, ALEX.
MY, THIS ONE'S BRAIN IS A WRITHING CAULDRON. CAN HARDLY READ WHAT HE'S THINKING AT ALL.
N'T NEED YOU TO READ THING. IT'S ALL UNDER TROL. WHY DON'T YOU GO BACK TO THE MANSION?
BUT I'VE ONLY JUST GOT HERE, ALEX. YOU'VE BECOME VERY BRUSQUE SINCE YOU WERE MADE LEADER OF THIS LITTLE X-MEN SQUAD.
IT WAS SCOTT'S DECISION, WASN'T IT? I DON'T RECALL THERE BEING A PLEBISCITE. OR IS THAT THE CORRECT TERM WHEN IT'S MUTANTS INVOLVED?
RELAX, ALEX. SHE'S ONLY TRYING TO RILE YOU.
WHY IS THAT, EMMA? ANYONE WOULD THINK YOU HAD AN ULTERIOR MOTIVE.
DARLING, I'M NOT SURE IF I HAVE ANY KIND OF MOTIVE.
GGNNGGG!
HE'S GETTING UP! HOLD HIM!

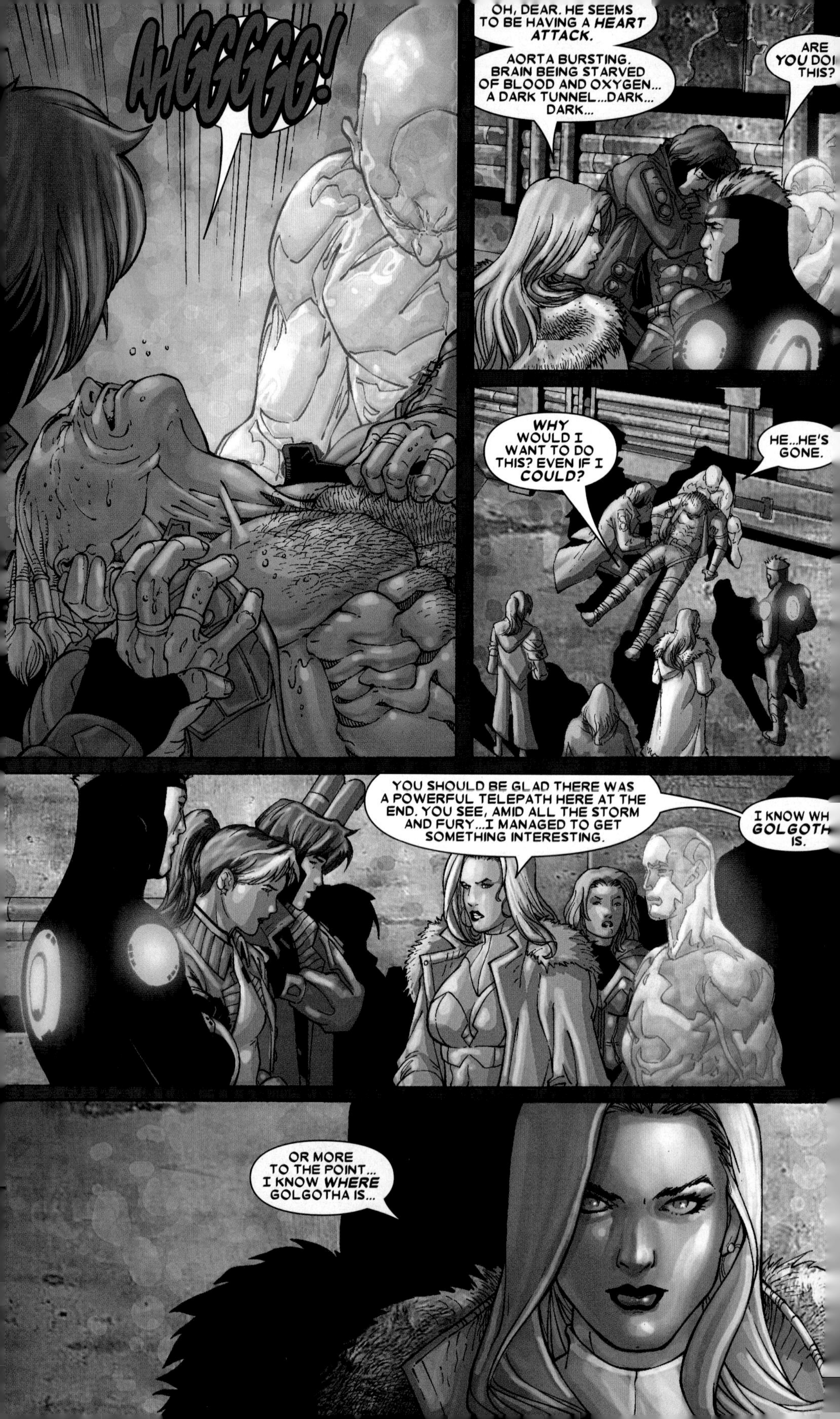
AHGGGGG!
OH, DEAR. HE SEEMS TO BE HAVING A *HEART ATTACK.*
AORTA BURSTING. BRAIN BEING STARVED OF BLOOD AND OXYGEN... A DARK TUNNEL...DARK... DARK...
ARE *YOU* DOI THIS?
*WHY* WOULD I WANT TO DO THIS? EVEN IF I *COULD?*
HE...HE'S GONE.
YOU SHOULD BE GLAD THERE WAS A POWERFUL TELEPATH HERE AT THE END. YOU SEE, AMID ALL THE STORM AND FURY...I MANAGED TO GET SOMETHING INTERESTING.
I KNOW WH *GOLGOTH* IS.
OR MORE TO THE POINT... I KNOW *WHERE* GOLGOTHA IS...

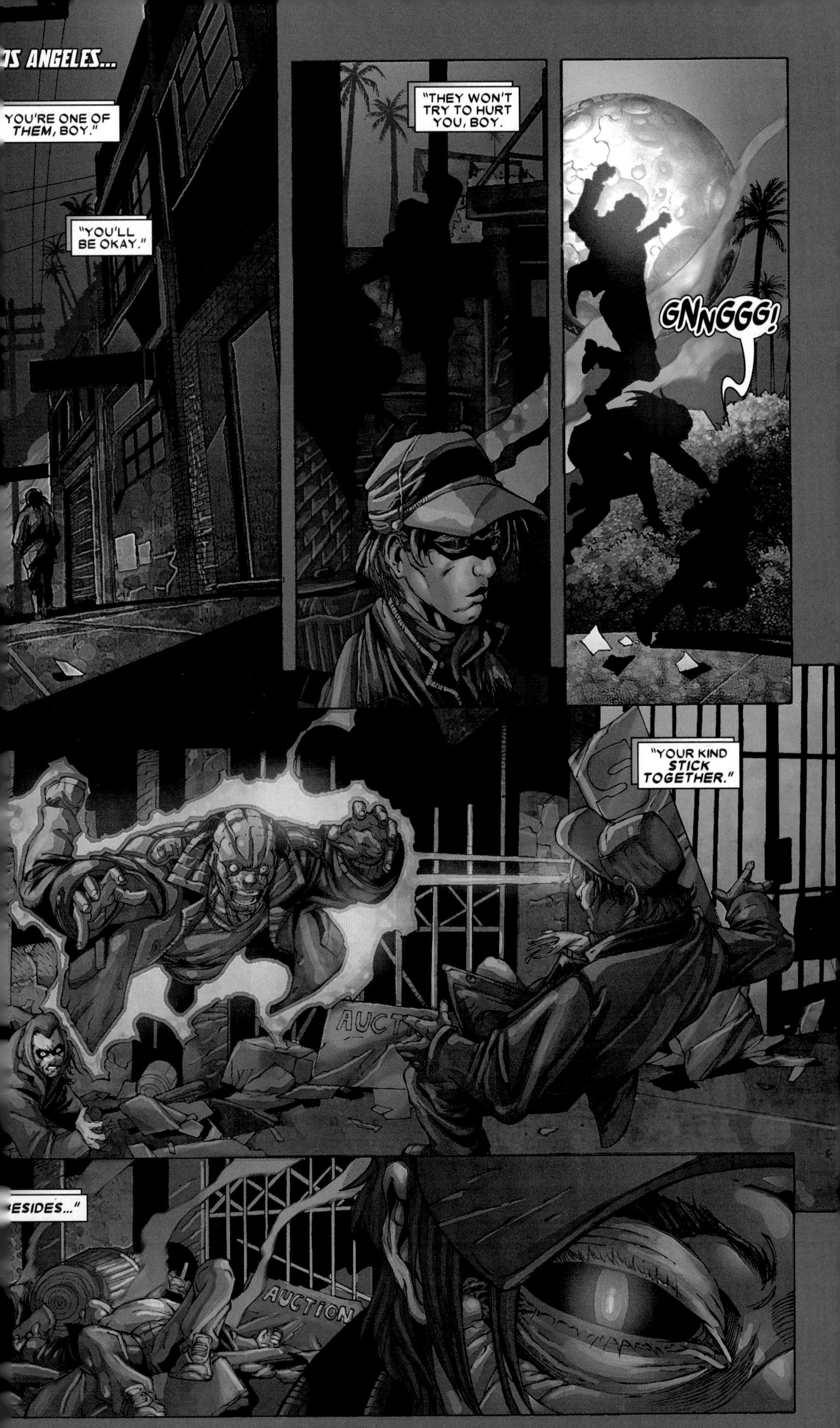

…OS ANGELES...
YOU'RE ONE OF THEM, BOY."
"YOU'LL BE OKAY."
"THEY WON'T TRY TO HURT YOU, BOY.
GNNGGG!
"YOUR KIND STICK TOGETHER."
AUCTI
…ESIDES..."
AUCTION

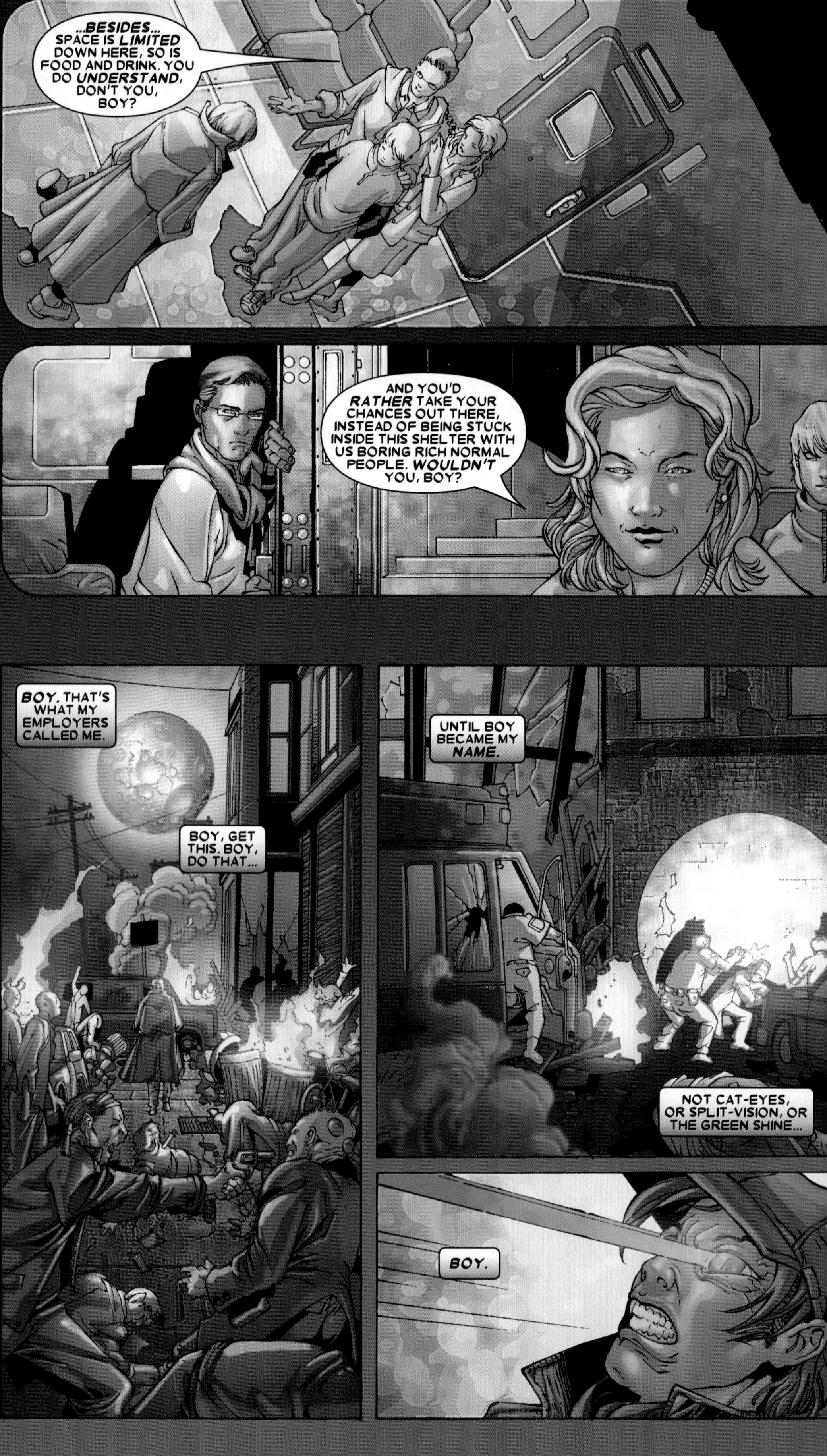
...BESIDES... SPACE IS LIMITED DOWN HERE, SO IS FOOD AND DRINK. YOU DO UNDERSTAND, DON'T YOU, BOY?
AND YOU'D RATHER TAKE YOUR CHANCES OUT THERE, INSTEAD OF BEING STUCK INSIDE THIS SHELTER WITH US BORING RICH NORMAL PEOPLE. WOULDN'T YOU, BOY?
BOY. THAT'S WHAT MY EMPLOYERS CALLED ME.
BOY, GET THIS. BOY, DO THAT...
UNTIL BOY BECAME MY NAME.
NOT CAT-EYES, OR SPLIT-VISION, OR THE GREEN SHINE...
BOY.

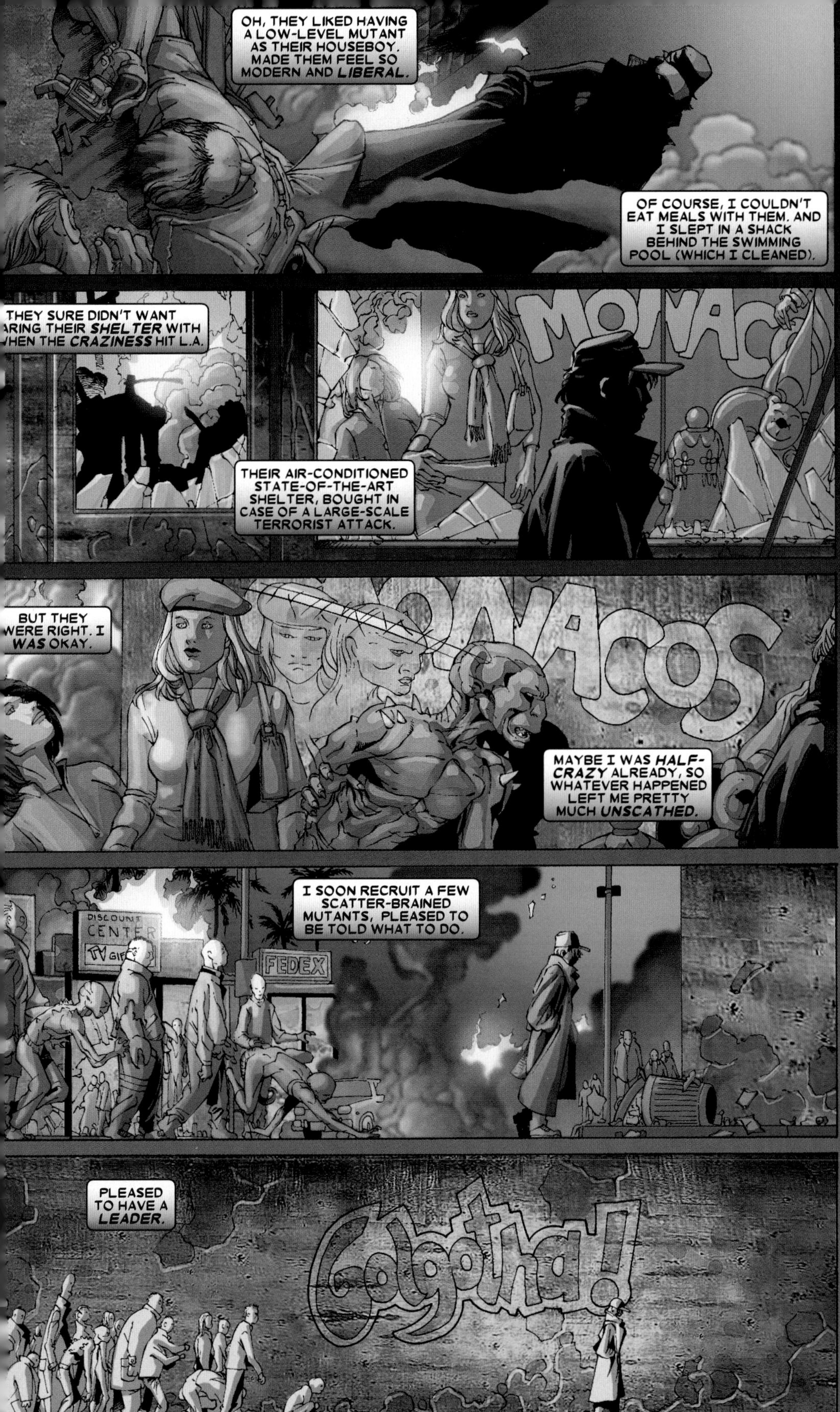

OH, THEY LIKED HAVING A LOW-LEVEL MUTANT AS THEIR HOUSEBOY. MADE THEM FEEL SO MODERN AND *LIBERAL*.
OF COURSE, I COULDN'T EAT MEALS WITH THEM. AND I SLEPT IN A SHACK BEHIND THE SWIMMING POOL (WHICH I CLEANED).
THEY SURE DIDN'T WANT ARING THEIR *SHELTER* WITH WHEN THE *CRAZINESS* HIT L.A.
MONACO
THEIR AIR-CONDITIONED STATE-OF-THE-ART SHELTER, BOUGHT IN CASE OF A LARGE-SCALE TERRORIST ATTACK.
BUT THEY WERE RIGHT. I *WAS* OKAY.
MONACOS
MAYBE I WAS *HALF-CRAZY* ALREADY, SO WHATEVER HAPPENED LEFT ME PRETTY MUCH *UNSCATHED*.
I SOON RECRUIT A FEW SCATTER-BRAINED MUTANTS, PLEASED TO BE TOLD WHAT TO DO.
DISCOUNT CENTER
FEDEX
PLEASED TO HAVE A *LEADER*.
Golgotha!

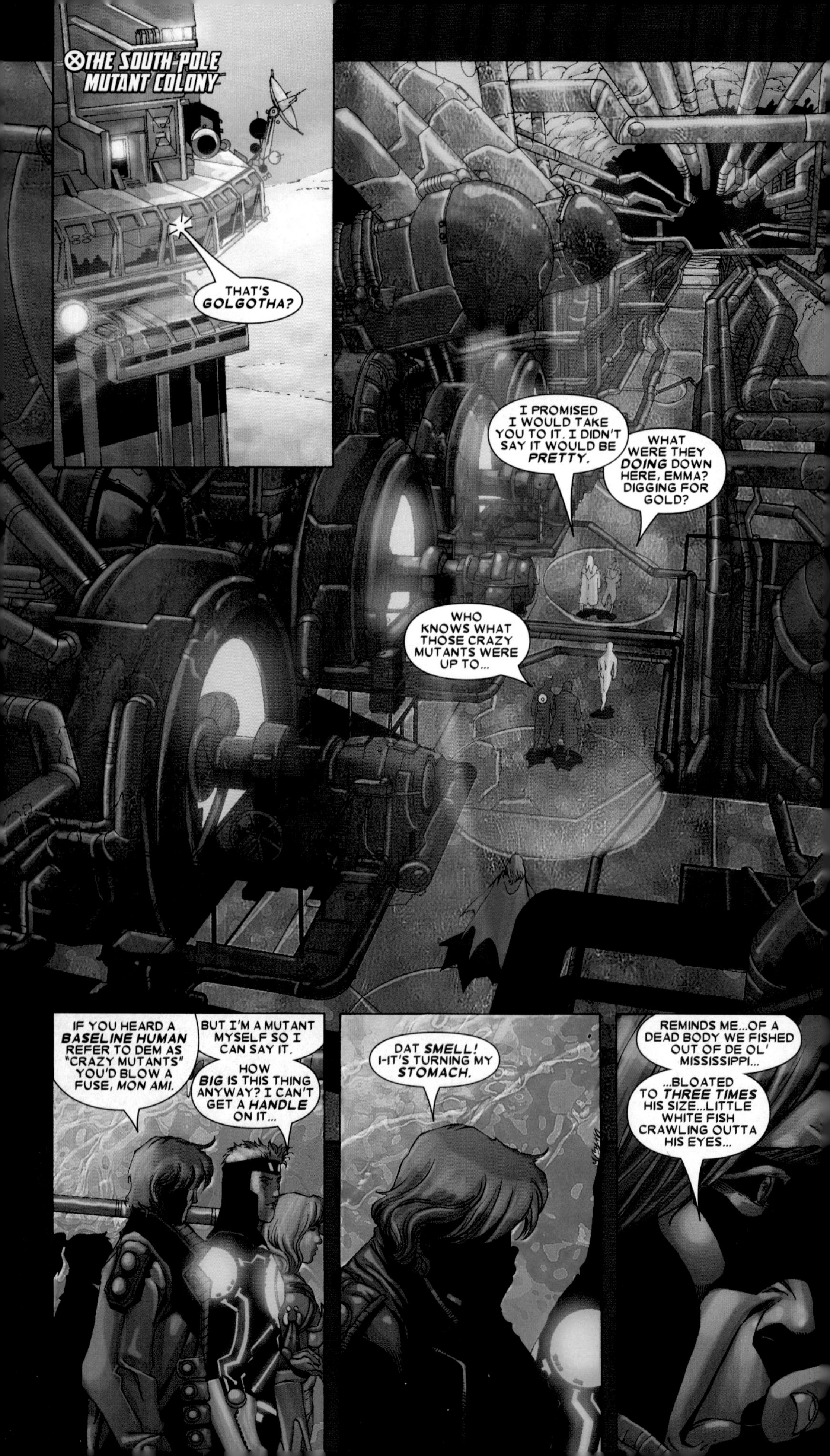
THE SOUTH POLE MUTANT COLONY
THAT'S GOLGOTHA?
I PROMISED I WOULD TAKE YOU TO IT. I DIDN'T SAY IT WOULD BE PRETTY.
WHAT WERE THEY DOING DOWN HERE, EMMA? DIGGING FOR GOLD?
WHO KNOWS WHAT THOSE CRAZY MUTANTS WERE UP TO...
IF YOU HEARD A BASELINE HUMAN REFER TO DEM AS "CRAZY MUTANTS" YOU'D BLOW A FUSE, MON AMI.
BUT I'M A MUTANT MYSELF SO I CAN SAY IT.
HOW BIG IS THIS THING ANYWAY? I CAN'T GET A HANDLE ON IT...
DAT SMELL! I-IT'S TURNING MY STOMACH.
REMINDS ME...OF A DEAD BODY WE FISHED OUT OF DE OL' MISSISSIPPI...
...BLOATED TO THREE TIMES HIS SIZE...LITTLE WHITE FISH CRAWLING OUTTA HIS EYES...

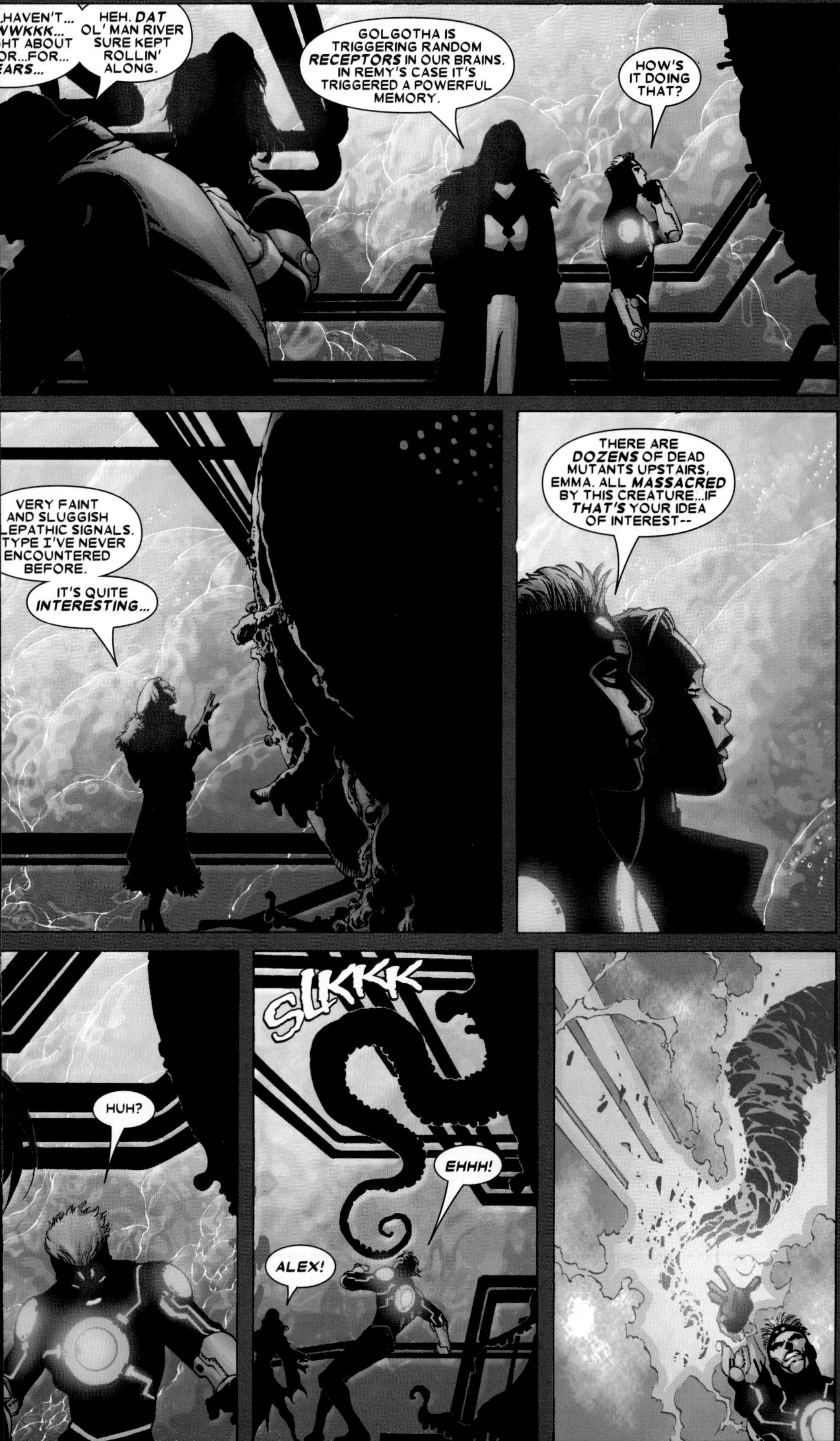

...HAVEN'T... ...WKKK... ...GHT ABOUT ...OR...FOR... ...EARS...
HEH. DAT OL' MAN RIVER SURE KEPT ROLLIN' ALONG.
GOLGOTHA IS TRIGGERING RANDOM RECEPTORS IN OUR BRAINS. IN REMY'S CASE IT'S TRIGGERED A POWERFUL MEMORY.
HOW'S IT DOING THAT?
VERY FAINT AND SLUGGISH ...LEPATHIC SIGNALS. ...TYPE I'VE NEVER ENCOUNTERED BEFORE.
IT'S QUITE INTERESTING...
THERE ARE DOZENS OF DEAD MUTANTS UPSTAIRS, EMMA. ALL MASSACRED BY THIS CREATURE...IF THAT'S YOUR IDEA OF INTEREST--
HUH?
SLKKK
EHHH!
ALEX!

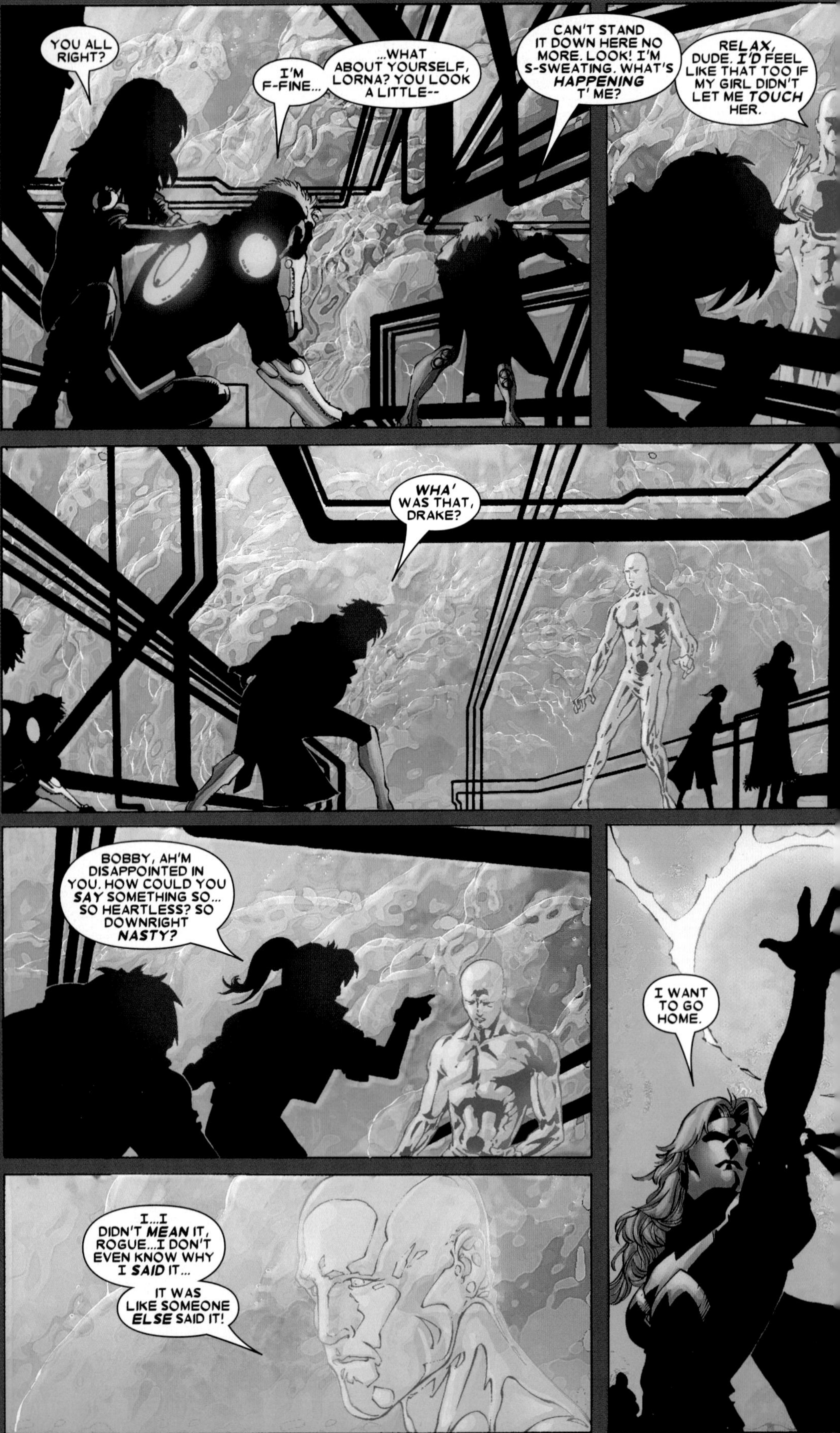

YOU ALL RIGHT?
I'M F-FINE...
...WHAT ABOUT YOURSELF, LORNA? YOU LOOK A LITTLE--
CAN'T STAND IT DOWN HERE NO MORE. LOOK! I'M S-SWEATING. WHAT'S HAPPENING T' ME?
RELAX, DUDE. I'D FEEL LIKE THAT TOO IF MY GIRL DIDN'T LET ME TOUCH HER.
WHA' WAS THAT, DRAKE?
BOBBY, AH'M DISAPPOINTED IN YOU. HOW COULD YOU SAY SOMETHING SO... SO HEARTLESS? SO DOWNRIGHT NASTY?
I WANT TO GO HOME.
I...I DIDN'T MEAN IT, ROGUE...I DON'T EVEN KNOW WHY I SAID IT...
IT WAS LIKE SOMEONE ELSE SAID IT!

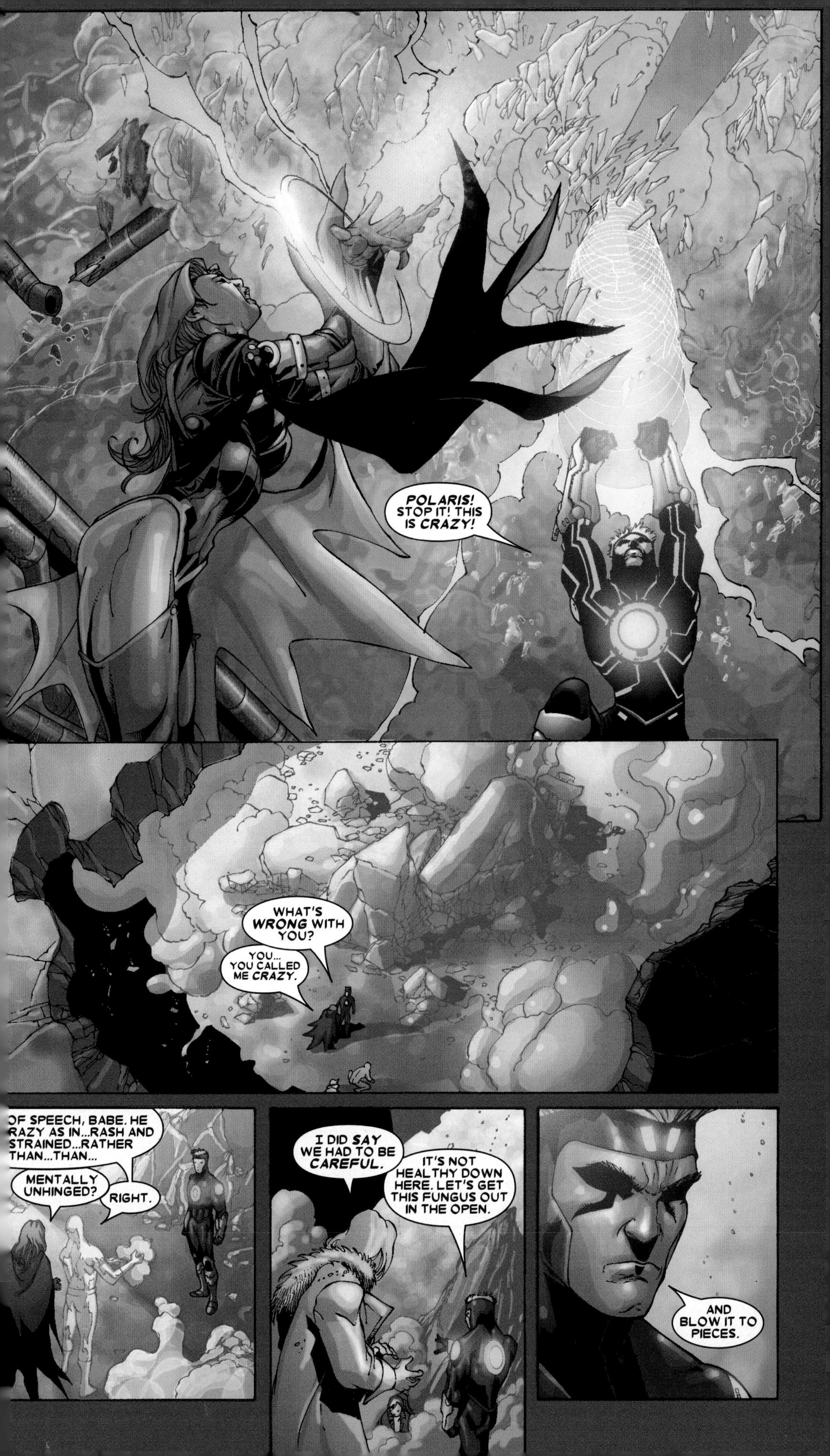
POLARIS! STOP IT! THIS IS CRAZY!
WHAT'S WRONG WITH YOU?
YOU... YOU CALLED ME CRAZY.
OF SPEECH, BABE. HE RAZY AS IN...RASH AND STRAINED...RATHER THAN...THAN...
MENTALLY UNHINGED?
RIGHT.
I DID SAY WE HAD TO BE CAREFUL.
IT'S NOT HEALTHY DOWN HERE. LET'S GET THIS FUNGUS OUT IN THE OPEN.
AND BLOW IT TO PIECES.

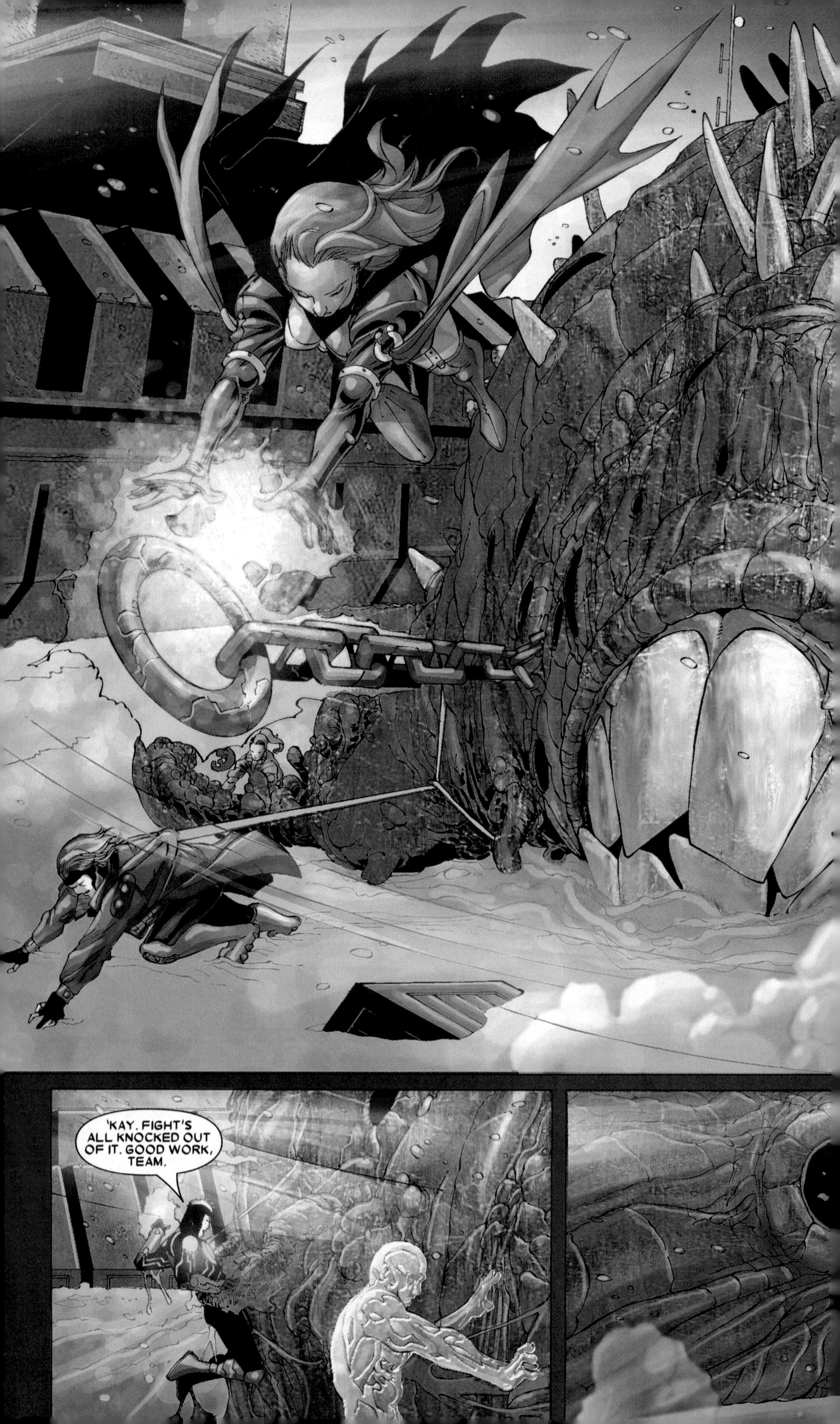
'KAY. FIGHT'S ALL KNOCKED OUT OF IT. GOOD WORK, TEAM.

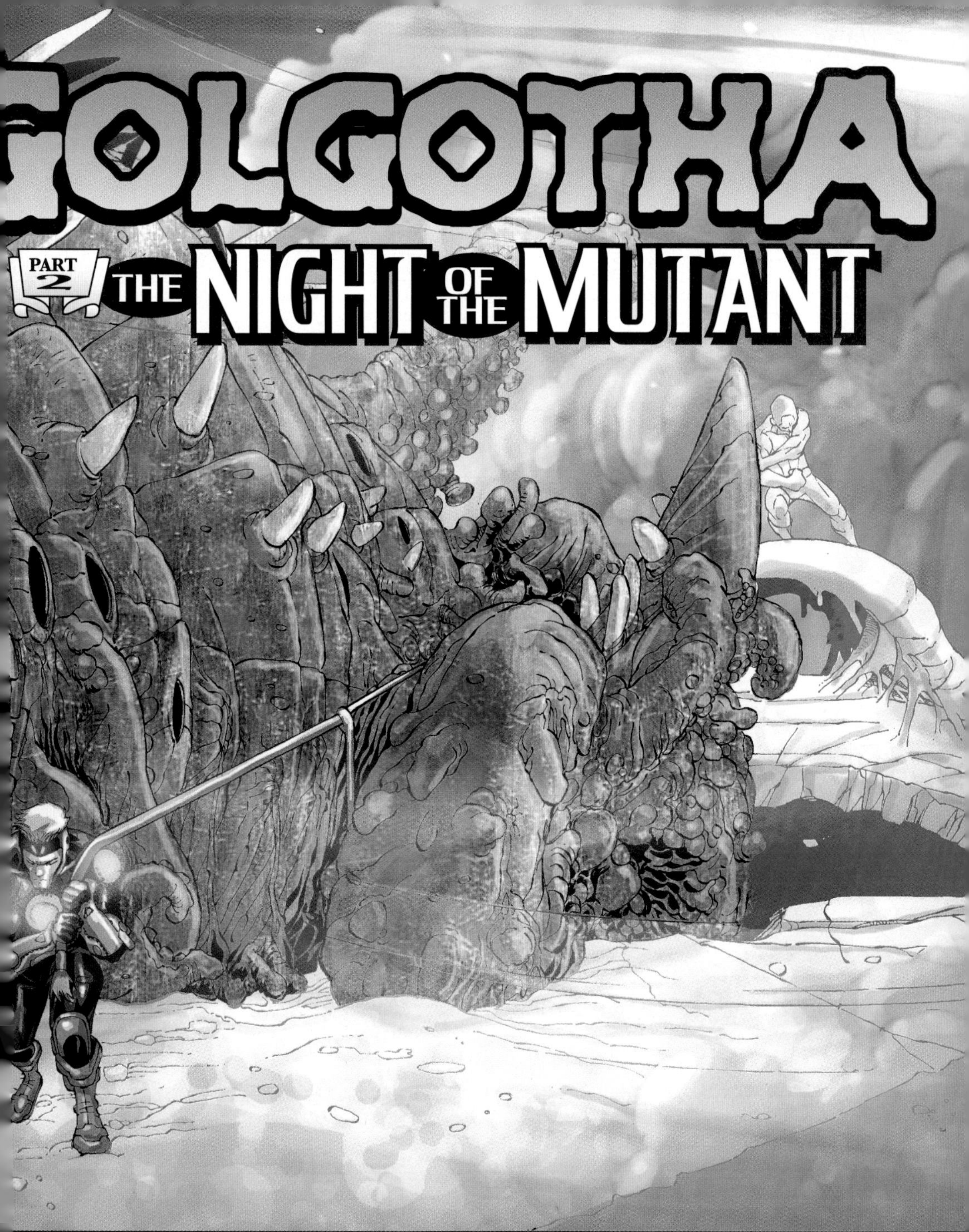
GOLGOTHA
PART 2
THE NIGHT OF THE MUTANT

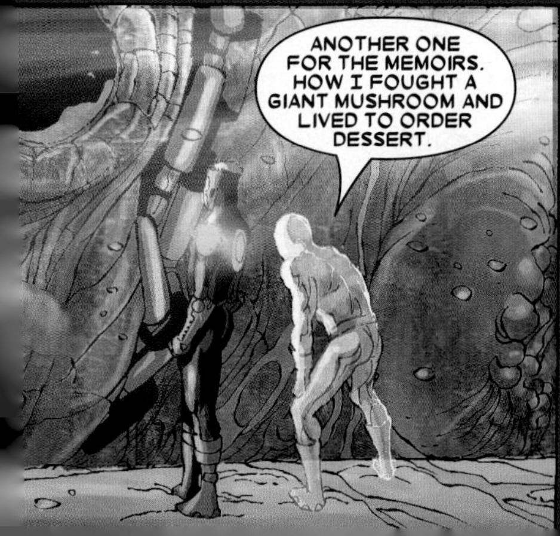
ANOTHER ONE FOR THE MEMOIRS. HOW I FOUGHT A GIANT MUSHROOM AND LIVED TO ORDER DESSERT.

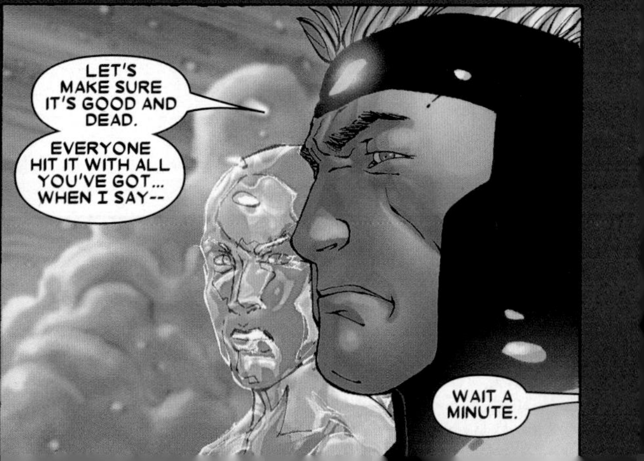
LET'S MAKE SURE IT'S GOOD AND DEAD.
EVERYONE HIT IT WITH ALL YOU'VE GOT... WHEN I SAY--
WAIT A MINUTE.

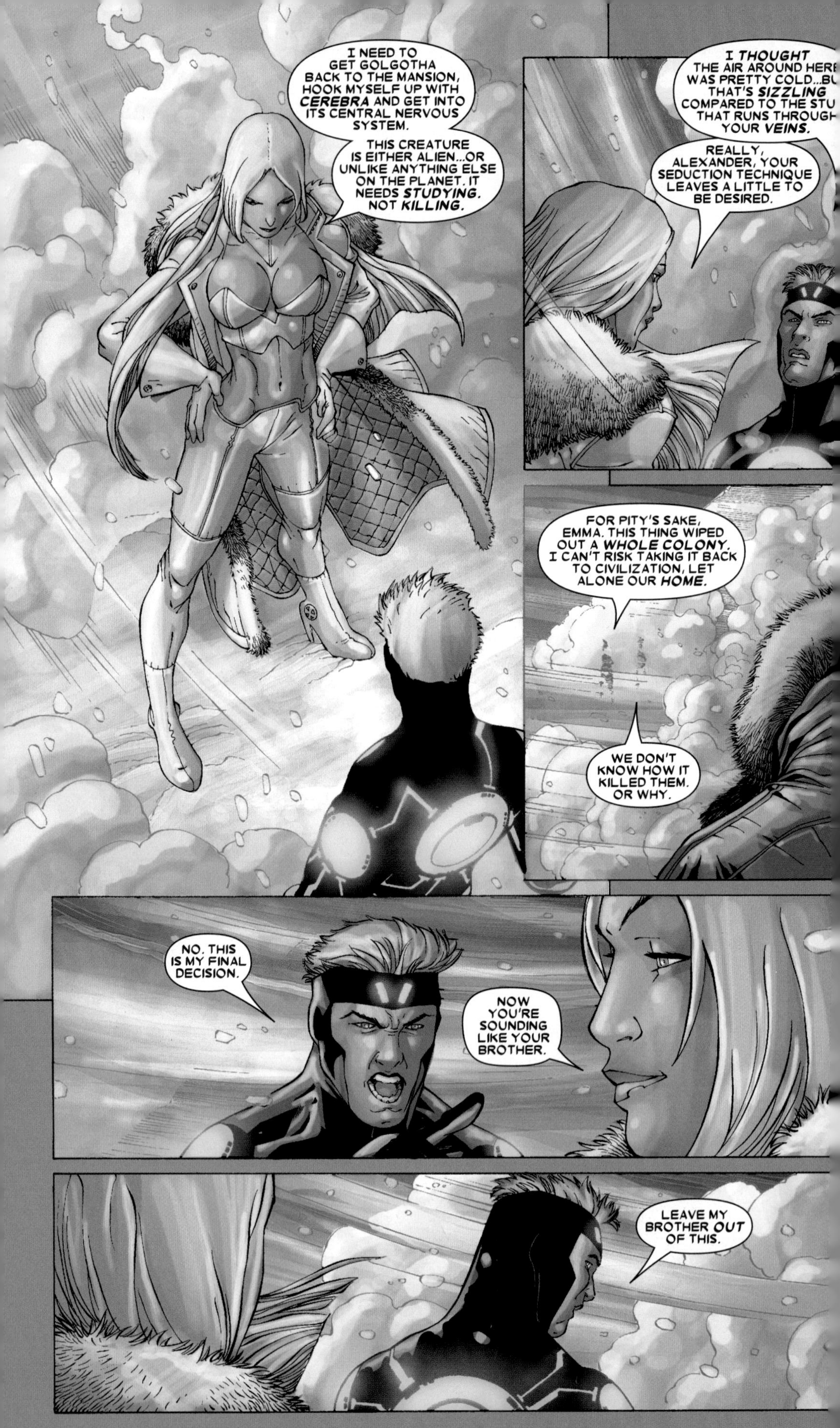
I NEED TO GET GOLGOTHA BACK TO THE MANSION, HOOK MYSELF UP WITH CEREBRA AND GET INTO ITS CENTRAL NERVOUS SYSTEM.
THIS CREATURE IS EITHER ALIEN...OR UNLIKE ANYTHING ELSE ON THE PLANET. IT NEEDS STUDYING. NOT KILLING.
I THOUGHT THE AIR AROUND HERE WAS PRETTY COLD...BU THAT'S SIZZLING COMPARED TO THE STU THAT RUNS THROUGH YOUR VEINS.
REALLY, ALEXANDER, YOUR SEDUCTION TECHNIQUE LEAVES A LITTLE TO BE DESIRED.
FOR PITY'S SAKE, EMMA. THIS THING WIPED OUT A WHOLE COLONY. I CAN'T RISK TAKING IT BACK TO CIVILIZATION, LET ALONE OUR HOME.
WE DON'T KNOW HOW IT KILLED THEM. OR WHY.
NO. THIS IS MY FINAL DECISION.
NOW YOU'RE SOUNDING LIKE YOUR BROTHER.
LEAVE MY BROTHER OUT OF THIS.

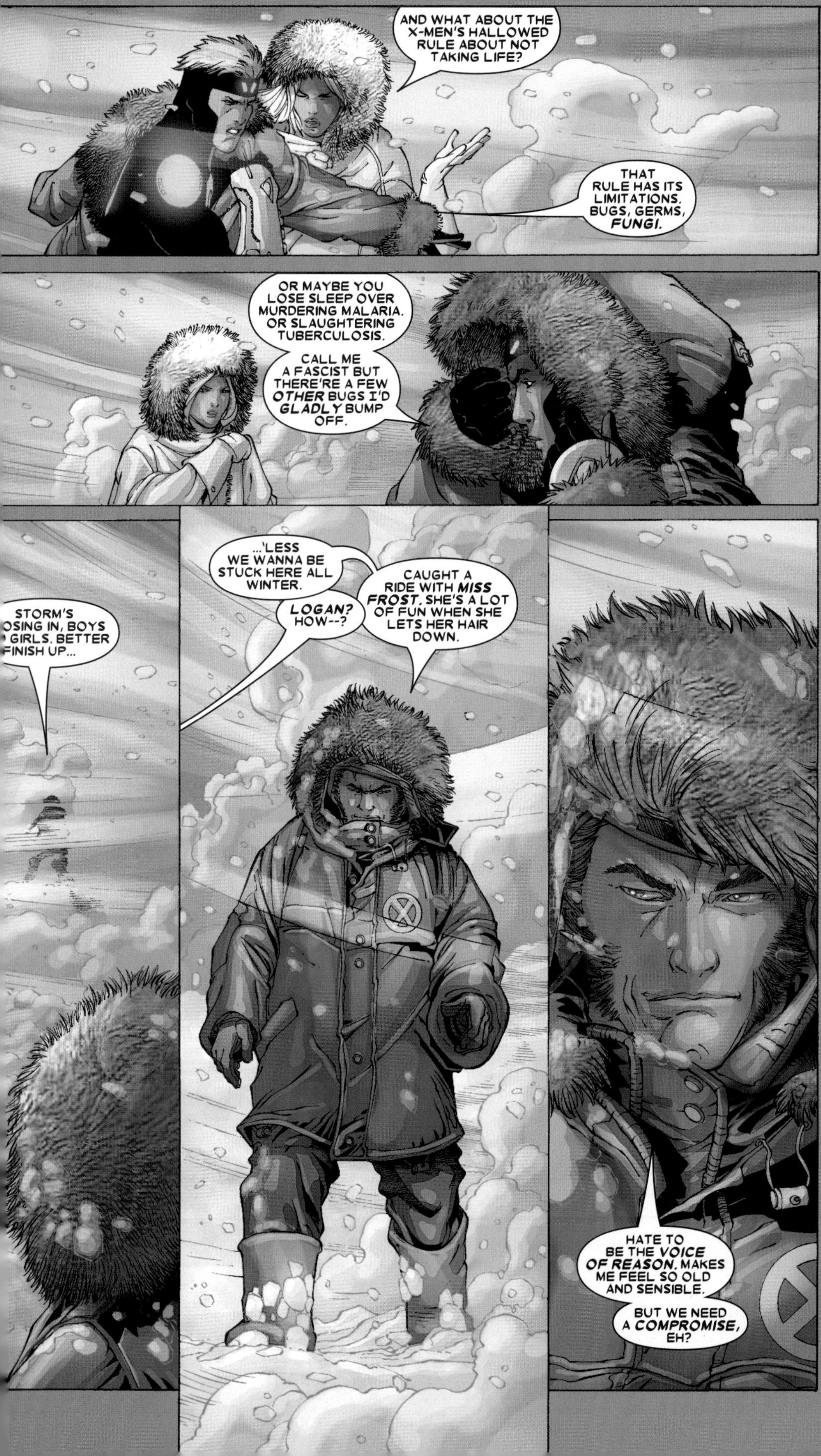
AND WHAT ABOUT THE X-MEN'S HALLOWED RULE ABOUT NOT TAKING LIFE?
THAT RULE HAS ITS LIMITATIONS. BUGS, GERMS, FUNGI.
OR MAYBE YOU LOSE SLEEP OVER MURDERING MALARIA. OR SLAUGHTERING TUBERCULOSIS.
CALL ME A FASCIST BUT THERE'RE A FEW OTHER BUGS I'D GLADLY BUMP OFF.
STORM'S OSING IN, BOYS GIRLS. BETTER FINISH UP...
...'LESS WE WANNA BE STUCK HERE ALL WINTER.
LOGAN? HOW--?
CAUGHT A RIDE WITH MISS FROST. SHE'S A LOT OF FUN WHEN SHE LETS HER HAIR DOWN.
HATE TO BE THE VOICE OF REASON. MAKES ME FEEL SO OLD AND SENSIBLE.
BUT WE NEED A COMPROMISE, EH?

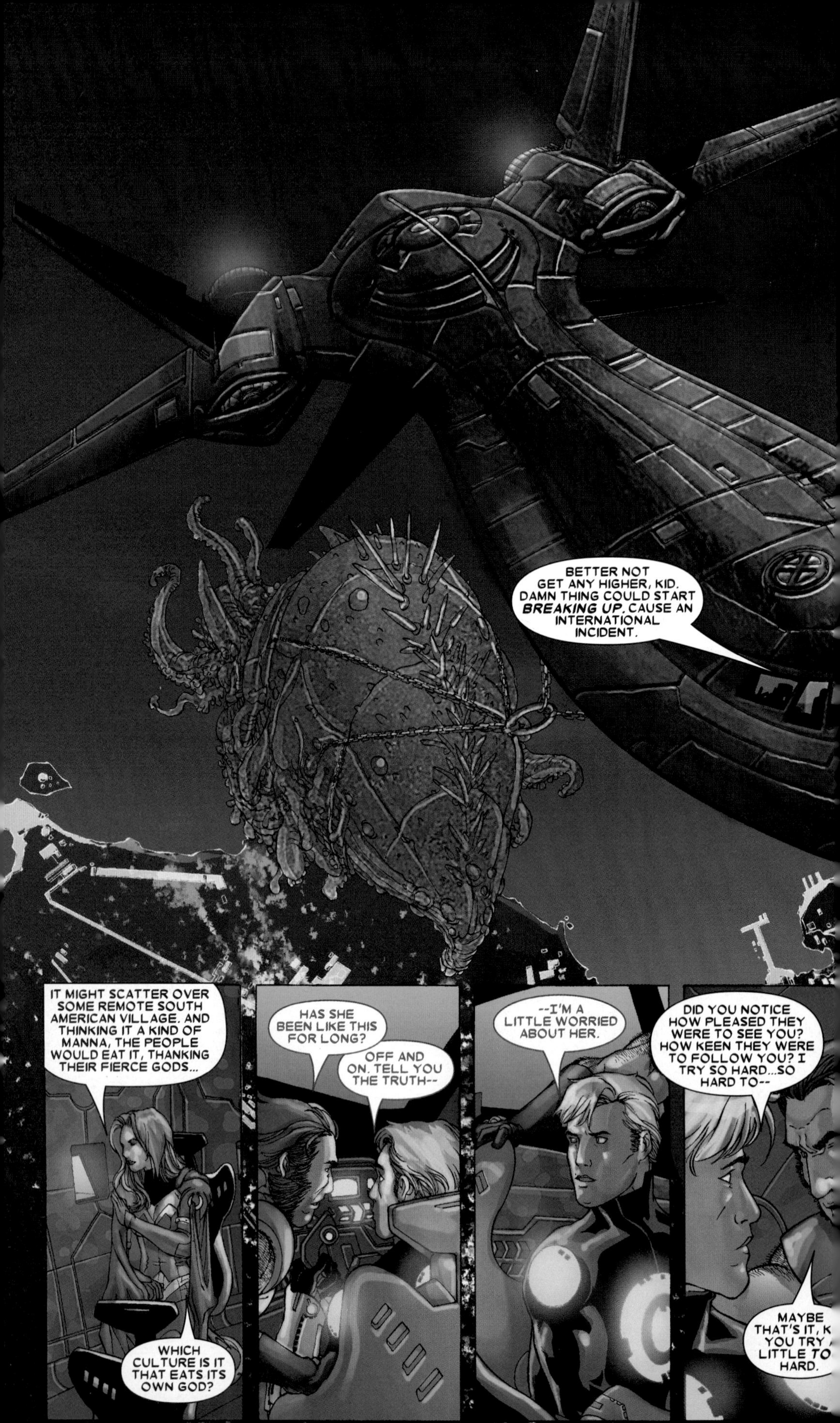
BETTER NOT GET ANY HIGHER, KID. DAMN THING COULD START *BREAKING UP.* CAUSE AN INTERNATIONAL INCIDENT.
IT MIGHT SCATTER OVER SOME REMOTE SOUTH AMERICAN VILLAGE. AND THINKING IT A KIND OF MANNA, THE PEOPLE WOULD EAT IT, THANKING THEIR FIERCE GODS...
WHICH CULTURE IS IT THAT EATS ITS OWN GOD?
HAS SHE BEEN LIKE THIS FOR LONG?
OFF AND ON. TELL YOU THE TRUTH--
--I'M A LITTLE WORRIED ABOUT HER.
DID YOU NOTICE HOW PLEASED THEY WERE TO SEE YOU? HOW KEEN THEY WERE TO FOLLOW YOU? I TRY SO HARD...SO HARD TO--
MAYBE THAT'S IT, K YOU TRY LITTLE *TO* HARD.

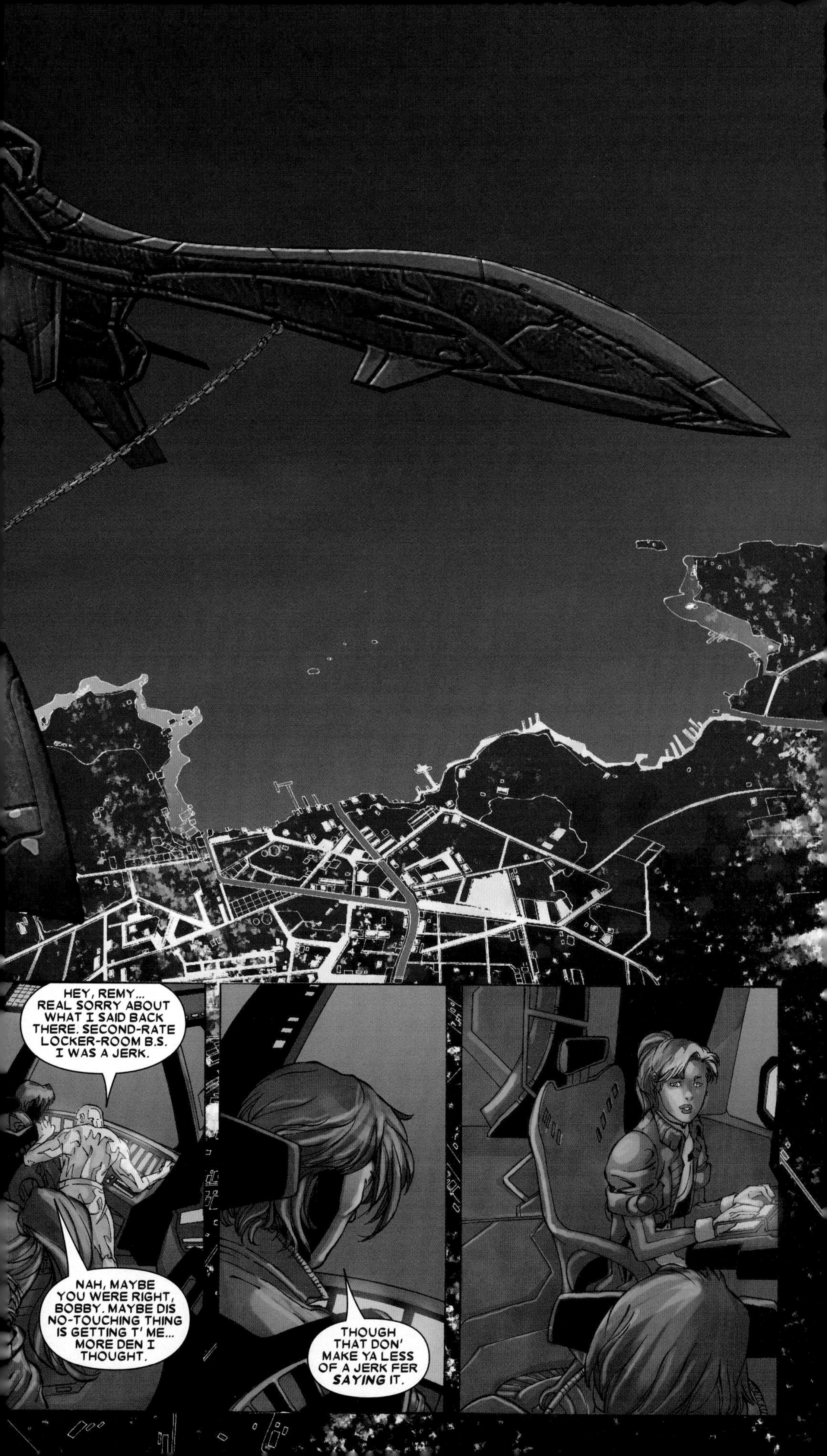
HEY, REMY... REAL SORRY ABOUT WHAT I SAID BACK THERE. SECOND-RATE LOCKER-ROOM B.S. I WAS A JERK.
NAH, MAYBE YOU WERE RIGHT, BOBBY. MAYBE DIS NO-TOUCHING THING IS GETTING T' ME... MORE DEN I THOUGHT.
THOUGH THAT DON' MAKE YA LESS OF A JERK FER SAYING IT.

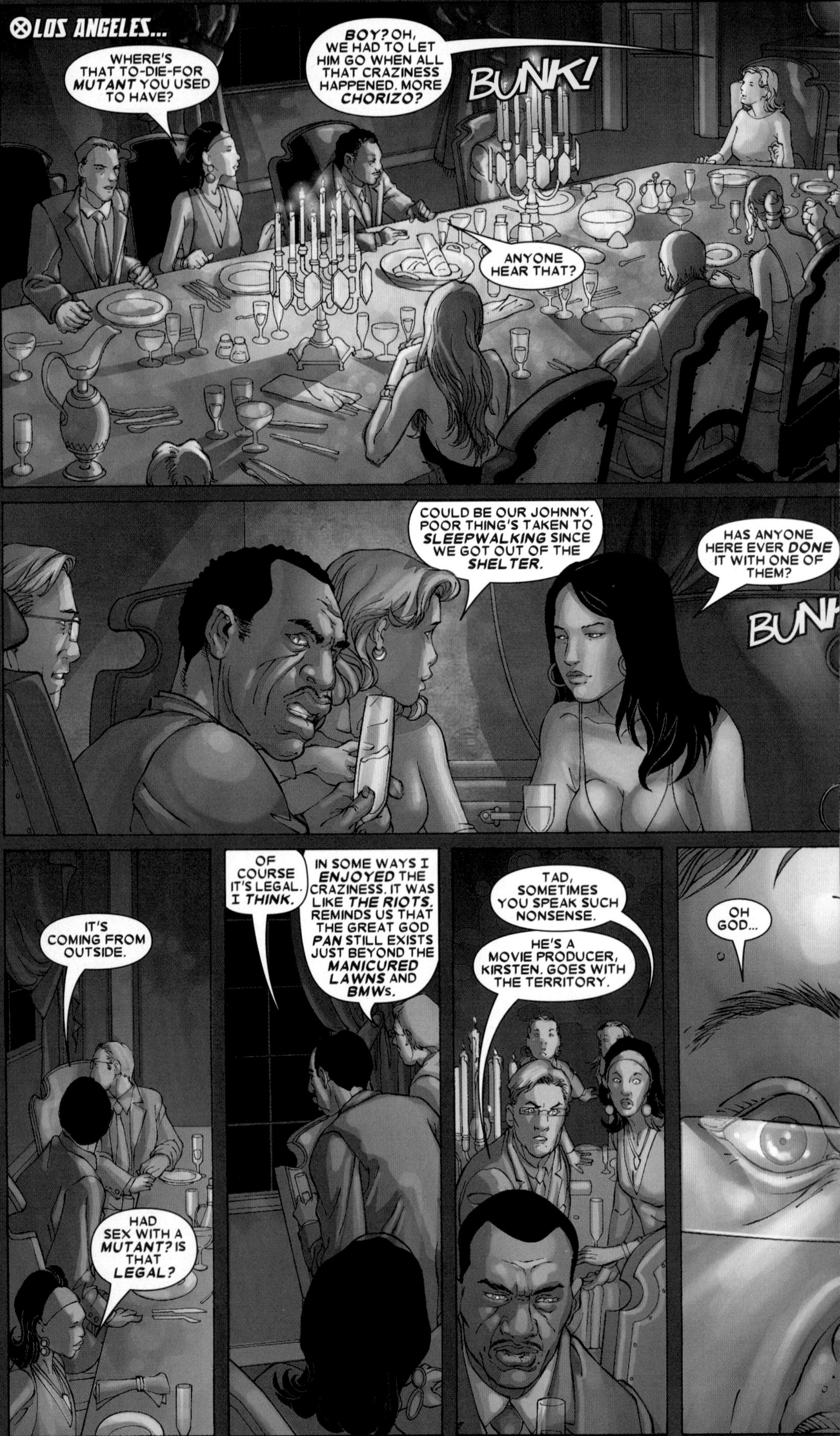

LOS ANGELES...
WHERE'S THAT TO-DIE-FOR MUTANT YOU USED TO HAVE?
BOY? OH, WE HAD TO LET HIM GO WHEN ALL THAT CRAZINESS HAPPENED. MORE CHORIZO?
BUNK!
ANYONE HEAR THAT?
COULD BE OUR JOHNNY. POOR THING'S TAKEN TO SLEEPWALKING SINCE WE GOT OUT OF THE SHELTER.
HAS ANYONE HERE EVER DONE IT WITH ONE OF THEM?
BUNK
IT'S COMING FROM OUTSIDE.
HAD SEX WITH A MUTANT? IS THAT LEGAL?
OF COURSE IT'S LEGAL. I THINK.
IN SOME WAYS I ENJOYED THE CRAZINESS. IT WAS LIKE THE RIOTS. REMINDS US THAT THE GREAT GOD PAN STILL EXISTS JUST BEYOND THE MANICURED LAWNS AND BMWs.
TAD, SOMETIMES YOU SPEAK SUCH NONSENSE.
HE'S A MOVIE PRODUCER, KIRSTEN. GOES WITH THE TERRITORY.
OH GOD...

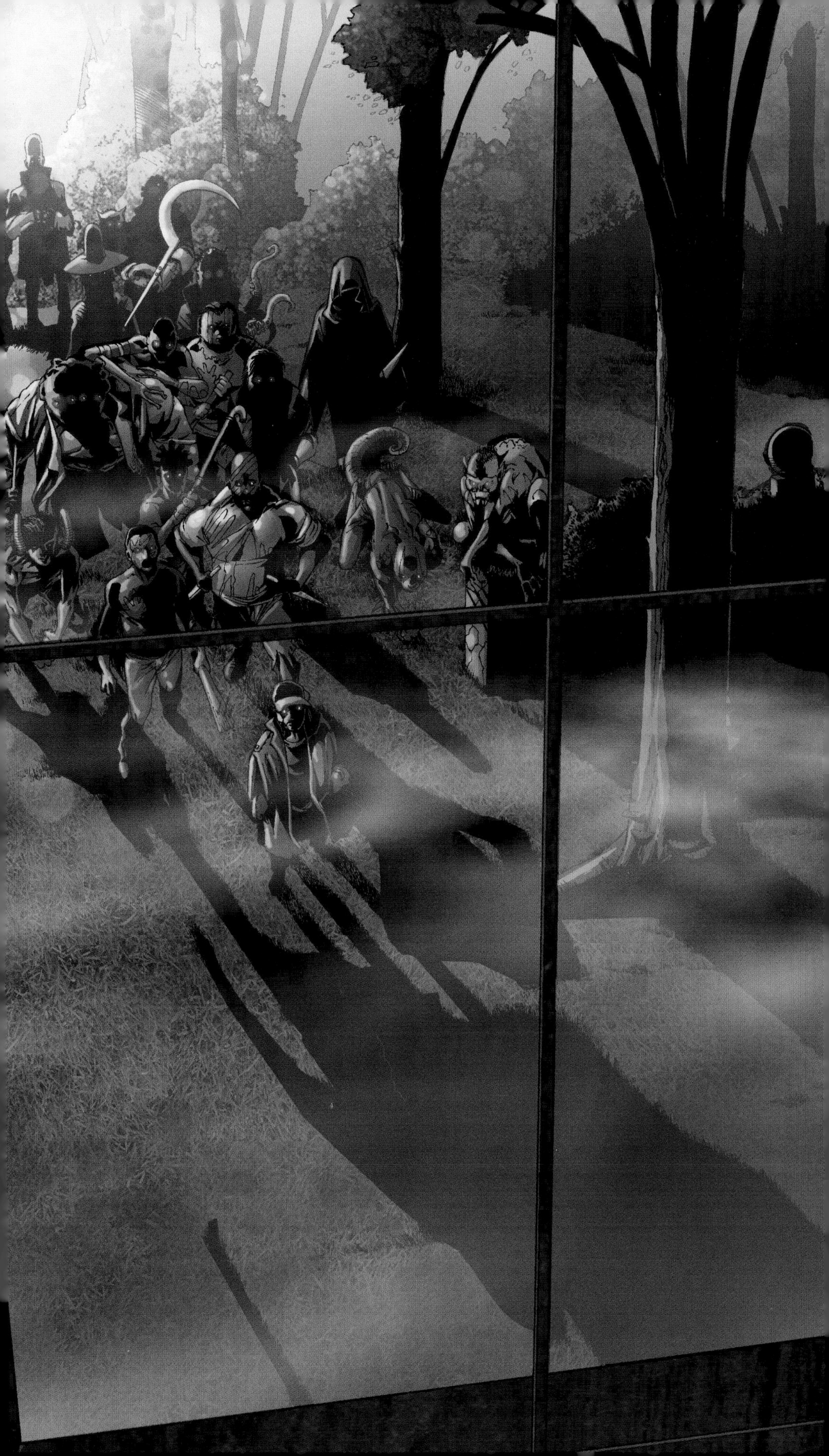

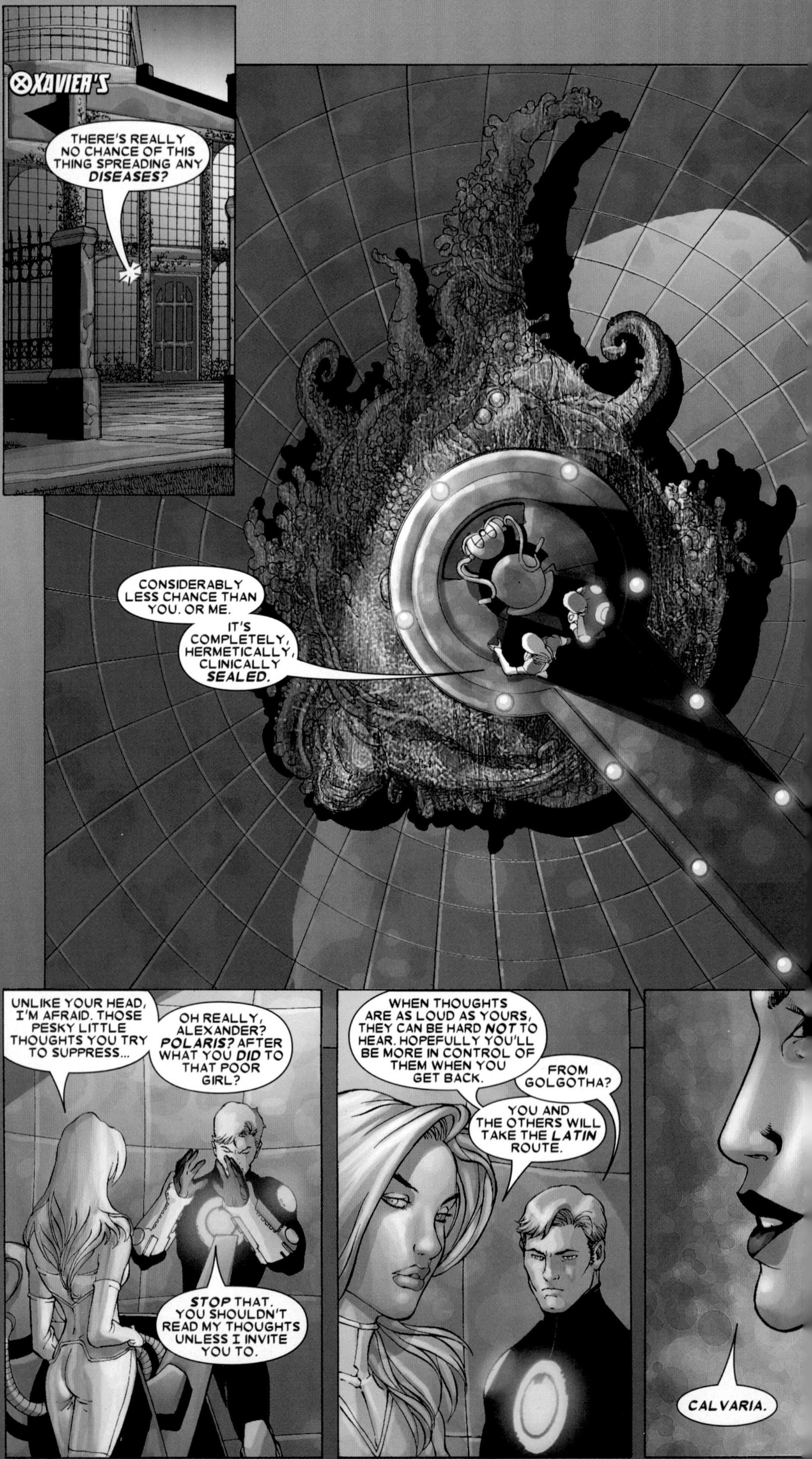
XAVIER'S
THERE'S REALLY NO CHANCE OF THIS THING SPREADING ANY DISEASES?
CONSIDERABLY LESS CHANCE THAN YOU. OR ME.
IT'S COMPLETELY, HERMETICALLY, CLINICALLY SEALED.
UNLIKE YOUR HEAD, I'M AFRAID. THOSE PESKY LITTLE THOUGHTS YOU TRY TO SUPPRESS...
OH REALLY, ALEXANDER? POLARIS? AFTER WHAT YOU DID TO THAT POOR GIRL?
STOP THAT. YOU SHOULDN'T READ MY THOUGHTS UNLESS I INVITE YOU TO.
WHEN THOUGHTS ARE AS LOUD AS YOURS, THEY CAN BE HARD NOT TO HEAR. HOPEFULLY YOU'LL BE MORE IN CONTROL OF THEM WHEN YOU GET BACK.
FROM GOLGOTHA?
YOU AND THE OTHERS WILL TAKE THE LATIN ROUTE.
CALVARIA.

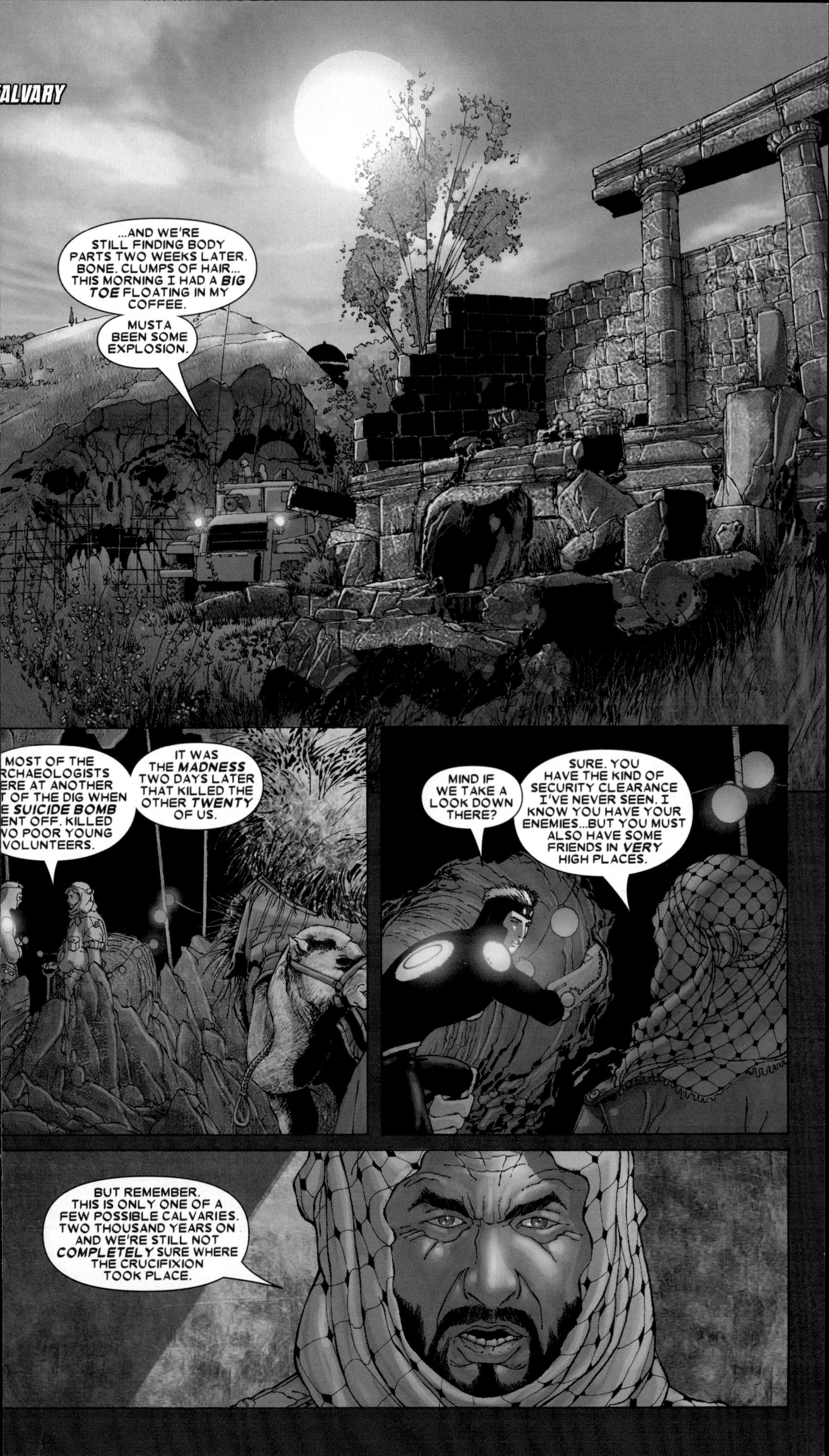

ALVARY
...AND WE'RE STILL FINDING BODY PARTS TWO WEEKS LATER. BONE. CLUMPS OF HAIR... THIS MORNING I HAD A BIG TOE FLOATING IN MY COFFEE.
MUSTA BEEN SOME EXPLOSION.
MOST OF THE RCHAEOLOGISTS ERE AT ANOTHER T OF THE DIG WHEN E SUICIDE BOMB ENT OFF. KILLED VO POOR YOUNG VOLUNTEERS.
IT WAS THE MADNESS TWO DAYS LATER THAT KILLED THE OTHER TWENTY OF US.
MIND IF WE TAKE A LOOK DOWN THERE?
SURE. YOU HAVE THE KIND OF SECURITY CLEARANCE I'VE NEVER SEEN. I KNOW YOU HAVE YOUR ENEMIES...BUT YOU MUST ALSO HAVE SOME FRIENDS IN VERY HIGH PLACES.
BUT REMEMBER. THIS IS ONLY ONE OF A FEW POSSIBLE CALVARIES. TWO THOUSAND YEARS ON AND WE'RE STILL NOT COMPLETELY SURE WHERE THE CRUCIFIXION TOOK PLACE.

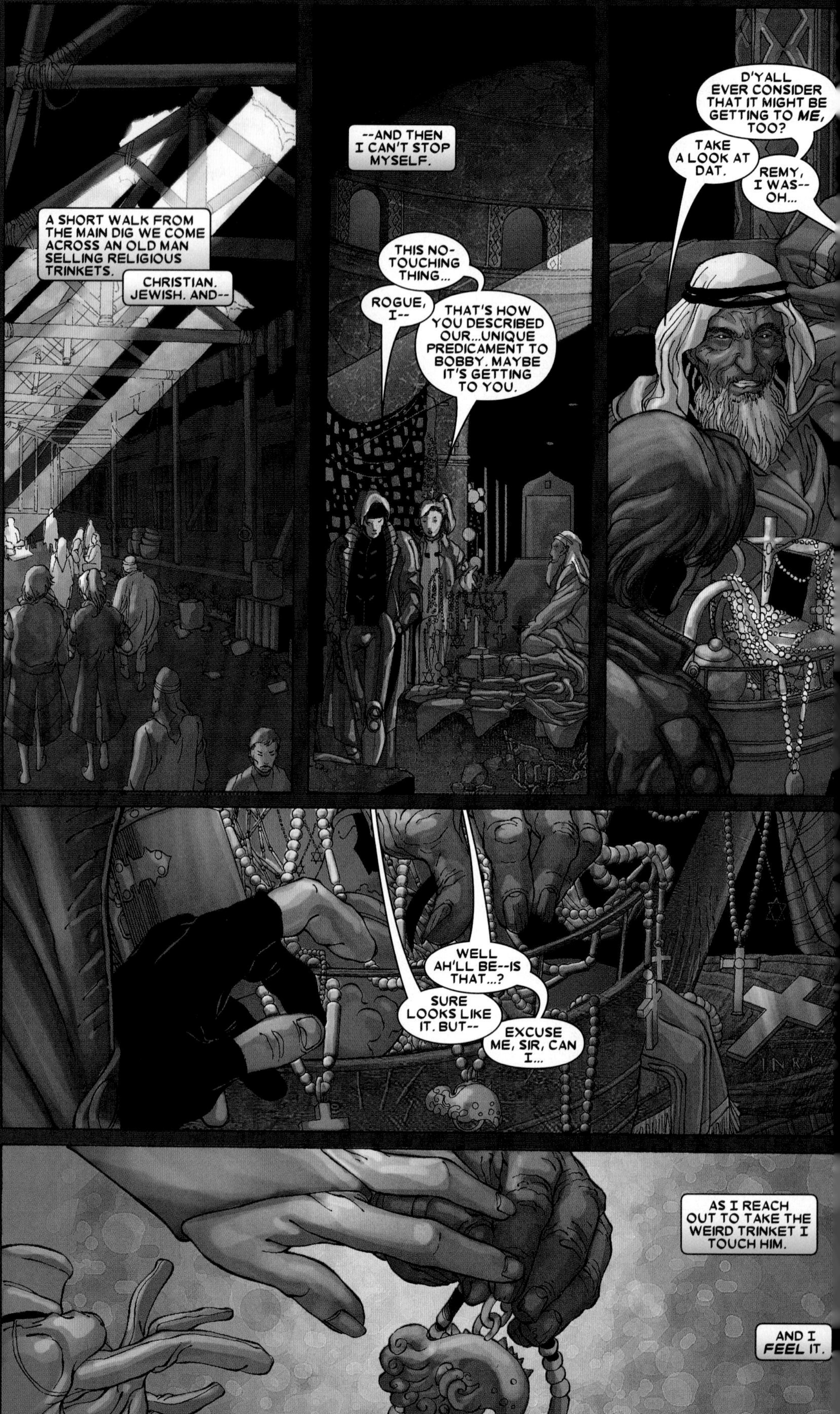
A SHORT WALK FROM THE MAIN DIG WE COME ACROSS AN OLD MAN SELLING RELIGIOUS TRINKETS.
CHRISTIAN. JEWISH. AND--
--AND THEN I CAN'T STOP MYSELF.
THIS NO-TOUCHING THING...
ROGUE, I--
THAT'S HOW YOU DESCRIBED OUR...UNIQUE PREDICAMENT TO BOBBY. MAYBE IT'S GETTING TO YOU.
D'YALL EVER CONSIDER THAT IT MIGHT BE GETTING TO *ME*, TOO?
TAKE A LOOK AT DAT.
REMY, I WAS-- OH...
WELL AH'LL BE--IS THAT...?
SURE LOOKS LIKE IT. BUT--
EXCUSE ME, SIR, CAN I...
AS I REACH OUT TO TAKE THE WEIRD TRINKET I TOUCH HIM.
AND I ***FEEL*** IT.

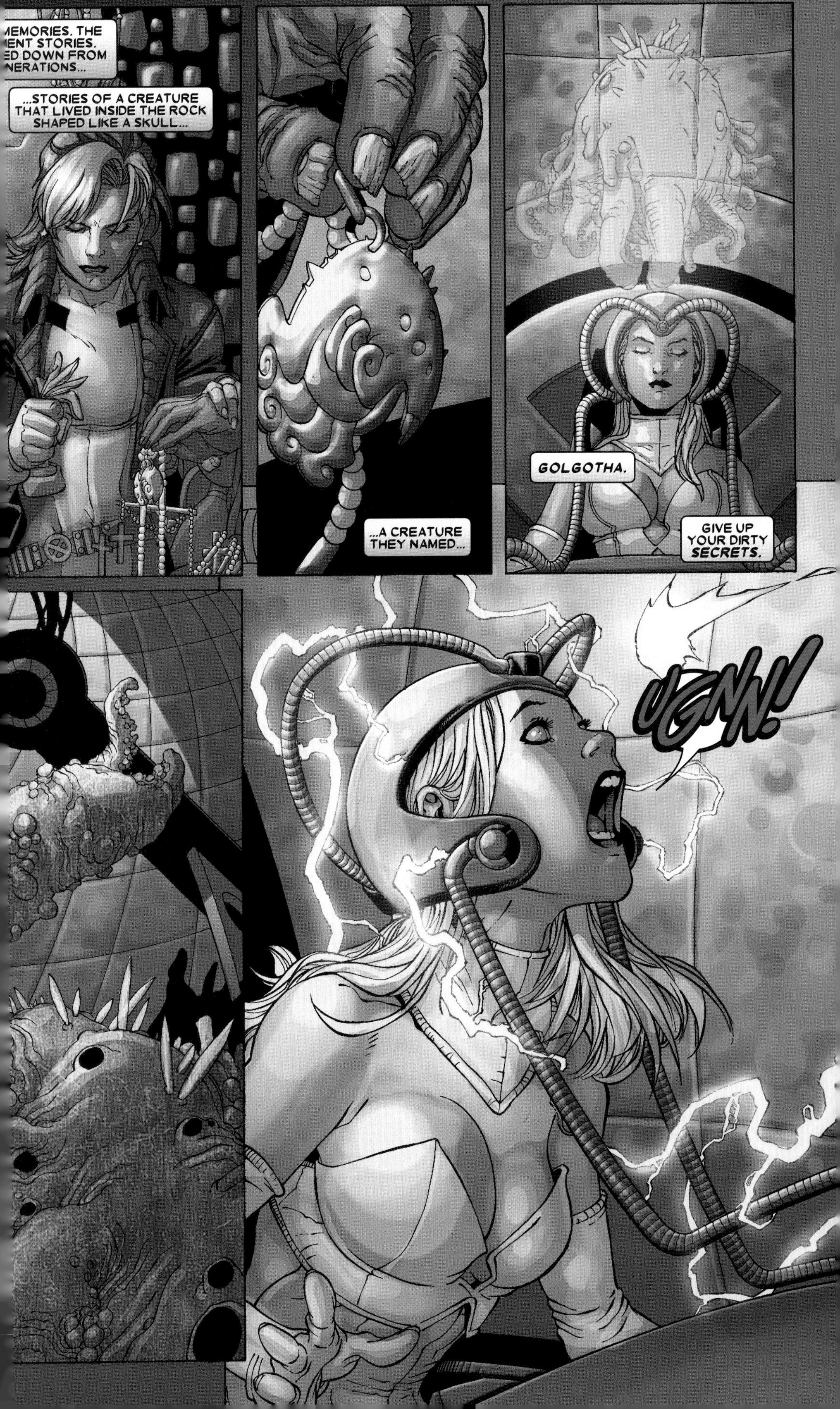

MEMORIES. THE
ENT STORIES.
ED DOWN FROM
NERATIONS...
...STORIES OF A CREATURE THAT LIVED INSIDE THE ROCK SHAPED LIKE A SKULL...
...A CREATURE THEY NAMED...
GOLGOTHA.
GIVE UP YOUR DIRTY SECRETS.
UGNN!

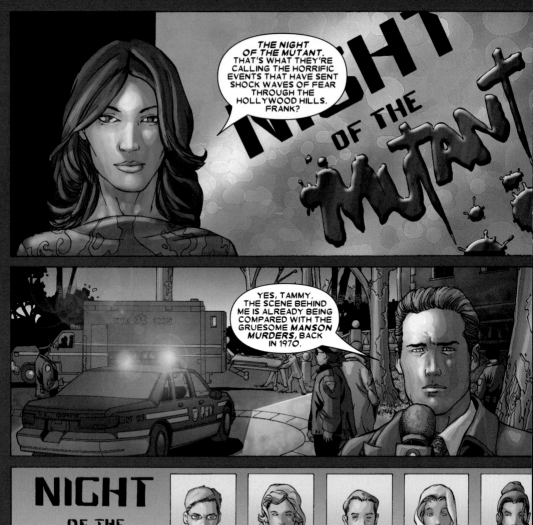

THE NIGHT OF THE MUTANT. THAT'S WHAT THEY'RE CALLING THE HORRIFIC EVENTS THAT HAVE SENT SHOCK WAVES OF FEAR THROUGH THE HOLLYWOOD HILLS. FRANK?

YES, TAMMY. THE SCENE BEHIND ME IS ALREADY BEING COMPARED WITH THE GRUESOME MANSON MURDERS, BACK IN 1970.

**NIGHT OF THE** *MUTANT*

"LAST NIGHT JIM COLLINS, HIS FAMILY AND GUESTS, WERE ALL BRUTALLY SLAIN IN HIS FIVE-MILLION-DOLLAR HOME, ONCE OWNED BY MOVIE LEGEND BURT REYNOLDS.

"POLICE HAVE RELEASED THIS SCENE-OF-THE-CRIME PHOTO FROM INSIDE THE LUXURY ABODE..."

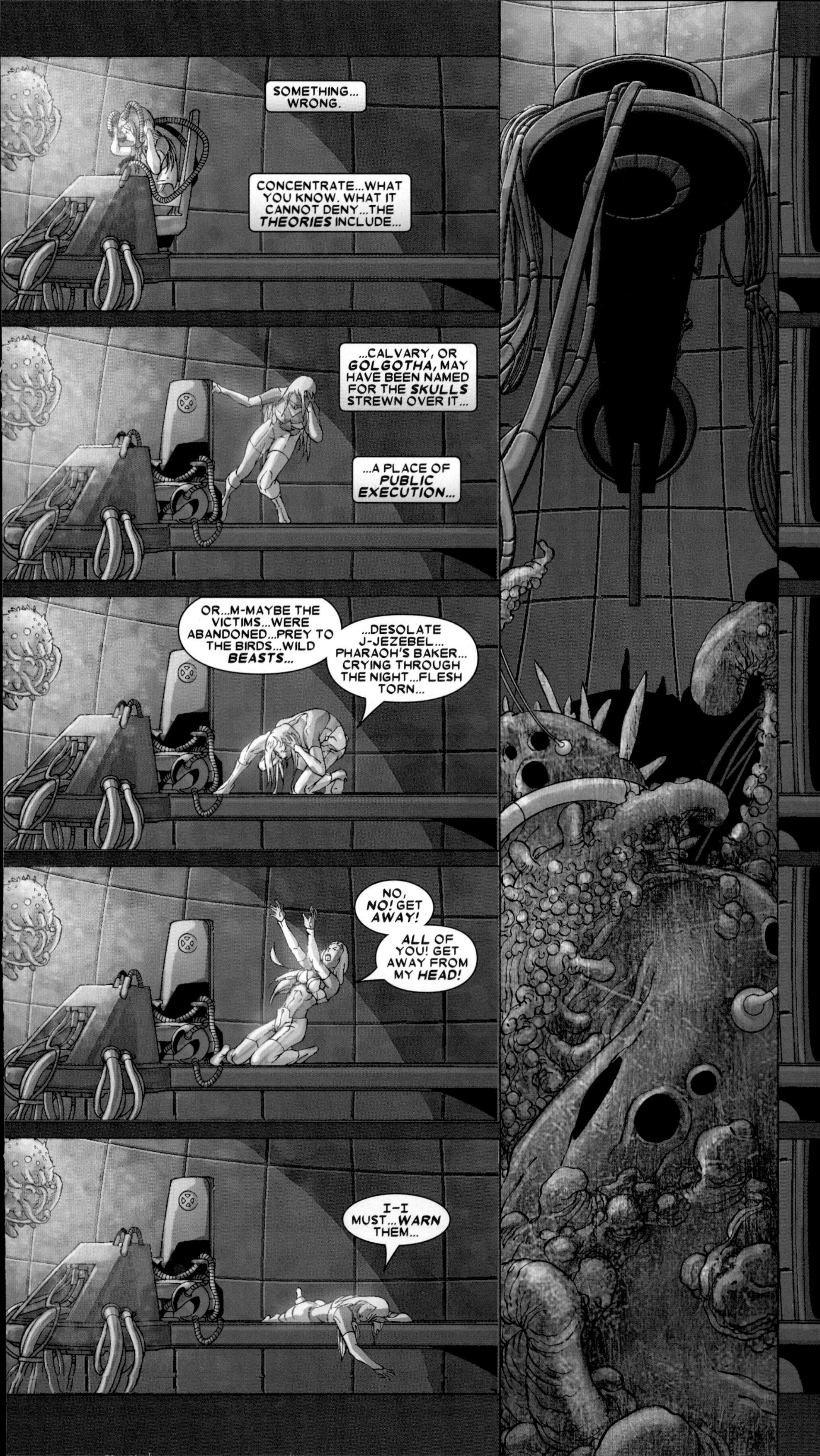
SOMETHING... WRONG.
CONCENTRATE...WHAT YOU KNOW. WHAT IT CANNOT DENY...THE THEORIES INCLUDE...
...CALVARY, OR GOLGOTHA, MAY HAVE BEEN NAMED FOR THE SKULLS STREWN OVER IT...
...A PLACE OF PUBLIC EXECUTION...
OR...M-MAYBE THE VICTIMS...WERE ABANDONED...PREY TO THE BIRDS...WILD BEASTS...
...DESOLATE J-JEZEBEL... PHARAOH'S BAKER... CRYING THROUGH THE NIGHT...FLESH TORN...
NO, NO! GET AWAY!
ALL OF YOU! GET AWAY FROM MY HEAD!
I-I MUST...WARN THEM...

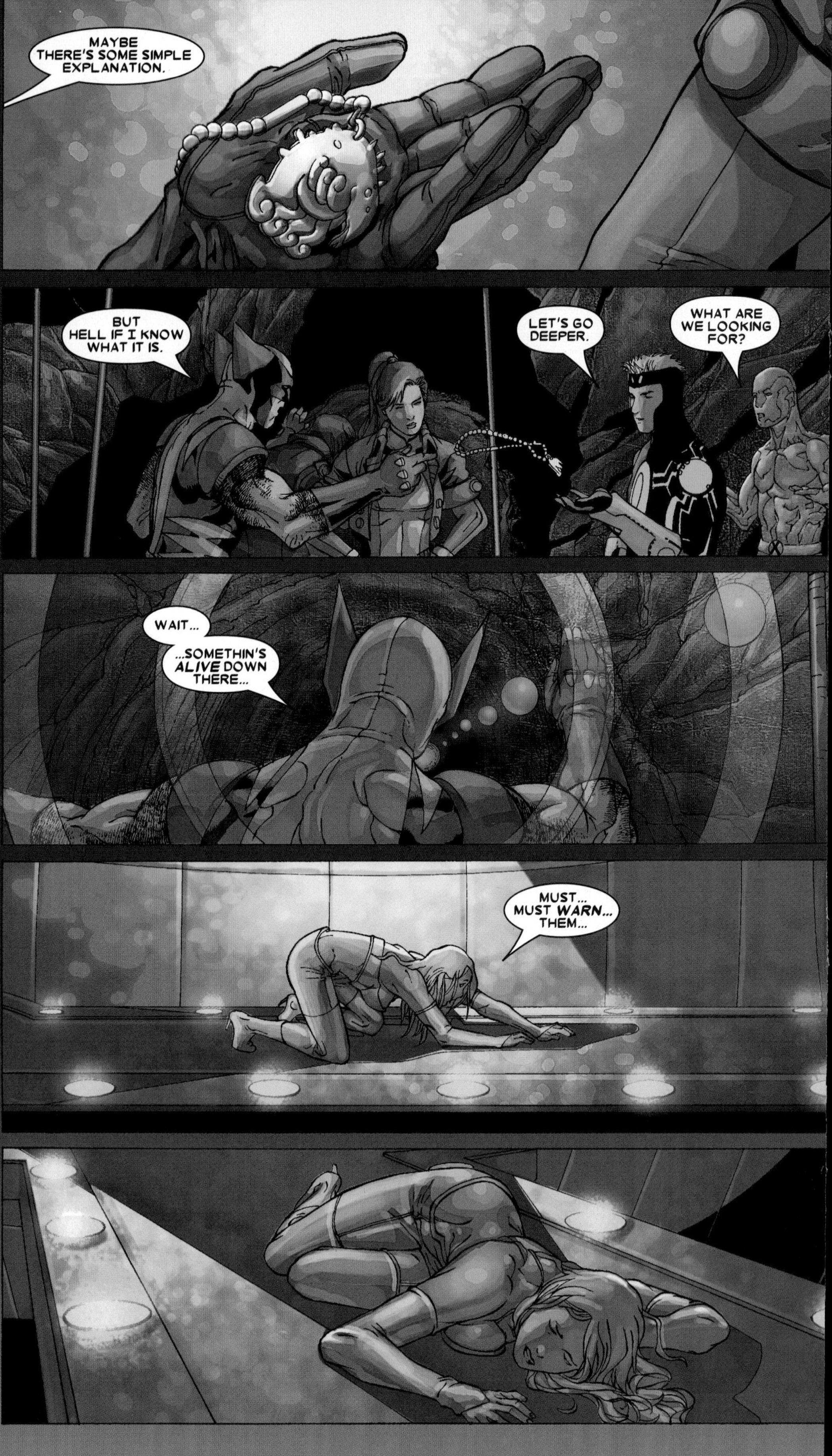
MAYBE THERE'S SOME SIMPLE EXPLANATION.
BUT HELL IF I KNOW WHAT IT IS.
LET'S GO DEEPER.
WHAT ARE WE LOOKING FOR?
WAIT...
...SOMETHIN'S *ALIVE* DOWN THERE...
MUST... MUST *WARN*... THEM...

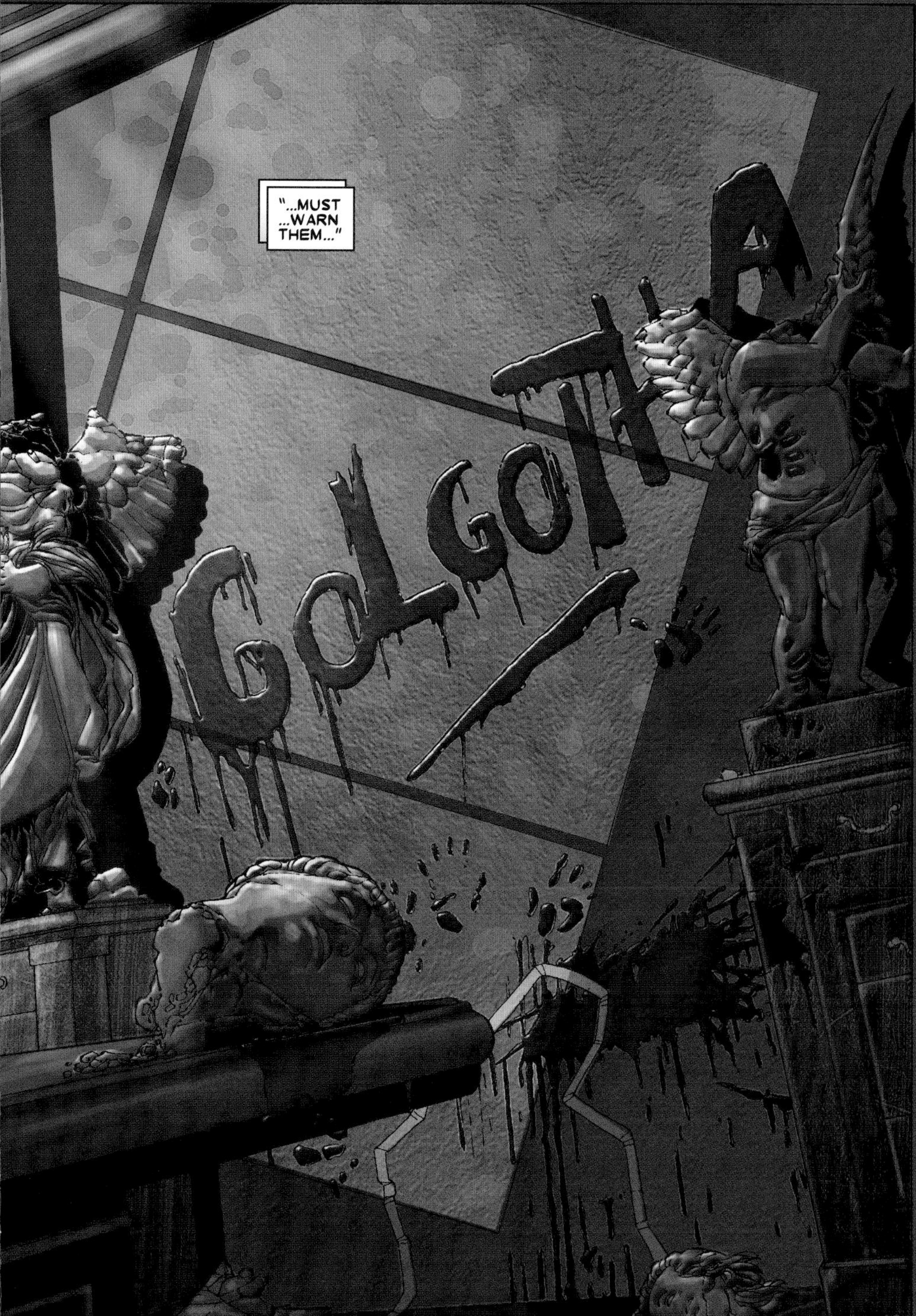
"...MUST ...WARN THEM..."
GOLGOTHA

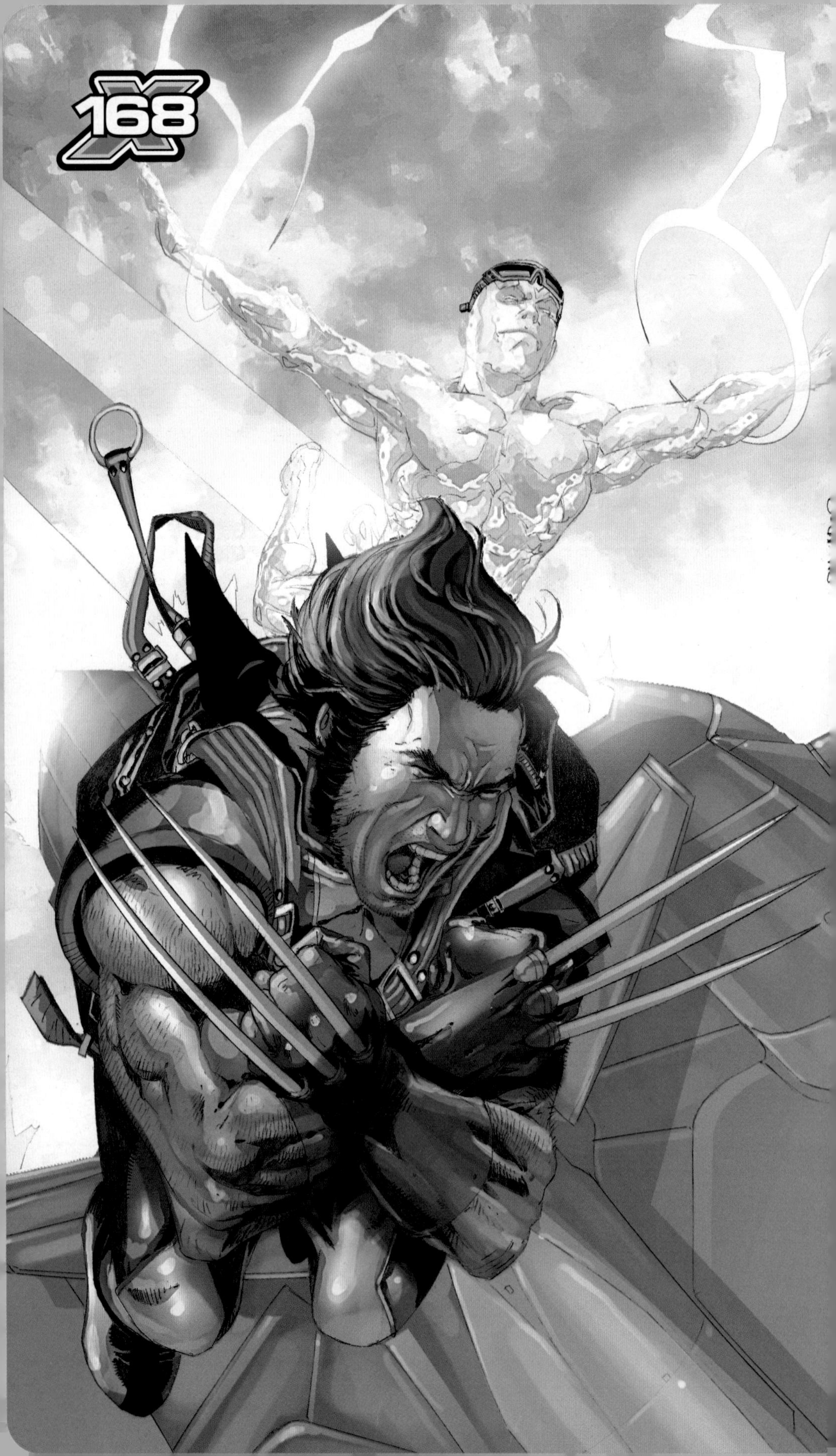
168

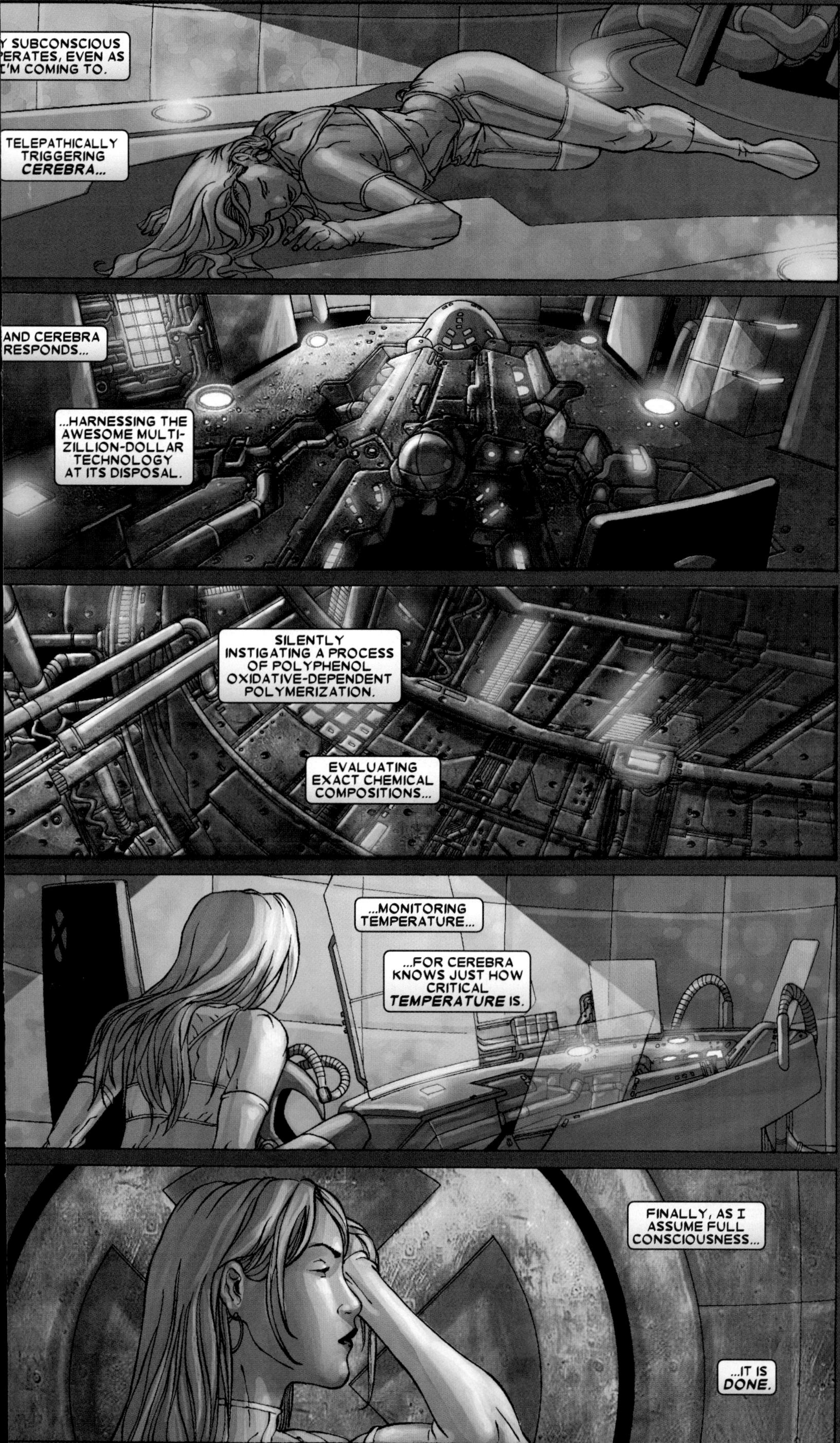

Y SUBCONSCIOUS PERATES, EVEN AS I'M COMING TO.
TELEPATHICALLY TRIGGERING *CEREBRA*...
AND CEREBRA RESPONDS...
...HARNESSING THE AWESOME MULTI-ZILLION-DOLLAR TECHNOLOGY AT ITS DISPOSAL.
SILENTLY INSTIGATING A PROCESS OF POLYPHENOL OXIDATIVE-DEPENDENT POLYMERIZATION.
EVALUATING EXACT CHEMICAL COMPOSITIONS...
...MONITORING TEMPERATURE...
...FOR CEREBRA KNOWS JUST HOW CRITICAL *TEMPERATURE* IS.
FINALLY, AS I ASSUME FULL CONSCIOUSNESS...
...IT IS *DONE*.

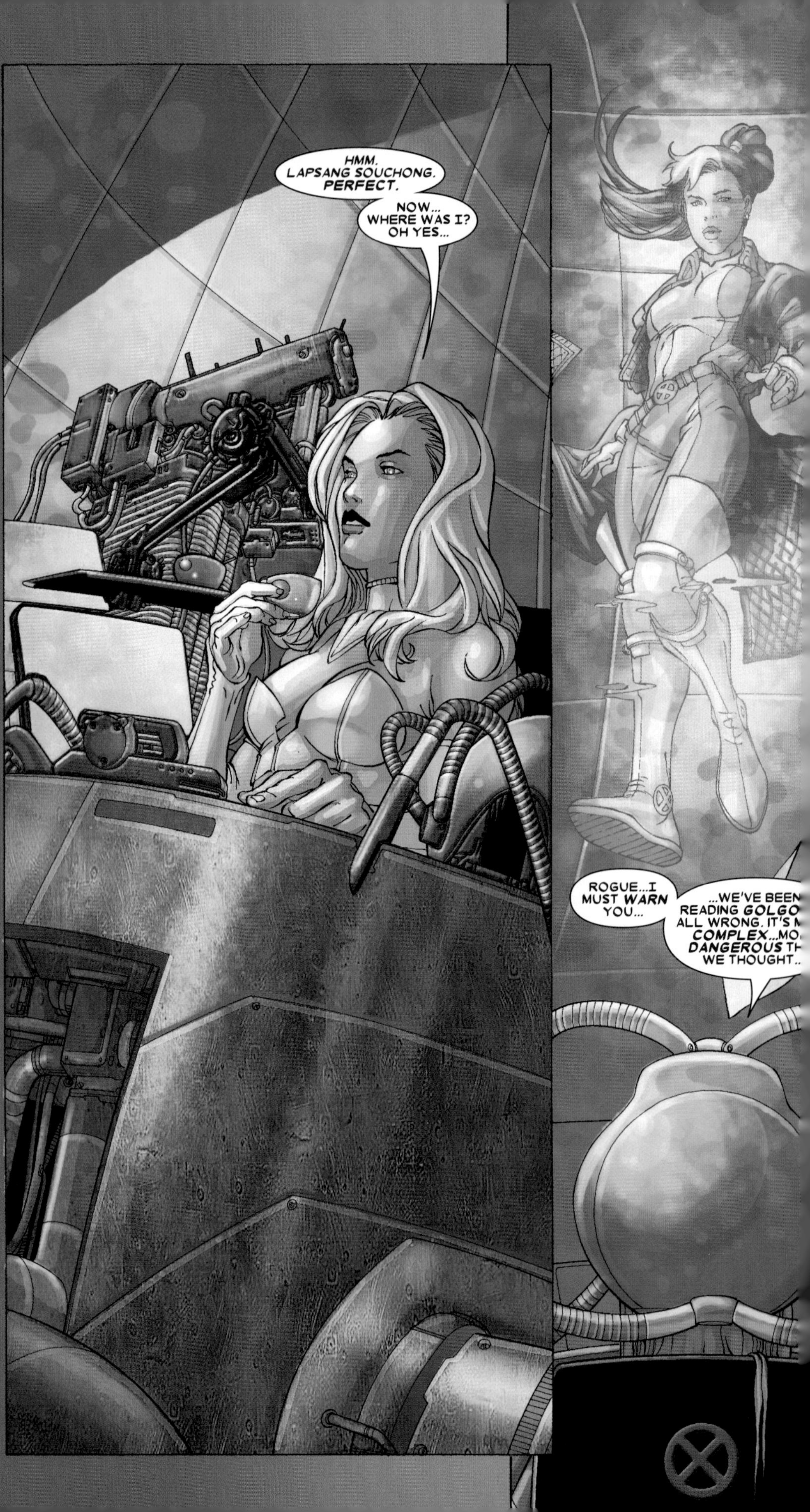
HMM. LAPSANG SOUCHONG. PERFECT.
NOW... WHERE WAS I? OH YES...
ROGUE...I MUST WARN YOU...
...WE'VE BEEN READING GOLGO ALL WRONG. IT'S COMPLEX...DANGEROUS WE THOUGHT...

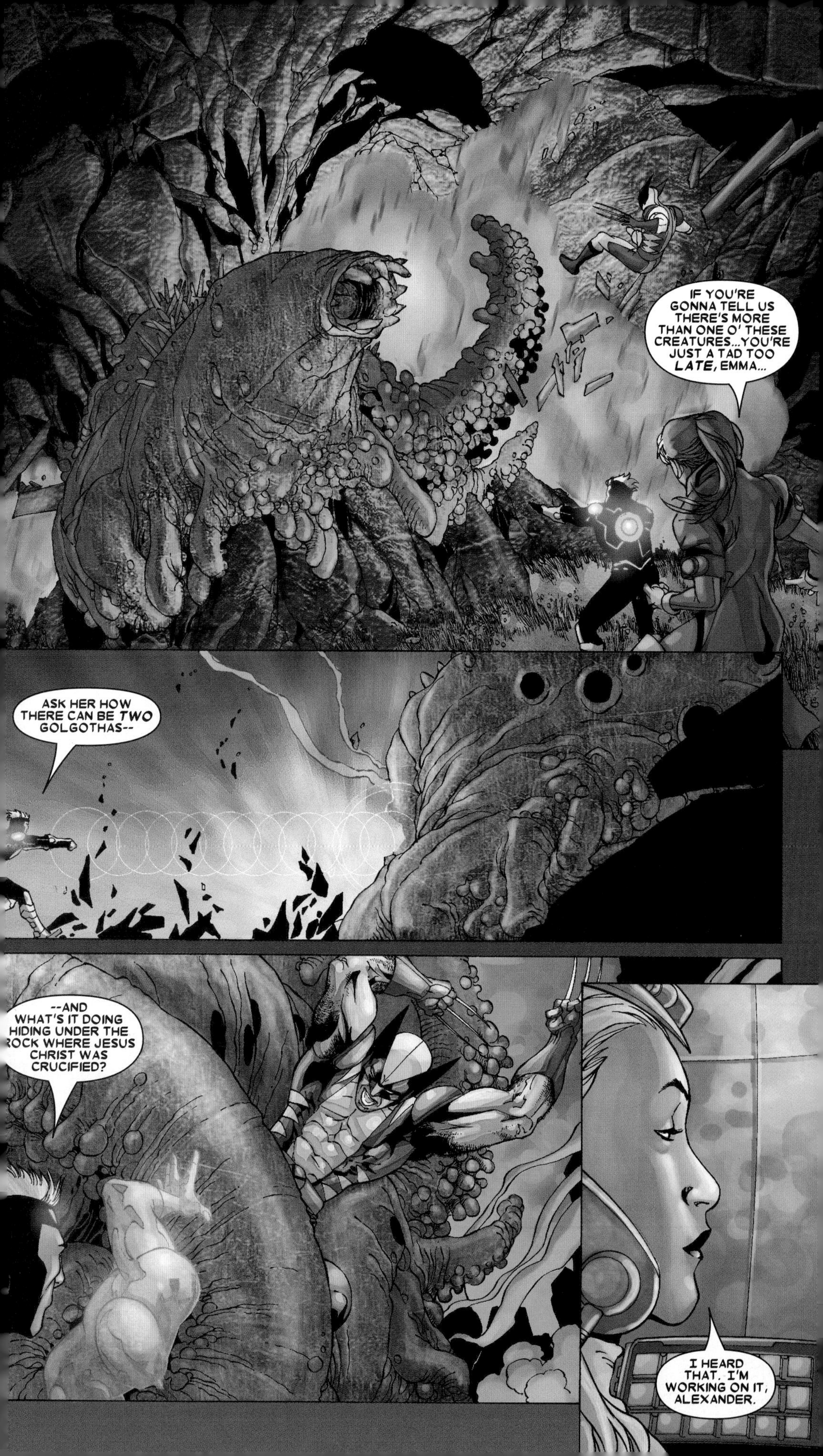
IF YOU'RE GONNA TELL US THERE'S MORE THAN ONE O' THESE CREATURES...YOU'RE JUST A TAD TOO LATE, EMMA...
ASK HER HOW THERE CAN BE TWO GOLGOTHAS--
--AND WHAT'S IT DOING HIDING UNDER THE ROCK WHERE JESUS CHRIST WAS CRUCIFIED?
I HEARD THAT. I'M WORKING ON IT, ALEXANDER.

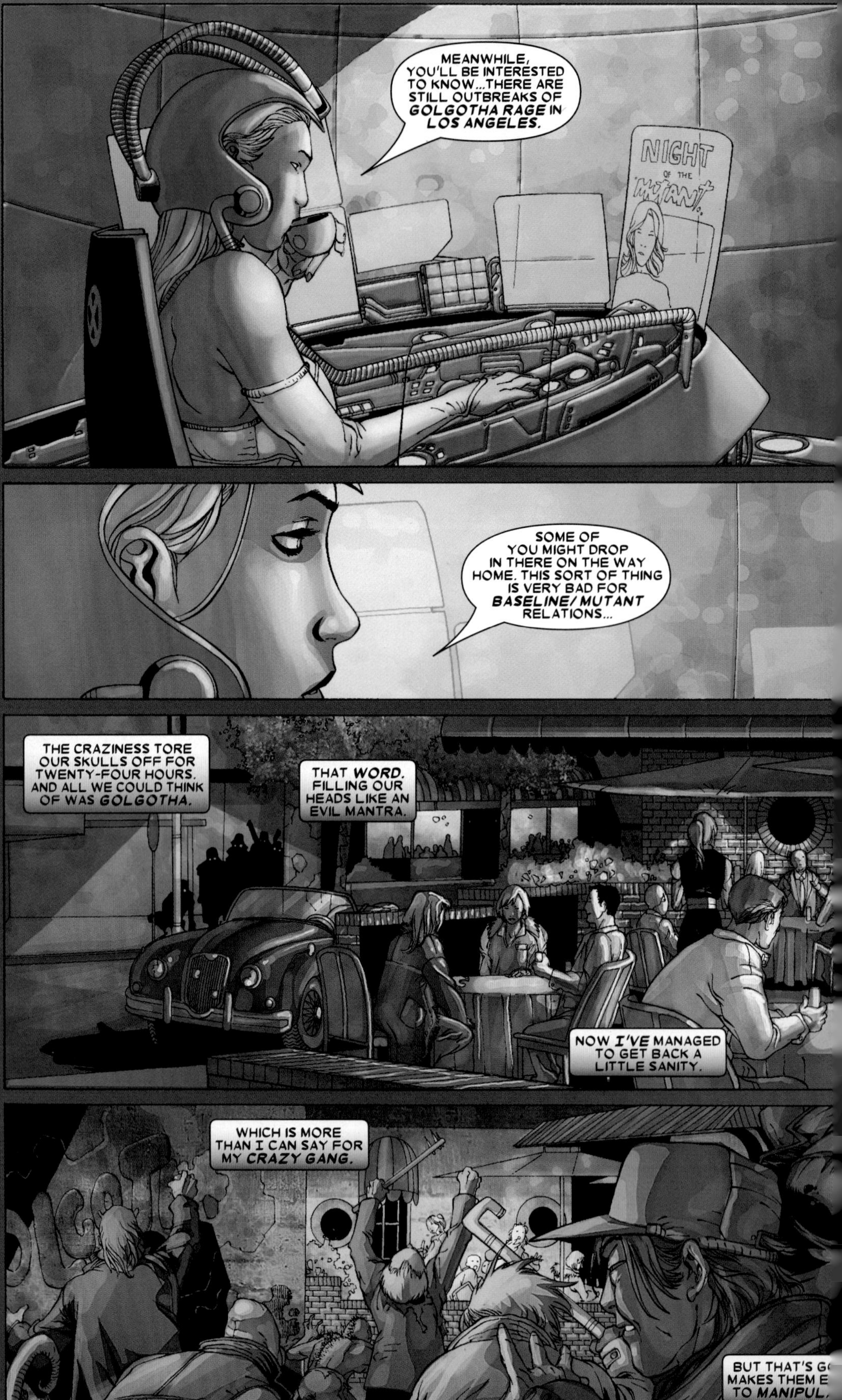

MEANWHILE, YOU'LL BE INTERESTED TO KNOW...THERE ARE STILL OUTBREAKS OF *GOLGOTHA RAGE* IN *LOS ANGELES.*
NIGHT OF THE MUTANT
SOME OF YOU MIGHT DROP IN THERE ON THE WAY HOME. THIS SORT OF THING IS VERY BAD FOR *BASELINE/MUTANT* RELATIONS...
THE CRAZINESS TORE OUR SKULLS OFF FOR TWENTY-FOUR HOURS. AND ALL WE COULD THINK OF WAS *GOLGOTHA.*
THAT *WORD.* FILLING OUR HEADS LIKE AN EVIL MANTRA.
NOW *I'VE* MANAGED TO GET BACK A LITTLE SANITY.
WHICH IS MORE THAN I CAN SAY FOR MY *CRAZY GANG.*
BUT THAT'S G
MAKES THEM E
TO *MANIPUL*

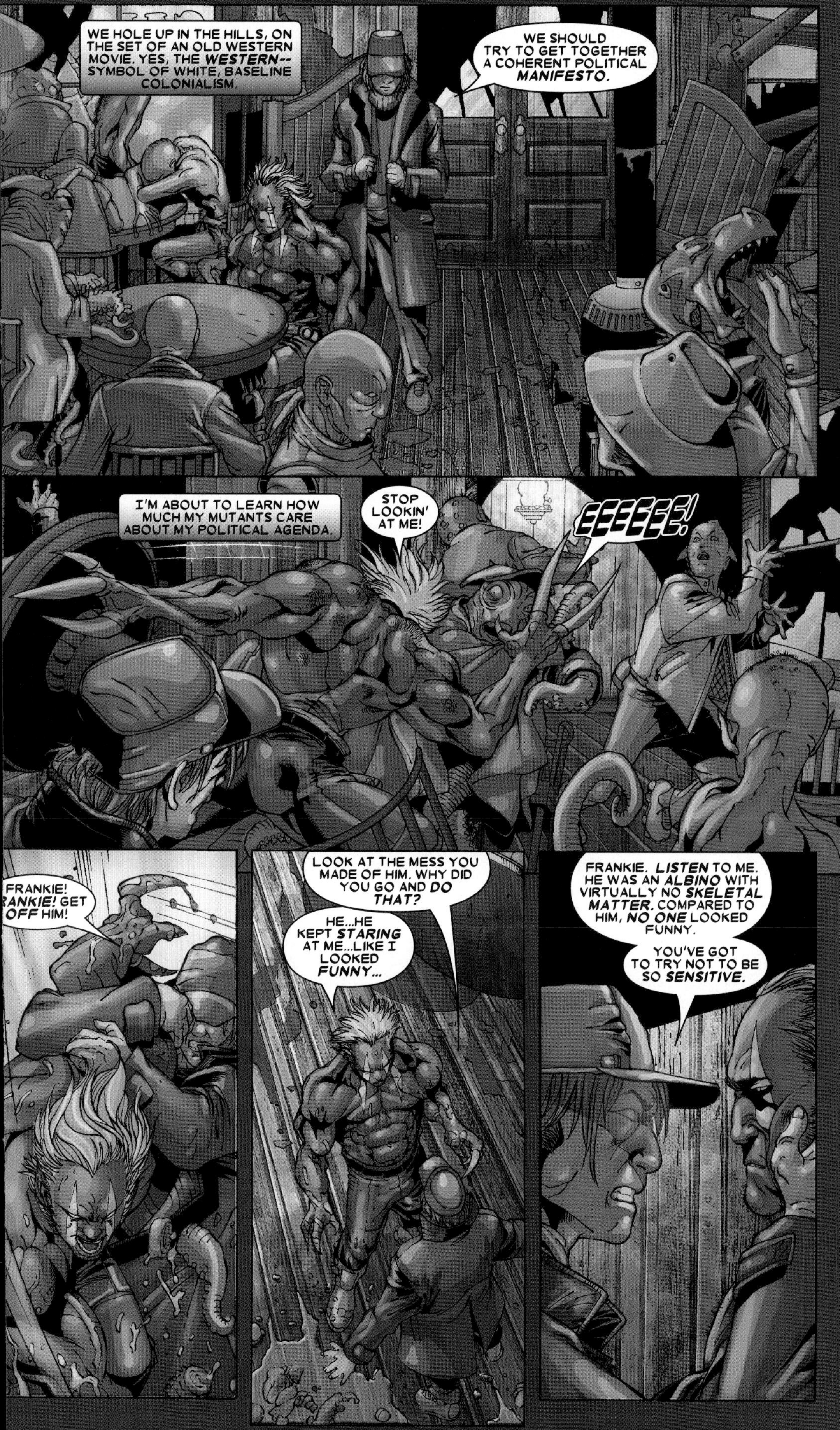
WE HOLE UP IN THE HILLS, ON THE SET OF AN OLD WESTERN MOVIE. YES, THE WESTERN-- SYMBOL OF WHITE, BASELINE COLONIALISM.
WE SHOULD TRY TO GET TOGETHER A COHERENT POLITICAL MANIFESTO.
I'M ABOUT TO LEARN HOW MUCH MY MUTANTS CARE ABOUT MY POLITICAL AGENDA.
STOP LOOKIN' AT ME!
EEEEEE!
FRANKIE! RANKIE! GET OFF HIM!
LOOK AT THE MESS YOU MADE OF HIM. WHY DID YOU GO AND DO THAT?
HE...HE KEPT STARING AT ME...LIKE I LOOKED FUNNY...
FRANKIE. LISTEN TO ME. HE WAS AN ALBINO WITH VIRTUALLY NO SKELETAL MATTER. COMPARED TO HIM, NO ONE LOOKED FUNNY.
YOU'VE GOT TO TRY NOT TO BE SO SENSITIVE.

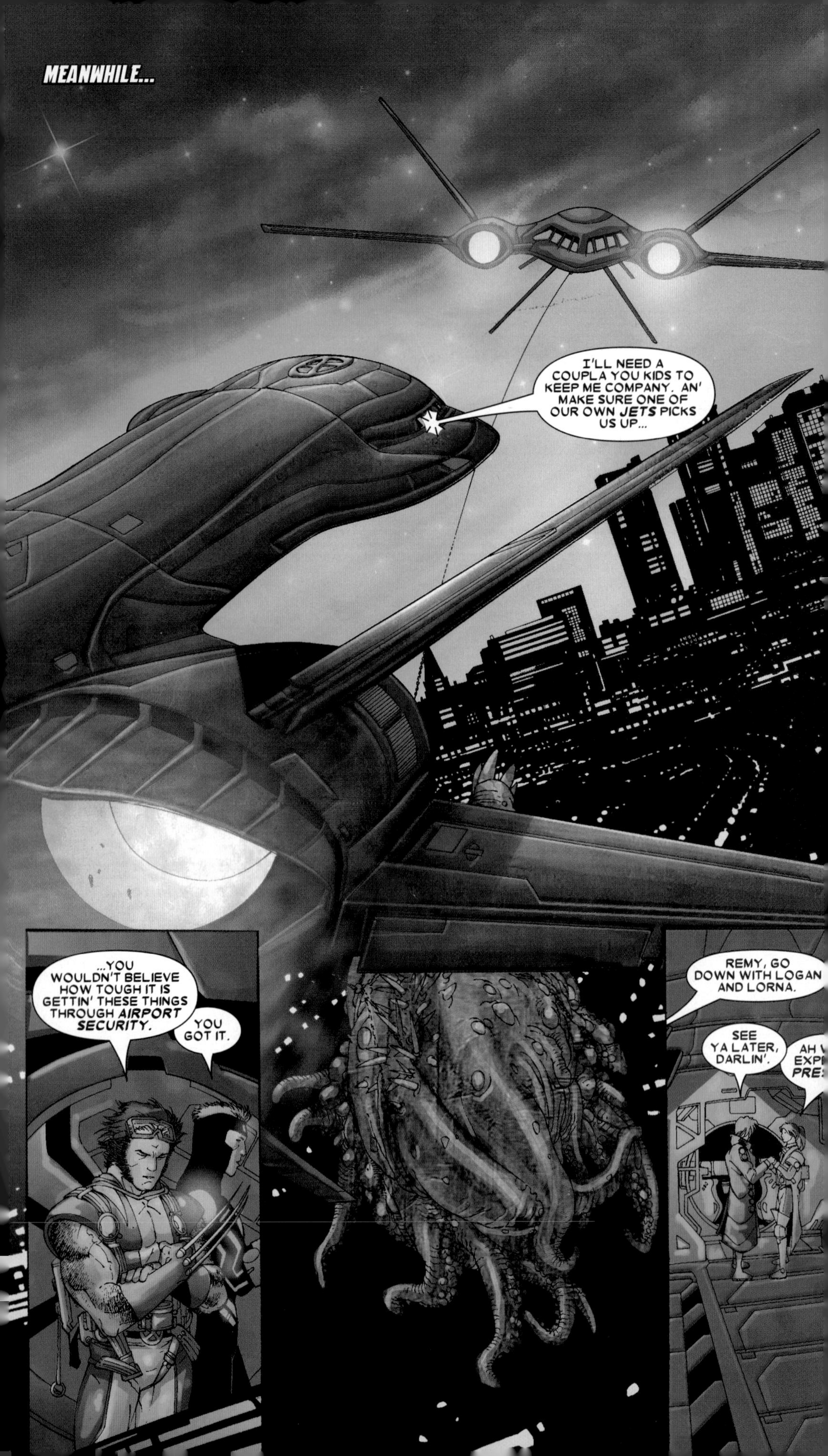

MEANWHILE...
I'LL NEED A COUPLA YOU KIDS TO KEEP ME COMPANY. AN' MAKE SURE ONE OF OUR OWN JETS PICKS US UP...
...YOU WOULDN'T BELIEVE HOW TOUGH IT IS GETTIN' THESE THINGS THROUGH AIRPORT SECURITY.
YOU GOT IT.
REMY, GO DOWN WITH LOGAN AND LORNA.
SEE YA LATER, DARLIN'.

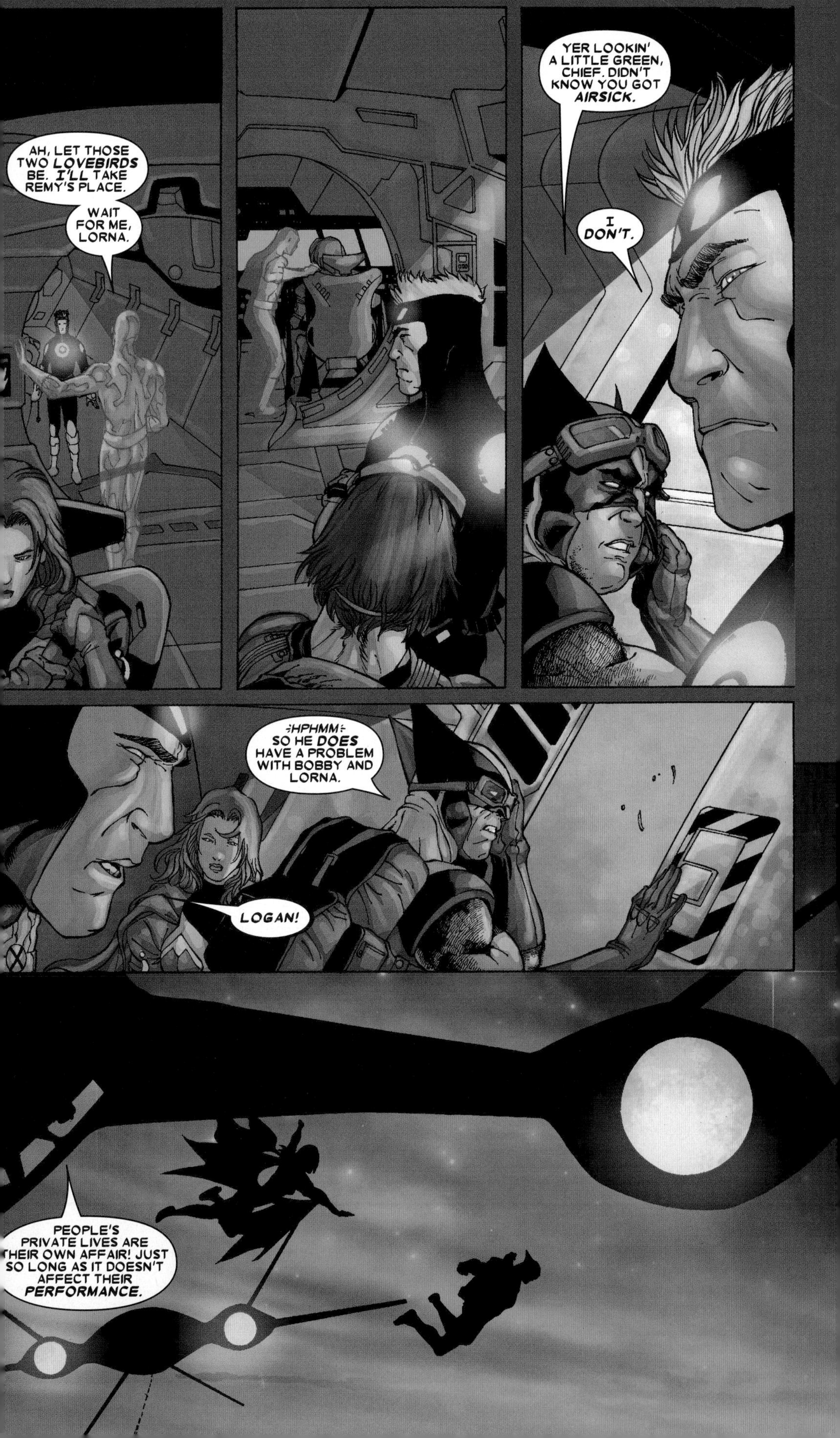
AH, LET THOSE TWO LOVEBIRDS BE. I'LL TAKE REMY'S PLACE.
WAIT FOR ME, LORNA.
YER LOOKIN' A LITTLE GREEN, CHIEF. DIDN'T KNOW YOU GOT AIRSICK.
I DON'T.
HPHMM SO HE DOES HAVE A PROBLEM WITH BOBBY AND LORNA.
LOGAN!
PEOPLE'S PRIVATE LIVES ARE THEIR OWN AFFAIR! JUST SO LONG AS IT DOESN'T AFFECT THEIR PERFORMANCE.

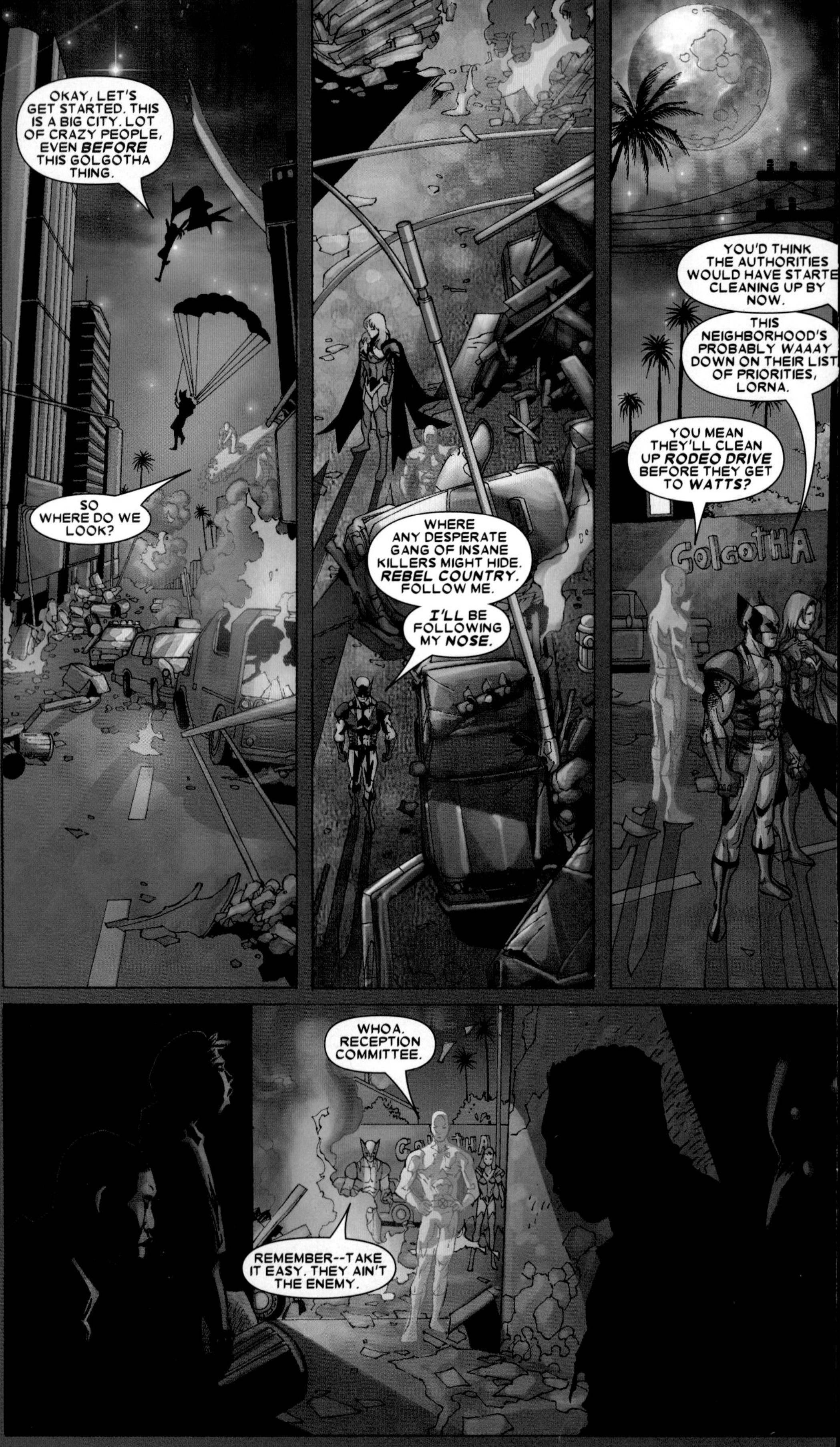
OKAY, LET'S GET STARTED. THIS IS A BIG CITY. LOT OF CRAZY PEOPLE, EVEN BEFORE THIS GOLGOTHA THING.
SO WHERE DO WE LOOK?
WHERE ANY DESPERATE GANG OF INSANE KILLERS MIGHT HIDE. REBEL COUNTRY. FOLLOW ME.
I'LL BE FOLLOWING MY NOSE.
YOU'D THINK THE AUTHORITIES WOULD HAVE STARTE CLEANING UP BY NOW.
THIS NEIGHBORHOOD'S PROBABLY WAAAY DOWN ON THEIR LIST OF PRIORITIES, LORNA.
YOU MEAN THEY'LL CLEAN UP RODEO DRIVE BEFORE THEY GET TO WATTS?
GOLGOTHA
WHOA. RECEPTION COMMITTEE.
REMEMBER--TAKE IT EASY. THEY AIN'T THE ENEMY.

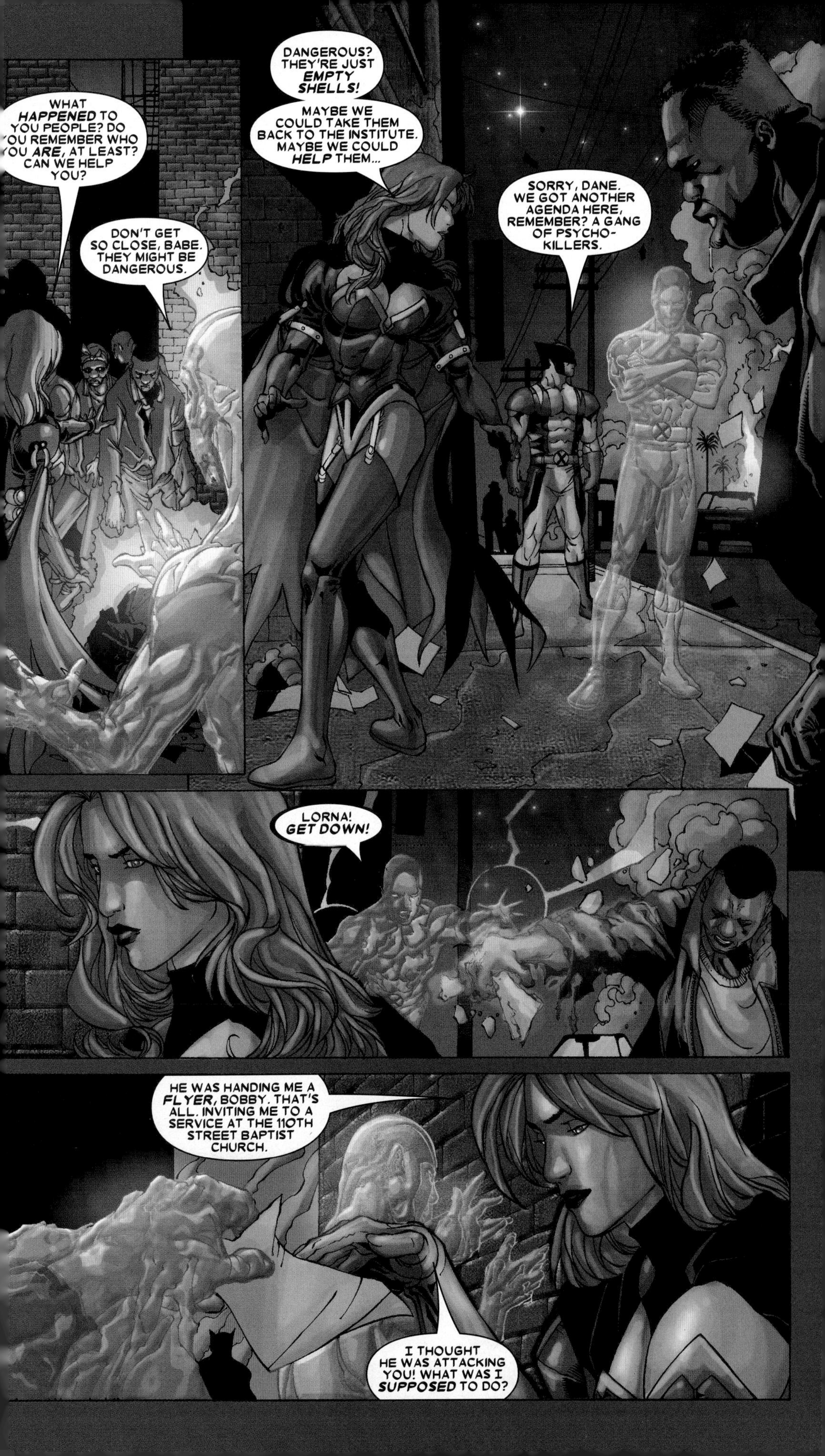
WHAT HAPPENED TO YOU PEOPLE? DO YOU REMEMBER WHO YOU ARE, AT LEAST? CAN WE HELP YOU?
DON'T GET SO CLOSE, BABE. THEY MIGHT BE DANGEROUS.
DANGEROUS? THEY'RE JUST EMPTY SHELLS!
MAYBE WE COULD TAKE THEM BACK TO THE INSTITUTE. MAYBE WE COULD HELP THEM...
SORRY, DANE. WE GOT ANOTHER AGENDA HERE, REMEMBER? A GANG OF PSYCHO-KILLERS.
LORNA! GET DOWN!
HE WAS HANDING ME A FLYER, BOBBY. THAT'S ALL. INVITING ME TO A SERVICE AT THE 110TH STREET BAPTIST CHURCH.
I THOUGHT HE WAS ATTACKING YOU! WHAT WAS I SUPPOSED TO DO?

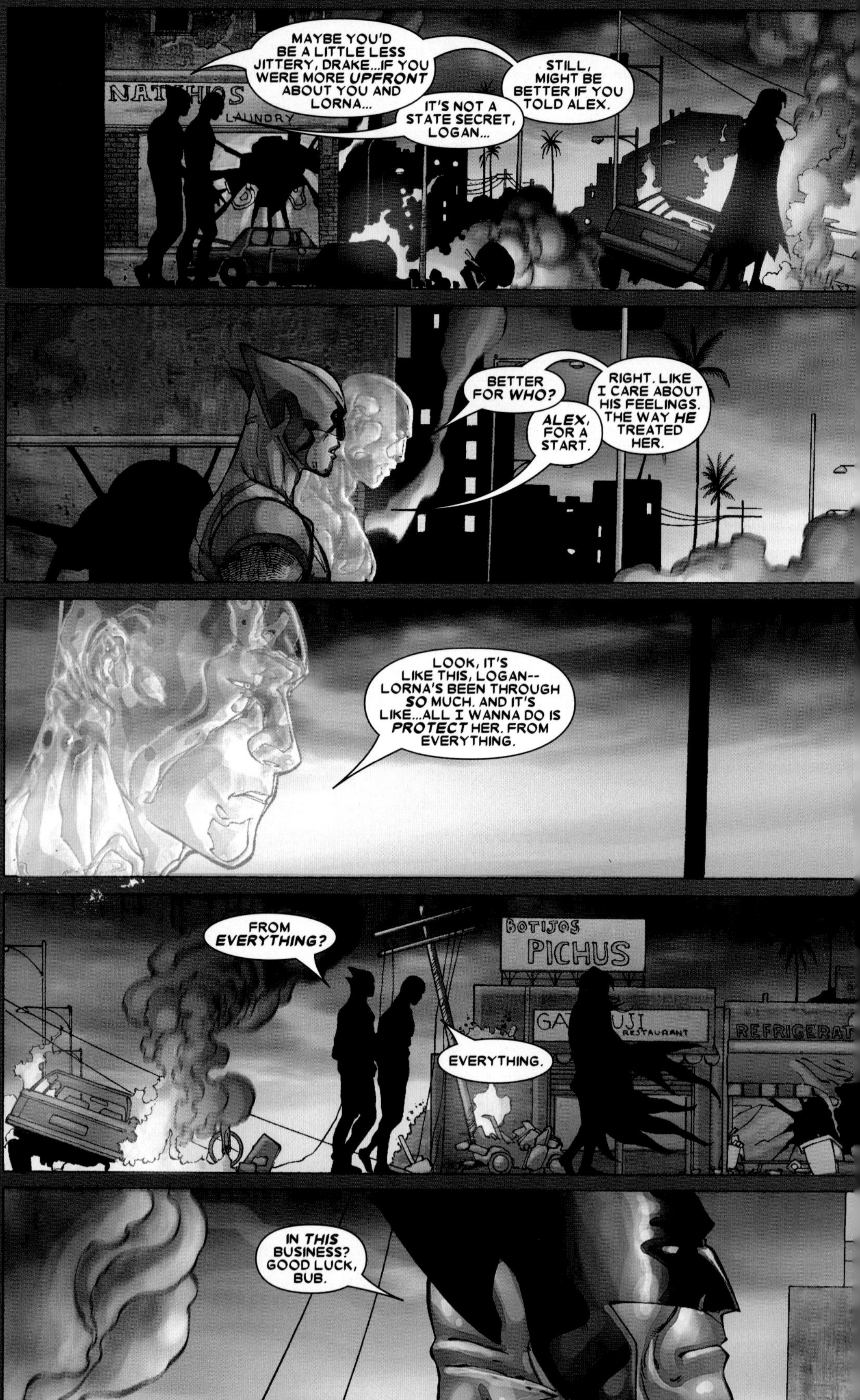
MAYBE YOU'D BE A LITTLE LESS JITTERY, DRAKE...IF YOU WERE MORE UPFRONT ABOUT YOU AND LORNA...
IT'S NOT A STATE SECRET, LOGAN...
STILL, MIGHT BE BETTER IF YOU TOLD ALEX.
NATIJOS
LAUNDRY
BETTER FOR WHO?
ALEX, FOR A START.
RIGHT. LIKE I CARE ABOUT HIS FEELINGS. THE WAY HE TREATED HER.
LOOK, IT'S LIKE THIS, LOGAN-- LORNA'S BEEN THROUGH SO MUCH. AND IT'S LIKE...ALL I WANNA DO IS PROTECT HER. FROM EVERYTHING.
FROM EVERYTHING?
EVERYTHING.
BOTIJOS
PICHUS
RESTAURANT
REFRIGERAT
IN THIS BUSINESS? GOOD LUCK, BUB.

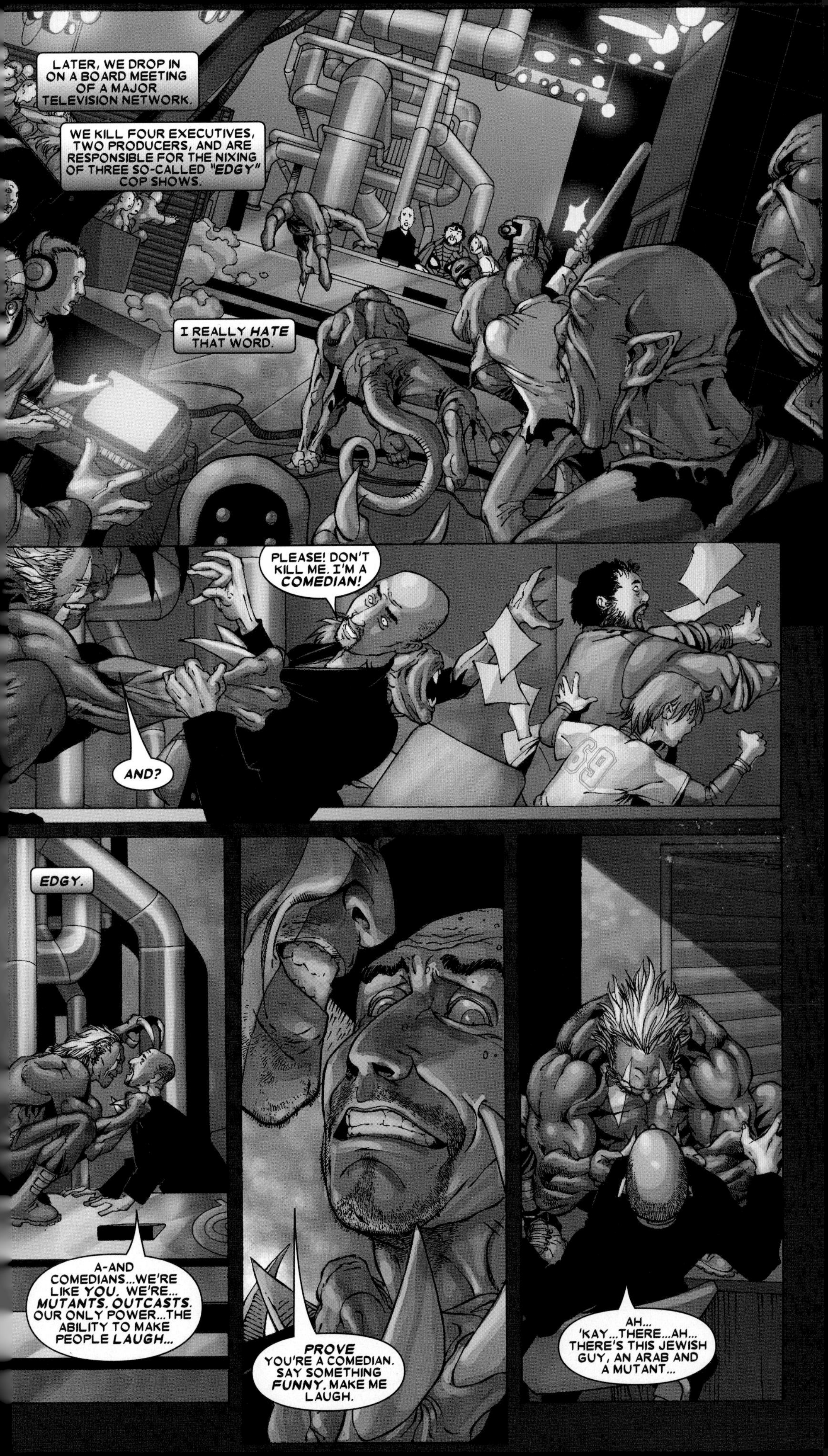
LATER, WE DROP IN ON A BOARD MEETING OF A MAJOR TELEVISION NETWORK.
WE KILL FOUR EXECUTIVES, TWO PRODUCERS, AND ARE RESPONSIBLE FOR THE NIXING OF THREE SO-CALLED "EDGY" COP SHOWS.
I REALLY HATE THAT WORD.
PLEASE! DON'T KILL ME. I'M A COMEDIAN!
AND?
69
EDGY.
A-AND COMEDIANS...WE'RE LIKE YOU. WE'RE... MUTANTS. OUTCASTS. OUR ONLY POWER...THE ABILITY TO MAKE PEOPLE LAUGH...
PROVE YOU'RE A COMEDIAN. SAY SOMETHING FUNNY. MAKE ME LAUGH.
AH... 'KAY...THERE...AH... THERE'S THIS JEWISH GUY, AN ARAB AND A MUTANT...

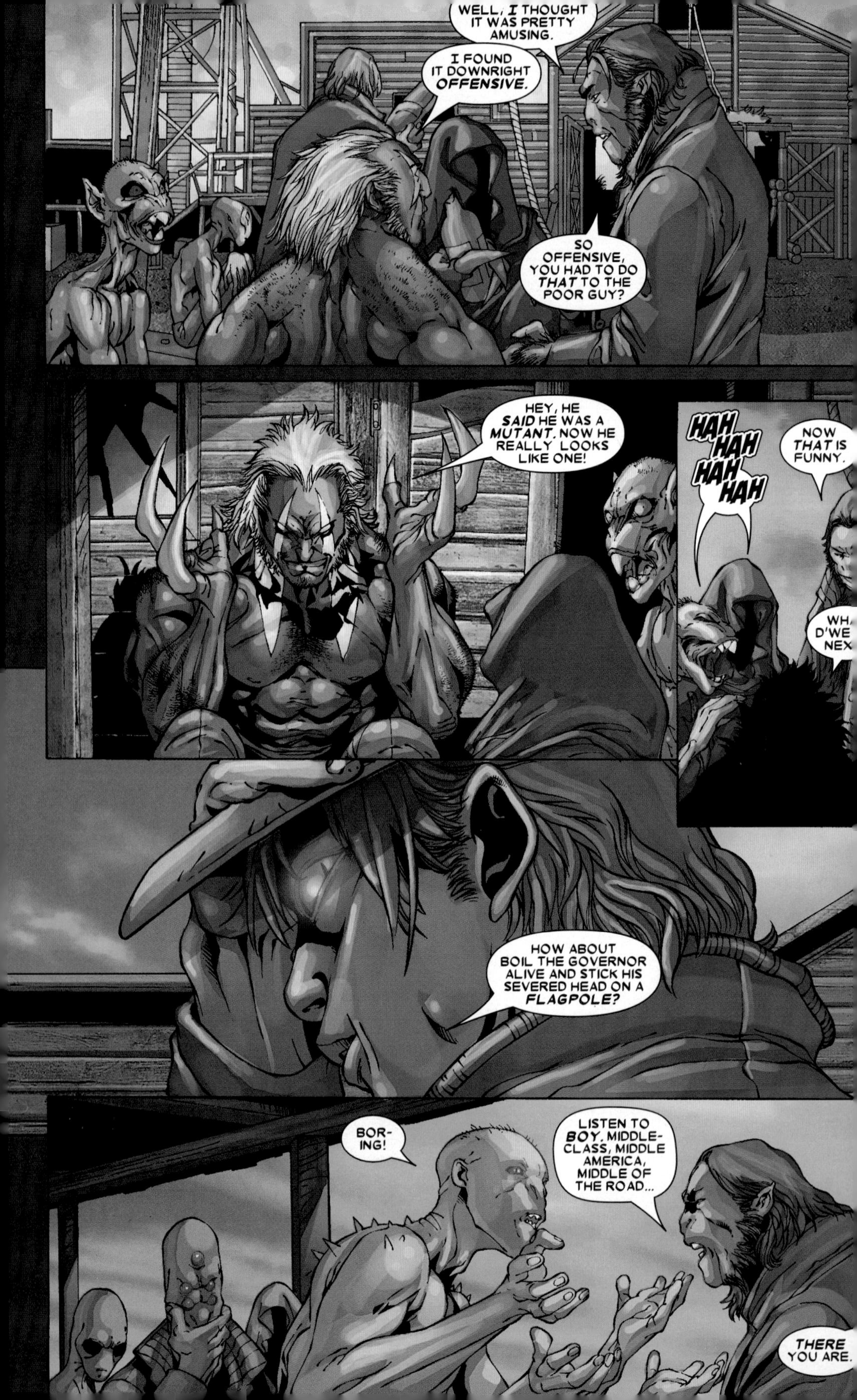

WELL, I THOUGHT IT WAS PRETTY AMUSING.
I FOUND IT DOWNRIGHT OFFENSIVE.
SO OFFENSIVE, YOU HAD TO DO THAT TO THE POOR GUY?
HEY, HE SAID HE WAS A MUTANT. NOW HE REALLY LOOKS LIKE ONE!
HAH HAH HAH HAH
NOW THAT IS FUNNY.
WH D'WE NEX
HOW ABOUT BOIL THE GOVERNOR ALIVE AND STICK HIS SEVERED HEAD ON A FLAGPOLE?
BOR-ING!
LISTEN TO BOY. MIDDLE-CLASS, MIDDLE AMERICA, MIDDLE OF THE ROAD...
THERE YOU ARE.

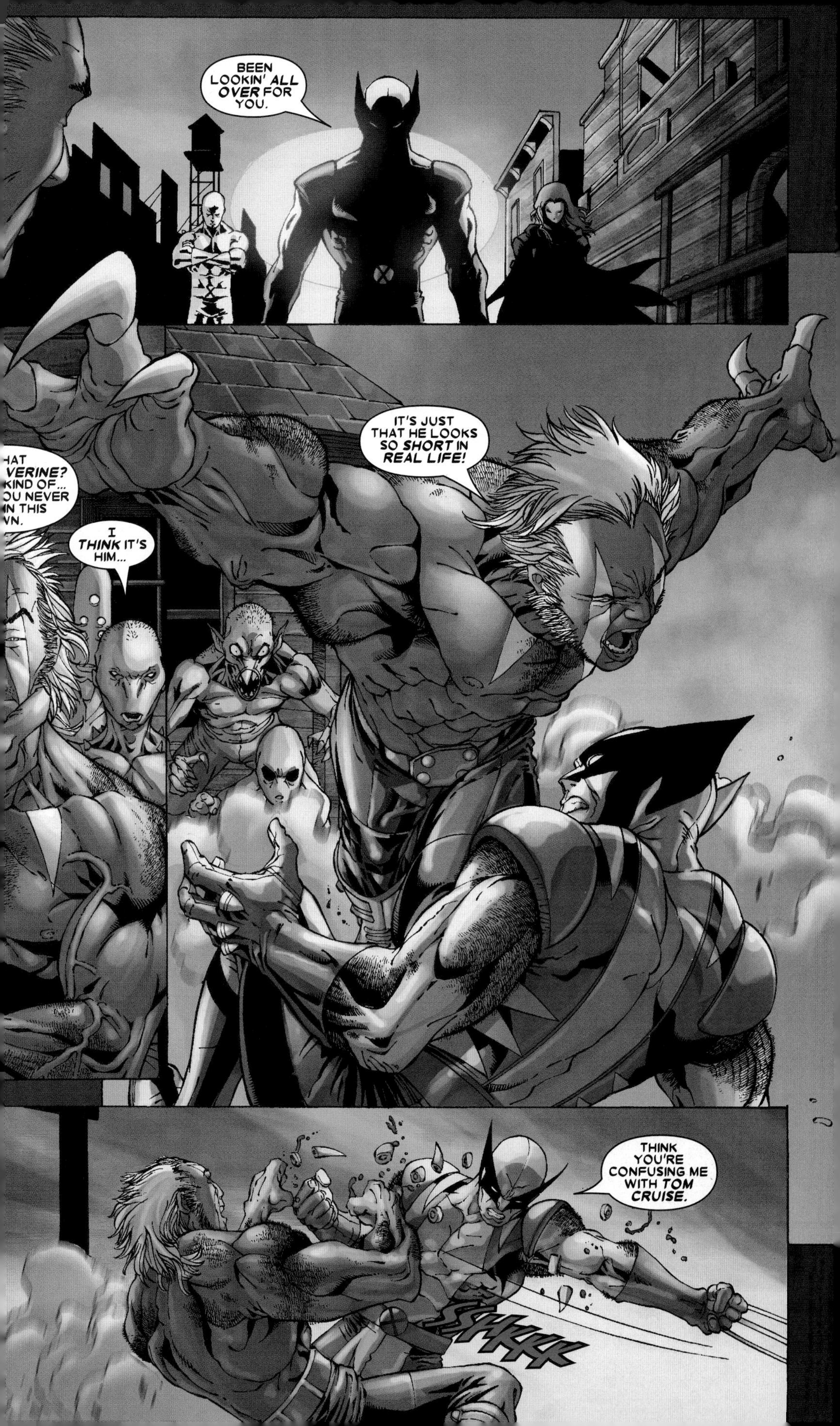
BEEN LOOKIN' ALL OVER FOR YOU.
I THINK IT'S HIM...
IT'S JUST THAT HE LOOKS SO SHORT IN REAL LIFE!
THINK YOU'RE CONFUSING ME WITH TOM CRUISE.
SSHKKK

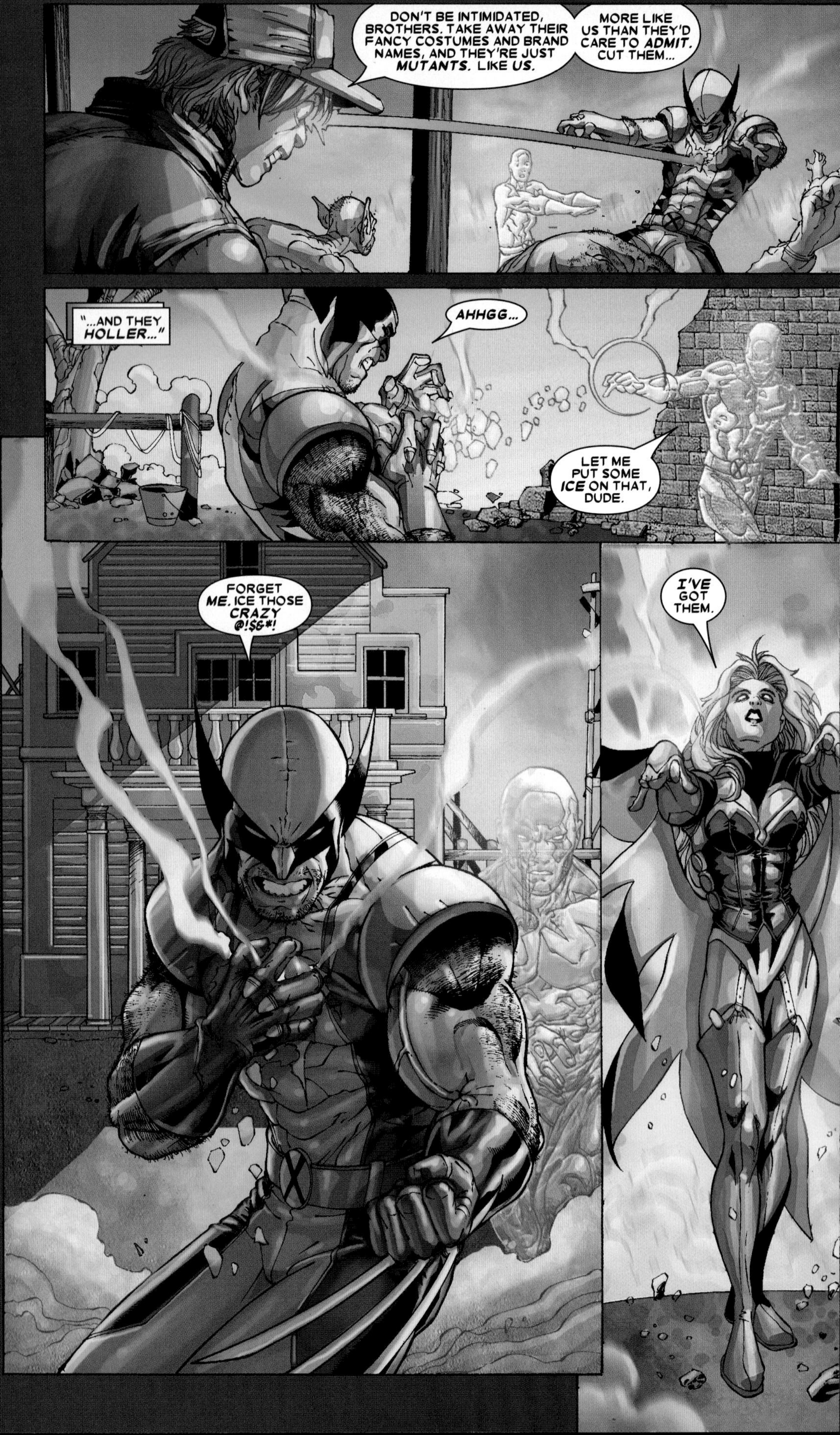
DON'T BE INTIMIDATED, BROTHERS. TAKE AWAY THEIR FANCY COSTUMES AND BRAND NAMES, AND THEY'RE JUST MUTANTS. LIKE US.
MORE LIKE US THAN THEY'D CARE TO ADMIT. CUT THEM...
"...AND THEY HOLLER..."
AHHGG...
LET ME PUT SOME ICE ON THAT, DUDE.
FORGET ME. ICE THOSE CRAZY @!$&*!
I'VE GOT THEM.

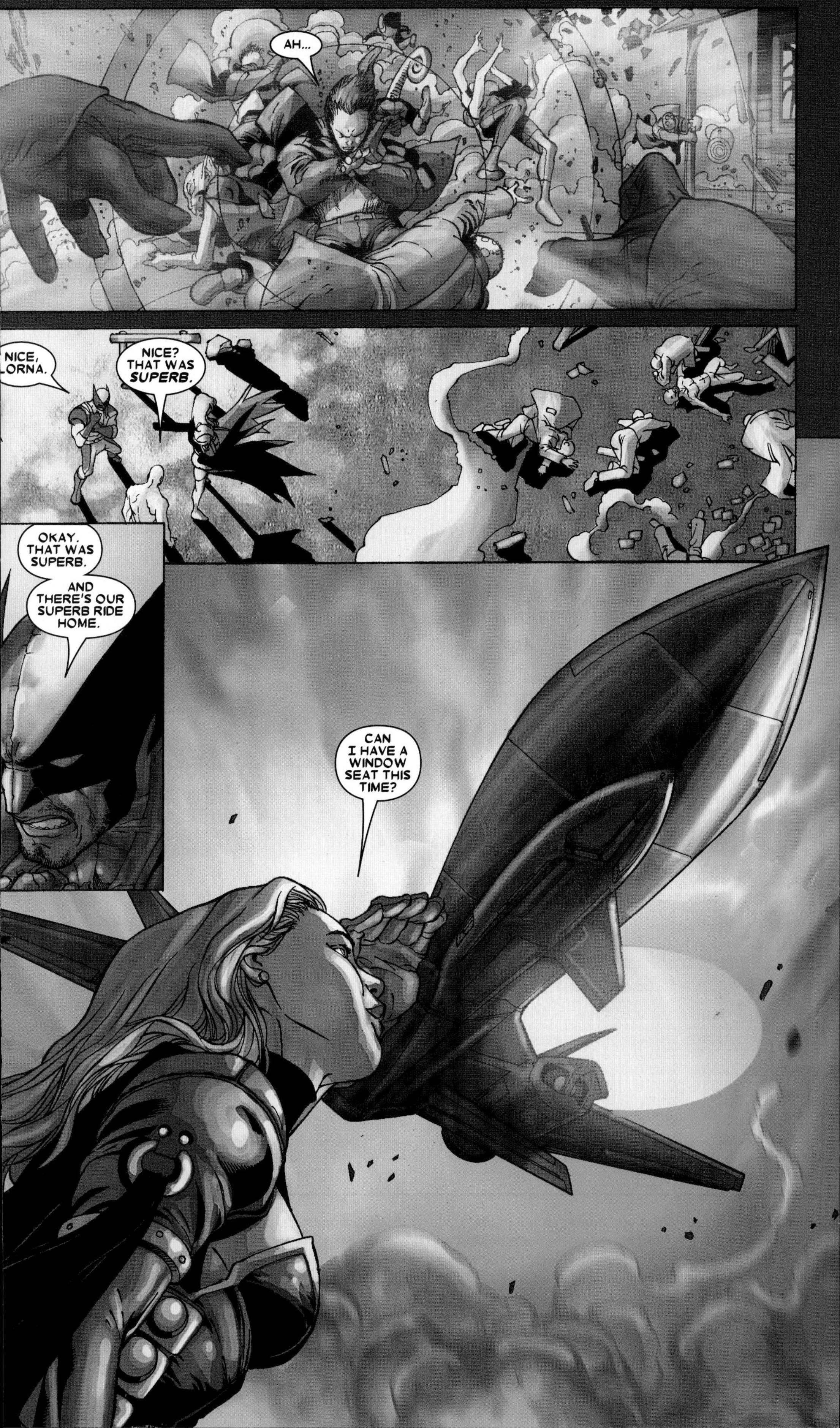
AH...
NICE, LORNA.
NICE? THAT WAS *SUPERB.*
OKAY. THAT WAS SUPERB.
AND THERE'S OUR SUPERB RIDE HOME.
CAN I HAVE A WINDOW SEAT THIS TIME?

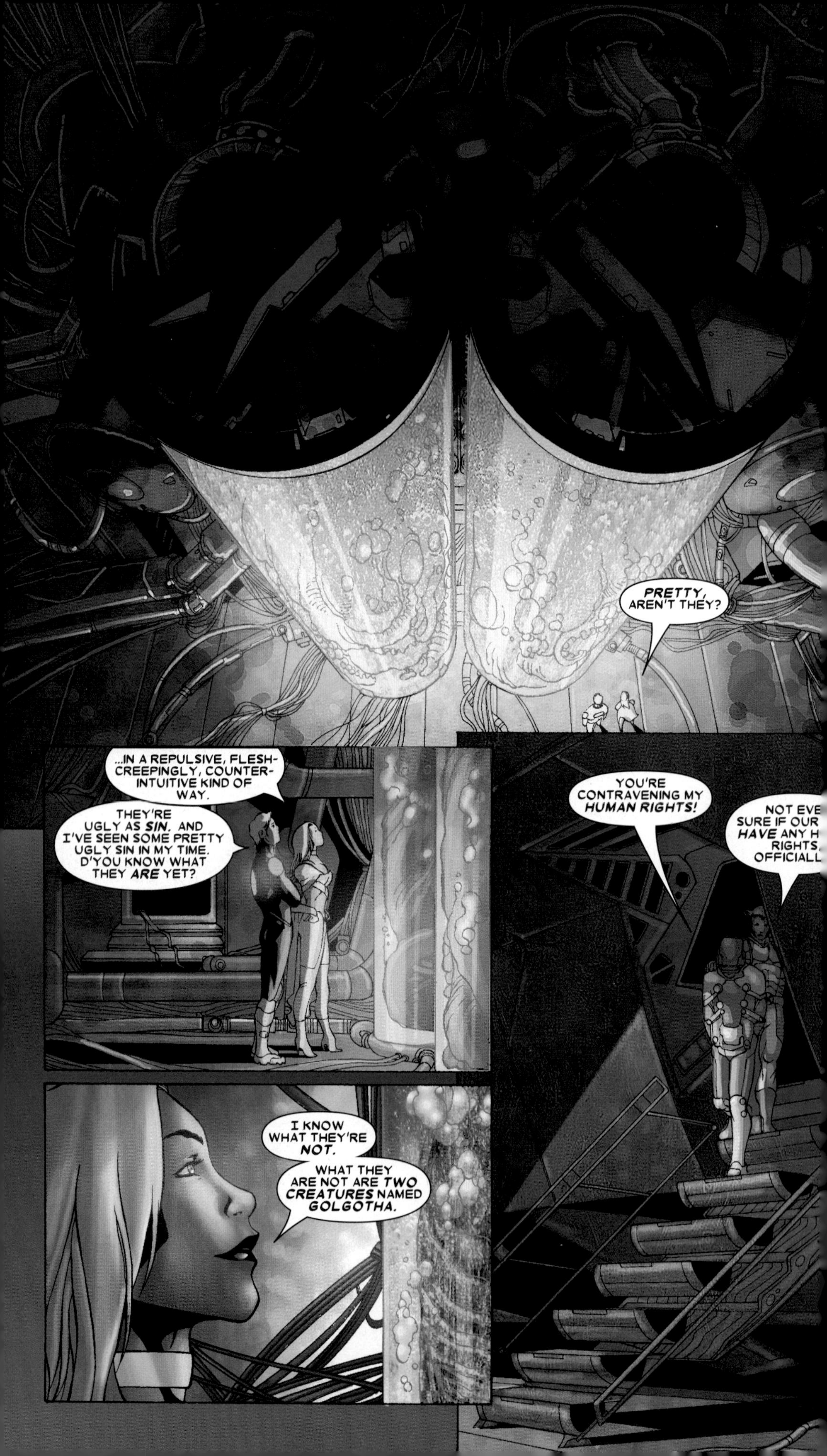
PRETTY, AREN'T THEY?
...IN A REPULSIVE, FLESH-CREEPINGLY, COUNTER-INTUITIVE KIND OF WAY.
THEY'RE UGLY AS SIN. AND I'VE SEEN SOME PRETTY UGLY SIN IN MY TIME. D'YOU KNOW WHAT THEY ARE YET?
I KNOW WHAT THEY'RE NOT.
WHAT THEY ARE NOT ARE TWO CREATURES NAMED GOLGOTHA.
YOU'RE CONTRAVENING MY HUMAN RIGHTS!

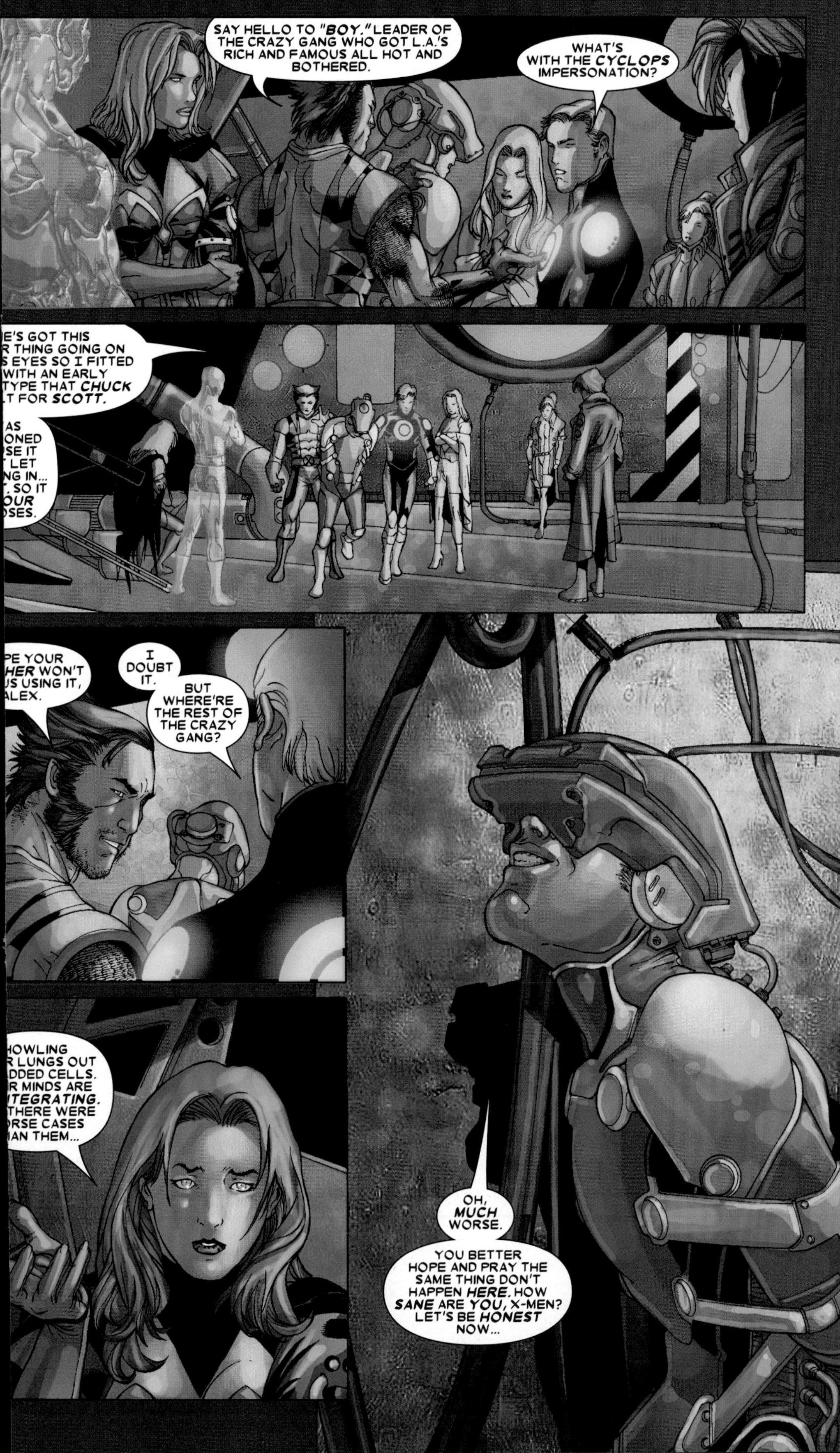
SAY HELLO TO "BOY," LEADER OF THE CRAZY GANG WHO GOT L.A.'S RICH AND FAMOUS ALL HOT AND BOTHERED.
WHAT'S WITH THE CYCLOPS IMPERSONATION?
GOT THIS THING GOING ON EYES SO I FITTED WITH AN EARLY TYPE THAT CHUCK FOR SCOTT.
WON'T USING IT, ALEX.
I DOUBT IT.
BUT WHERE'RE THE REST OF THE CRAZY GANG?
HOWLING LUNGS OUT CELLS. MINDS ARE THERE WERE CASES THEM...
OH, MUCH WORSE.
YOU BETTER HOPE AND PRAY THE SAME THING DON'T HAPPEN HERE. HOW SANE ARE YOU, X-MEN? LET'S BE HONEST NOW...

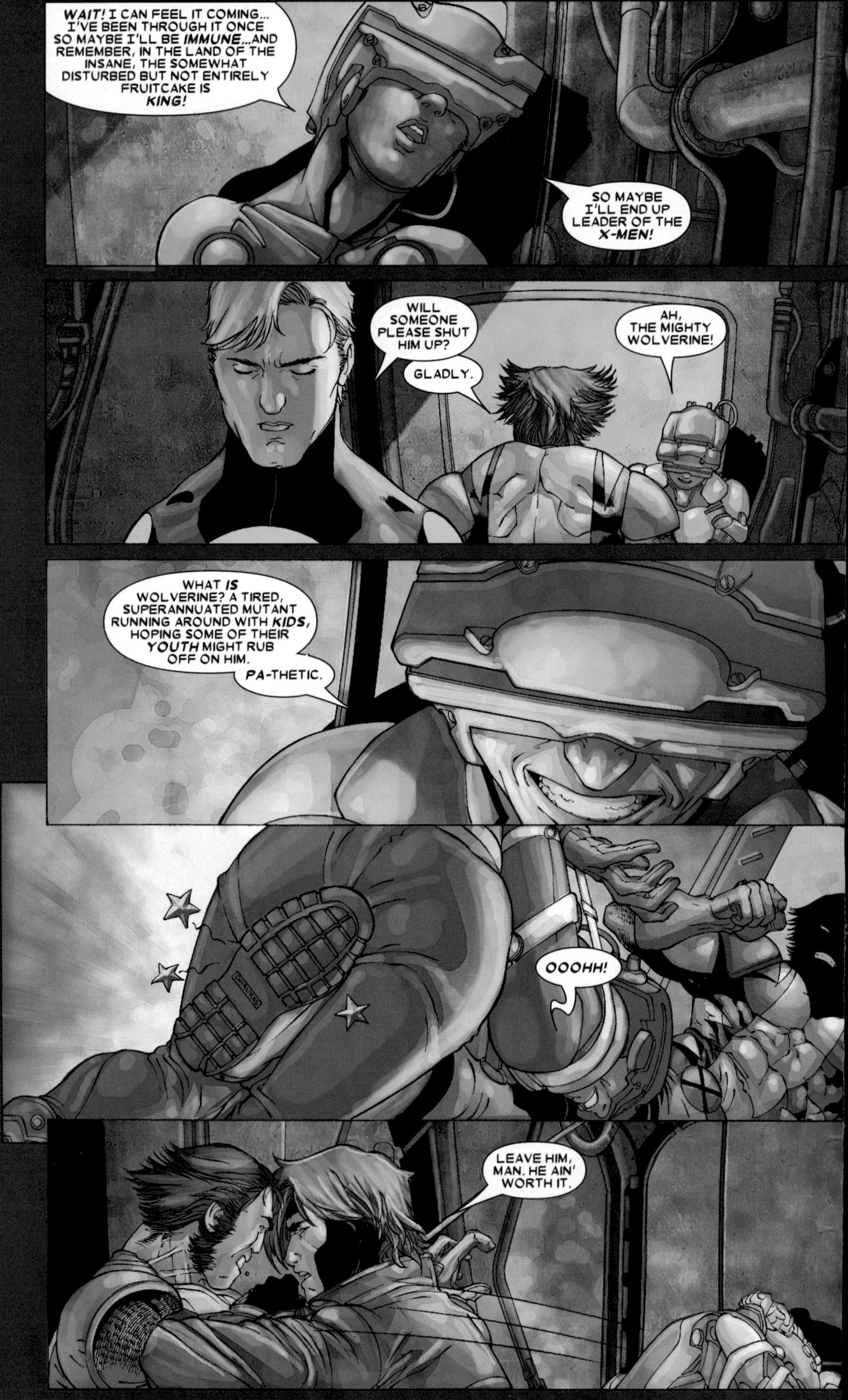
WAIT! I CAN FEEL IT COMING... I'VE BEEN THROUGH IT ONCE SO MAYBE I'LL BE IMMUNE...AND REMEMBER, IN THE LAND OF THE INSANE, THE SOMEWHAT DISTURBED BUT NOT ENTIRELY FRUITCAKE IS KING!
SO MAYBE I'LL END UP LEADER OF THE X-MEN!
WILL SOMEONE PLEASE SHUT HIM UP?
GLADLY.
AH, THE MIGHTY WOLVERINE!
WHAT IS WOLVERINE? A TIRED, SUPERANNUATED MUTANT RUNNING AROUND WITH KIDS, HOPING SOME OF THEIR YOUTH MIGHT RUB OFF ON HIM.
PA-THETIC.
OOOHH!
LEAVE HIM, MAN. HE AIN' WORTH IT.

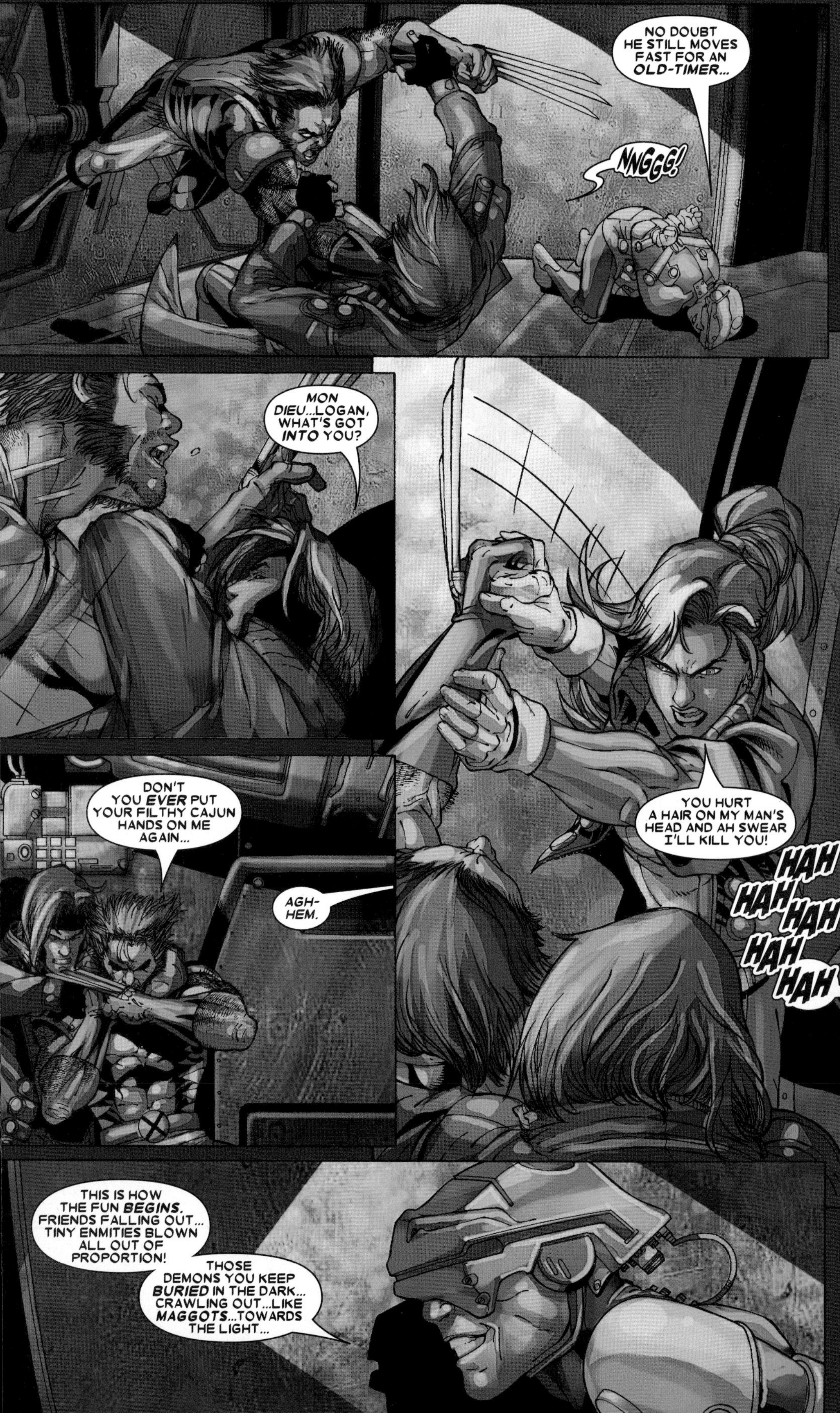
NO DOUBT HE STILL MOVES FAST FOR AN OLD-TIMER...
NNGGG!
MON DIEU...LOGAN, WHAT'S GOT INTO YOU?
YOU HURT A HAIR ON MY MAN'S HEAD AND AH SWEAR I'LL KILL YOU!
DON'T YOU EVER PUT YOUR FILTHY CAJUN HANDS ON ME AGAIN...
AGH-HEM.
HAH HAH HAH HAH HAH
THIS IS HOW THE FUN BEGINS. FRIENDS FALLING OUT... TINY ENMITIES BLOWN ALL OUT OF PROPORTION!
THOSE DEMONS YOU KEEP BURIED IN THE DARK... CRAWLING OUT...LIKE MAGGOTS...TOWARDS THE LIGHT...

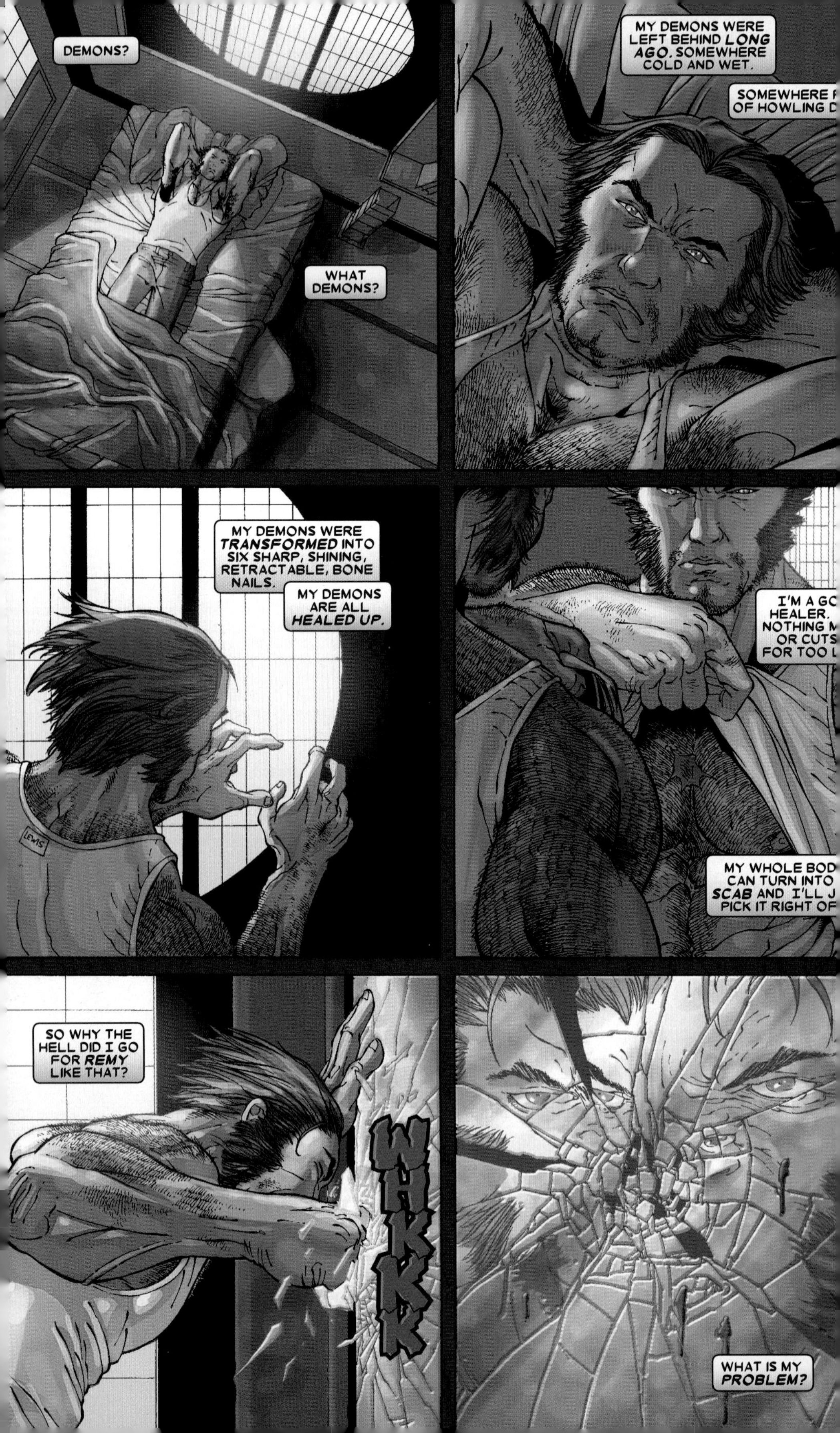
DEMONS?
WHAT DEMONS?
MY DEMONS WERE LEFT BEHIND *LONG AGO*. SOMEWHERE COLD AND WET.
SOMEWHERE OF HOWLING
MY DEMONS WERE *TRANSFORMED* INTO SIX SHARP, SHINING, RETRACTABLE, BONE NAILS.
MY DEMONS ARE ALL *HEALED UP.*
LEWIS
I'M A HEALER. NOTHING OR CUTS FOR TOO
MY WHOLE CAN TURN INTO *SCAB* AND I'LL PICK IT RIGHT
SO WHY THE HELL DID I GO FOR *REMY* LIKE THAT?
WHKKK
WHAT IS MY *PROBLEM?*

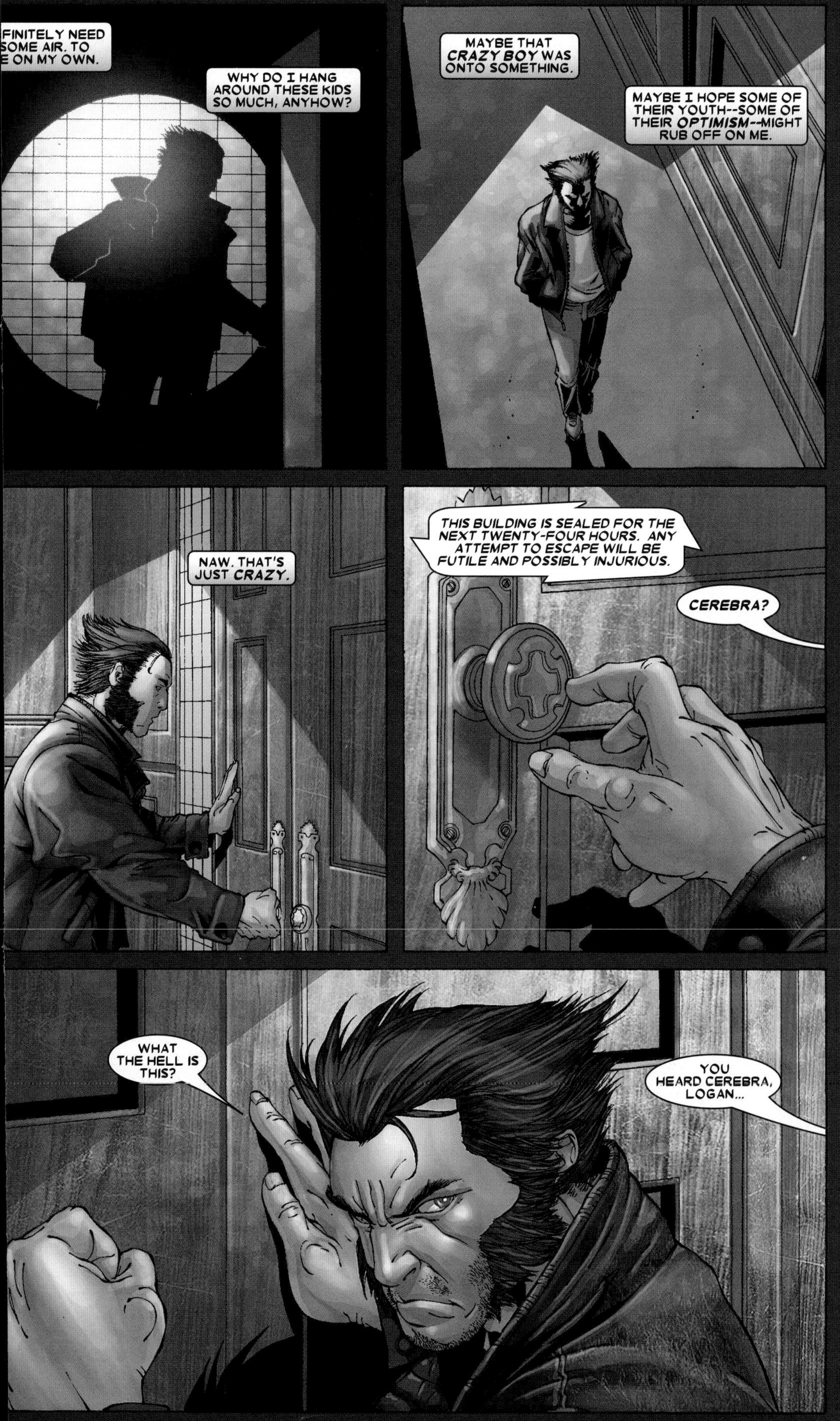
FINITELY NEED
SOME AIR. TO
E ON MY OWN.
WHY DO I HANG AROUND THESE KIDS SO MUCH, ANYHOW?
MAYBE THAT CRAZY BOY WAS ONTO SOMETHING.
MAYBE I HOPE SOME OF THEIR YOUTH--SOME OF THEIR OPTIMISM--MIGHT RUB OFF ON ME.
NAW. THAT'S JUST CRAZY.
THIS BUILDING IS SEALED FOR THE NEXT TWENTY-FOUR HOURS. ANY ATTEMPT TO ESCAPE WILL BE FUTILE AND POSSIBLY INJURIOUS.
CEREBRA?
WHAT THE HELL IS THIS?
YOU HEARD CEREBRA, LOGAN...

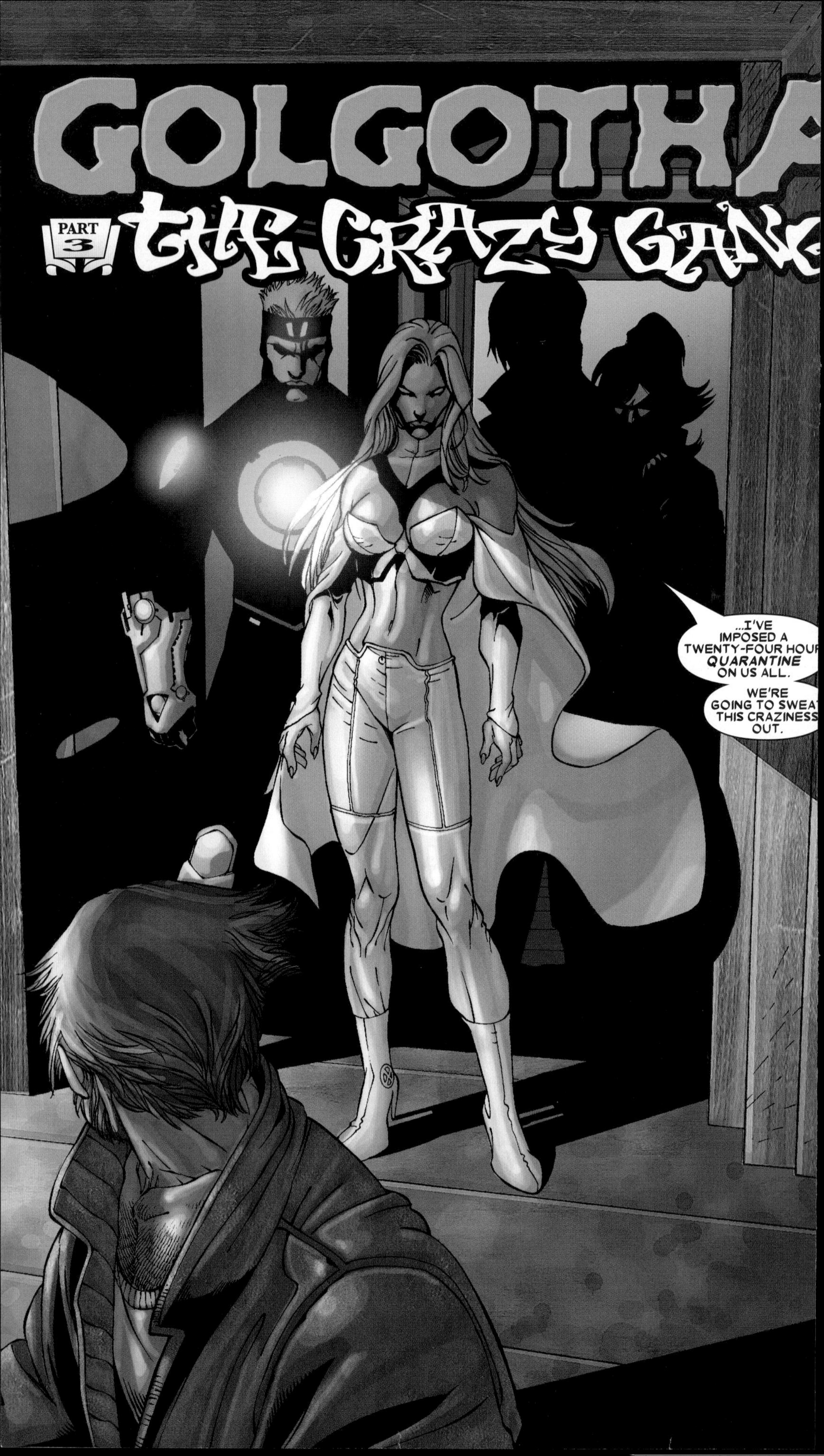
GOLGOTHA
PART 3
THE CRAZY GAN
...I'VE IMPOSED A TWENTY-FOUR HOUR QUARANTINE ON US ALL.
WE'RE GOING TO SWEAT THIS CRAZINESS OUT.

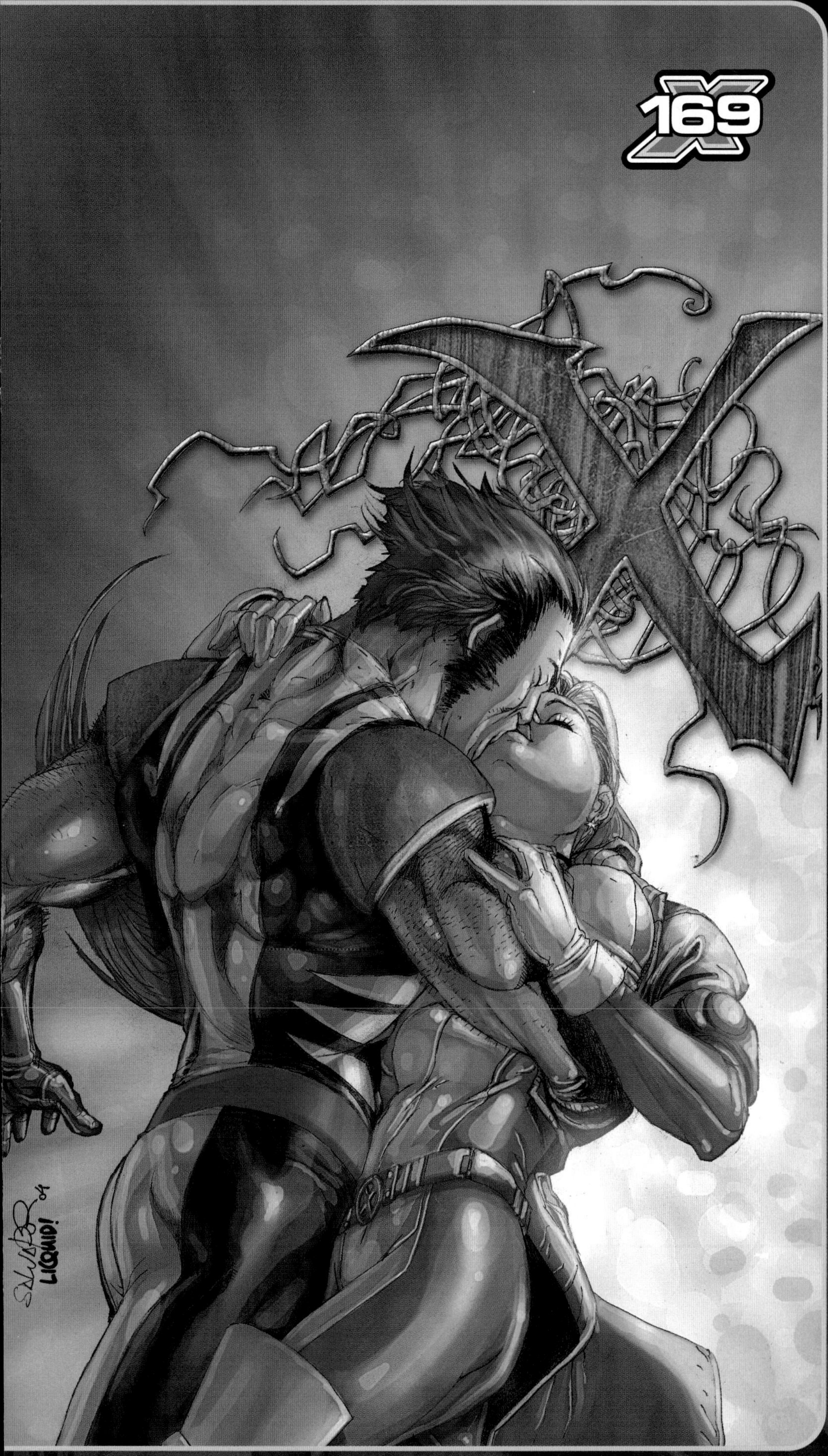
169
LIQUID!

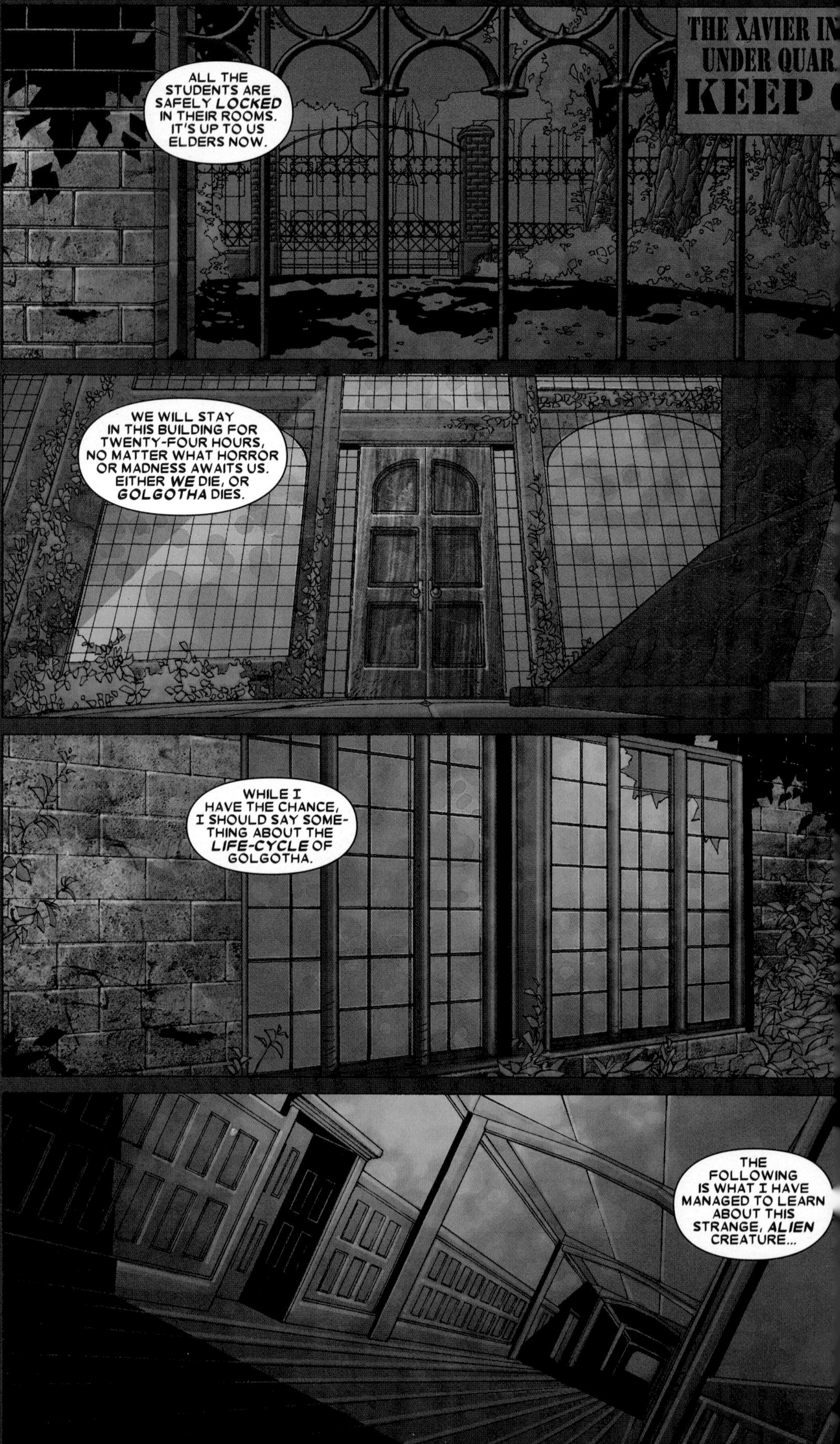
THE XAVIER IN
UNDER QUAR
KEEP
ALL THE STUDENTS ARE SAFELY LOCKED IN THEIR ROOMS. IT'S UP TO US ELDERS NOW.
WE WILL STAY IN THIS BUILDING FOR TWENTY-FOUR HOURS, NO MATTER WHAT HORROR OR MADNESS AWAITS US. EITHER WE DIE, OR GOLGOTHA DIES.
WHILE I HAVE THE CHANCE, I SHOULD SAY SOME-THING ABOUT THE LIFE-CYCLE OF GOLGOTHA.
THE FOLLOWING IS WHAT I HAVE MANAGED TO LEARN ABOUT THIS STRANGE, ALIEN CREATURE...

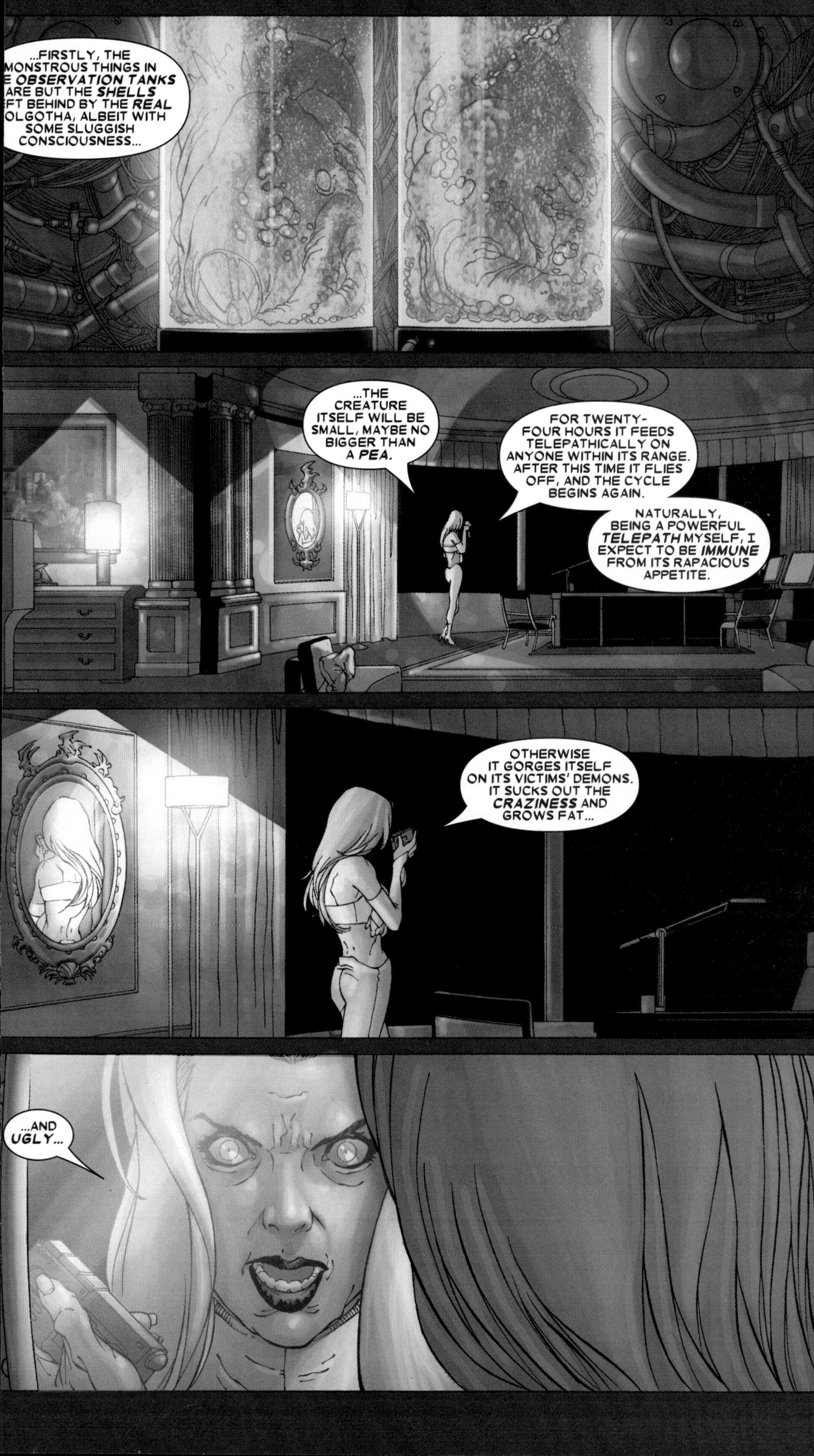
...FIRSTLY, THE MONSTROUS THINGS IN E OBSERVATION TANKS ARE BUT THE SHELLS EFT BEHIND BY THE REAL OLGOTHA, ALBEIT WITH SOME SLUGGISH CONSCIOUSNESS...
...THE CREATURE ITSELF WILL BE SMALL, MAYBE NO BIGGER THAN A PEA.
FOR TWENTY-FOUR HOURS IT FEEDS TELEPATHICALLY ON ANYONE WITHIN ITS RANGE. AFTER THIS TIME IT FLIES OFF, AND THE CYCLE BEGINS AGAIN.
NATURALLY, BEING A POWERFUL TELEPATH MYSELF, I EXPECT TO BE IMMUNE FROM ITS RAPACIOUS APPETITE.
OTHERWISE IT GORGES ITSELF ON ITS VICTIMS' DEMONS. IT SUCKS OUT THE CRAZINESS AND GROWS FAT...
...AND UGLY...

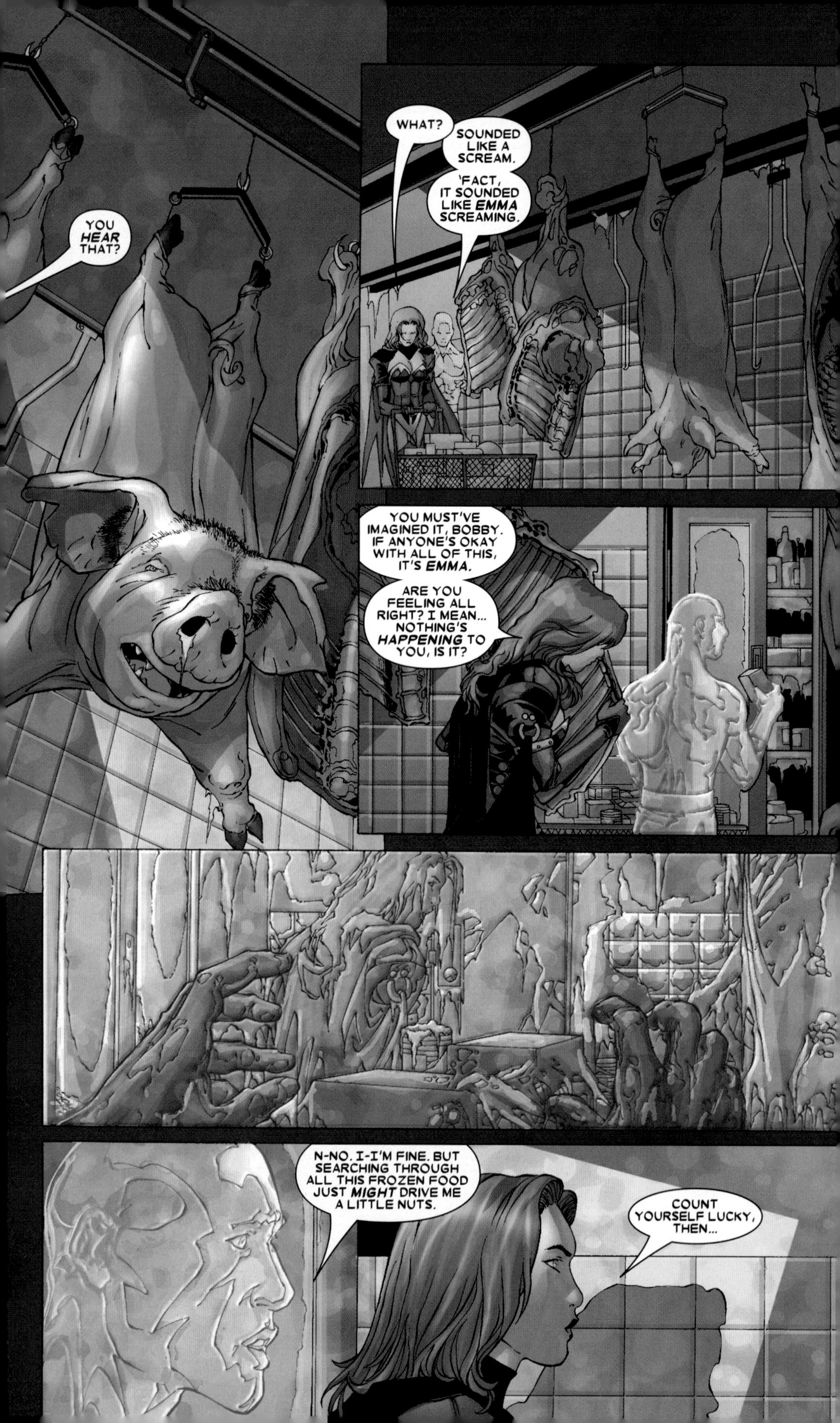

YOU HEAR THAT?
WHAT?
SOUNDED LIKE A SCREAM.
'FACT, IT SOUNDED LIKE EMMA SCREAMING.
YOU MUST'VE IMAGINED IT, BOBBY. IF ANYONE'S OKAY WITH ALL OF THIS, IT'S EMMA.
ARE YOU FEELING ALL RIGHT? I MEAN... NOTHING'S HAPPENING TO YOU, IS IT?
N-NO. I-I'M FINE. BUT SEARCHING THROUGH ALL THIS FROZEN FOOD JUST MIGHT DRIVE ME A LITTLE NUTS.
COUNT YOURSELF LUCKY, THEN...

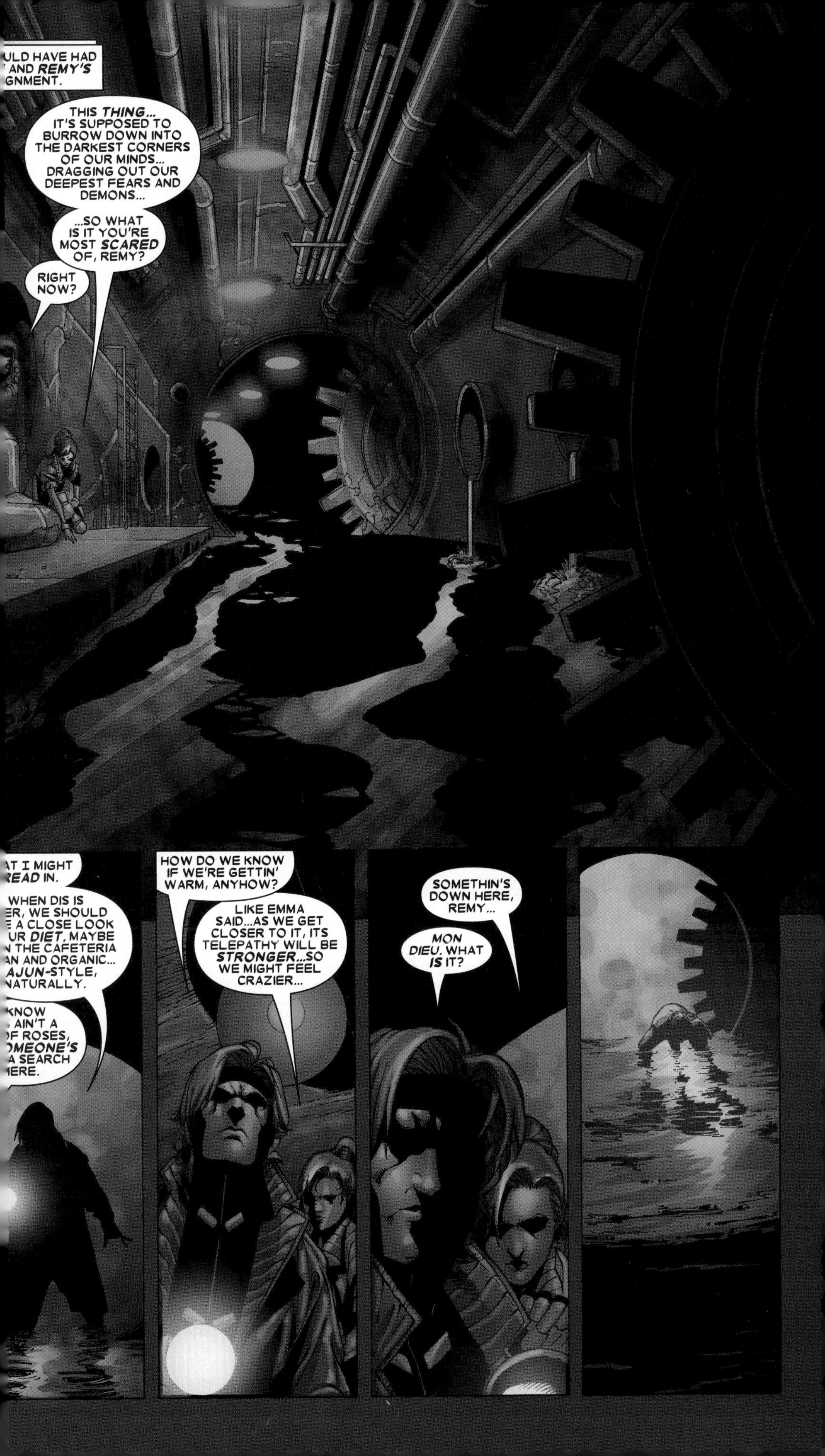
ULD HAVE HAD AND REMY'S GNMENT.
THIS THING... IT'S SUPPOSED TO BURROW DOWN INTO THE DARKEST CORNERS OF OUR MINDS... DRAGGING OUT OUR DEEPEST FEARS AND DEMONS...
...SO WHAT IS IT YOU'RE MOST SCARED OF, REMY?
RIGHT NOW?
AT I MIGHT READ IN.
WHEN DIS IS ER, WE SHOULD E A CLOSE LOOK UR DIET. MAYBE N THE CAFETERIA AN AND ORGANIC... AJUN-STYLE, NATURALLY.
KNOW AIN'T A OF ROSES, OMEONE'S A SEARCH HERE.
HOW DO WE KNOW IF WE'RE GETTIN' WARM, ANYHOW?
LIKE EMMA SAID...AS WE GET CLOSER TO IT, ITS TELEPATHY WILL BE STRONGER...SO WE MIGHT FEEL CRAZIER...
SOMETHIN'S DOWN HERE, REMY...
MON DIEU. WHAT IS IT?

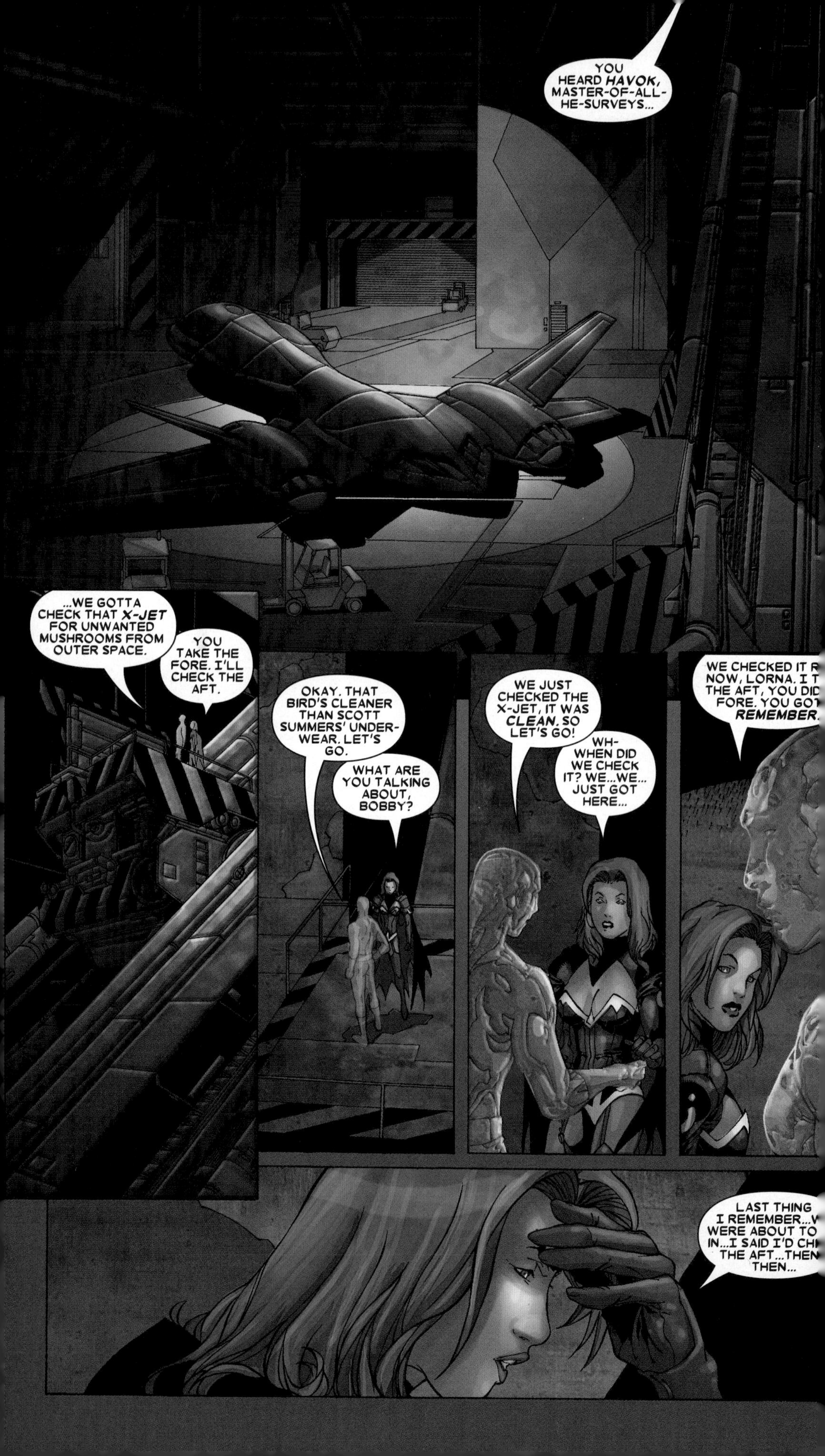
YOU HEARD HAVOK, MASTER-OF-ALL-HE-SURVEYS...
...WE GOTTA CHECK THAT X-JET FOR UNWANTED MUSHROOMS FROM OUTER SPACE.
YOU TAKE THE FORE. I'LL CHECK THE AFT.
OKAY. THAT BIRD'S CLEANER THAN SCOTT SUMMERS' UNDER-WEAR. LET'S GO.
WHAT ARE YOU TALKING ABOUT, BOBBY?
WE JUST CHECKED THE X-JET, IT WAS CLEAN. SO LET'S GO!
WH-WHEN DID WE CHECK IT? WE...WE... JUST GOT HERE...
WE CHECKED IT R NOW, LORNA. I T THE AFT, YOU DID FORE. YOU GOT REMEMBER.
LAST THING I REMEMBER...W WERE ABOUT TO IN...I SAID I'D CH THE AFT...THEN THEN...

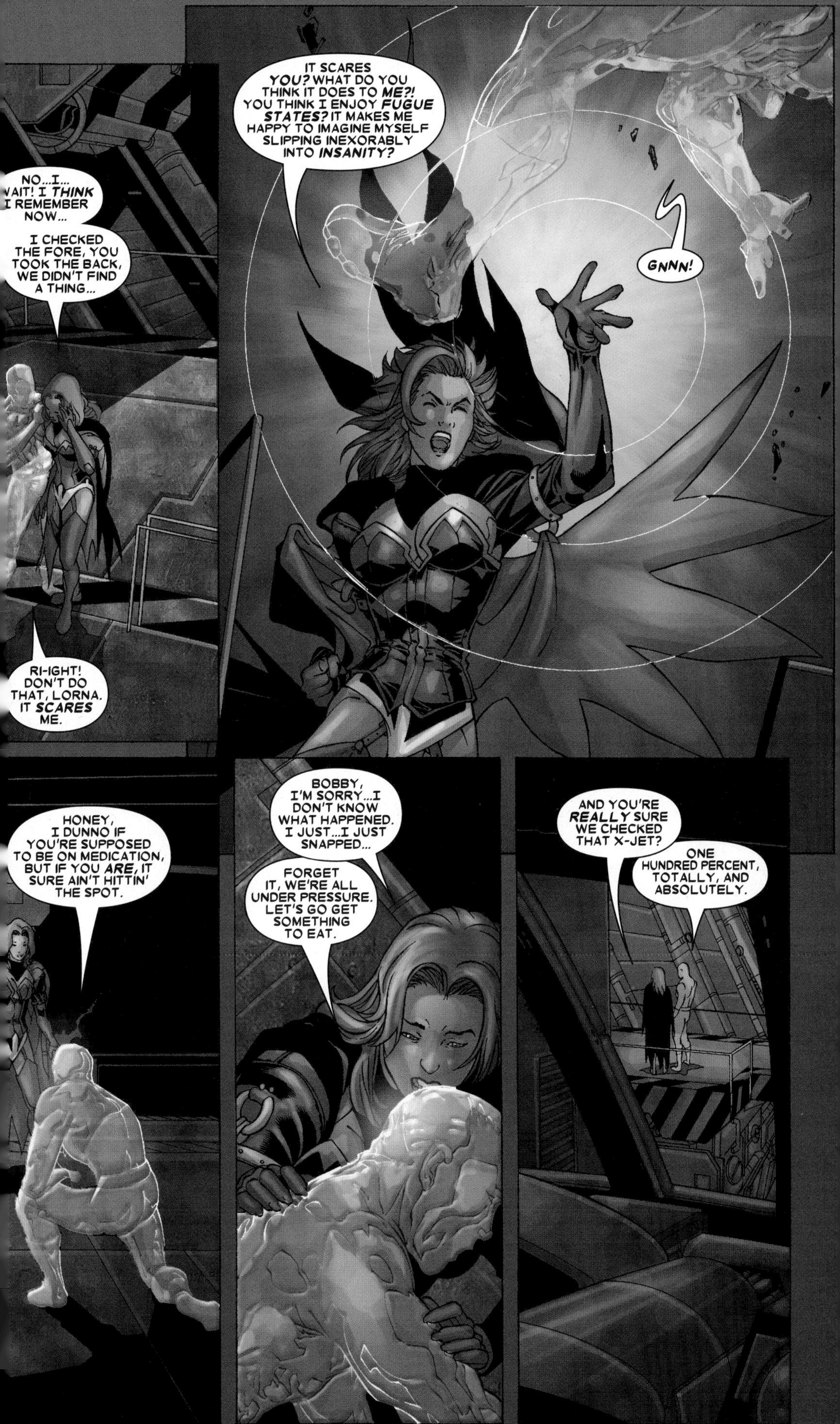
NO...I... WAIT! I THINK I REMEMBER NOW...
I CHECKED THE FORE, YOU TOOK THE BACK, WE DIDN'T FIND A THING...
RI-IGHT! DON'T DO THAT, LORNA. IT SCARES ME.
IT SCARES YOU? WHAT DO YOU THINK IT DOES TO ME?! YOU THINK I ENJOY FUGUE STATES? IT MAKES ME HAPPY TO IMAGINE MYSELF SLIPPING INEXORABLY INTO INSANITY?
GNNN!
HONEY, I DUNNO IF YOU'RE SUPPOSED TO BE ON MEDICATION, BUT IF YOU ARE, IT SURE AIN'T HITTIN' THE SPOT.
BOBBY, I'M SORRY...I DON'T KNOW WHAT HAPPENED. I JUST...I JUST SNAPPED...
FORGET IT, WE'RE ALL UNDER PRESSURE. LET'S GO GET SOMETHING TO EAT.
AND YOU'RE REALLY SURE WE CHECKED THAT X-JET?
ONE HUNDRED PERCENT, TOTALLY, AND ABSOLUTELY.

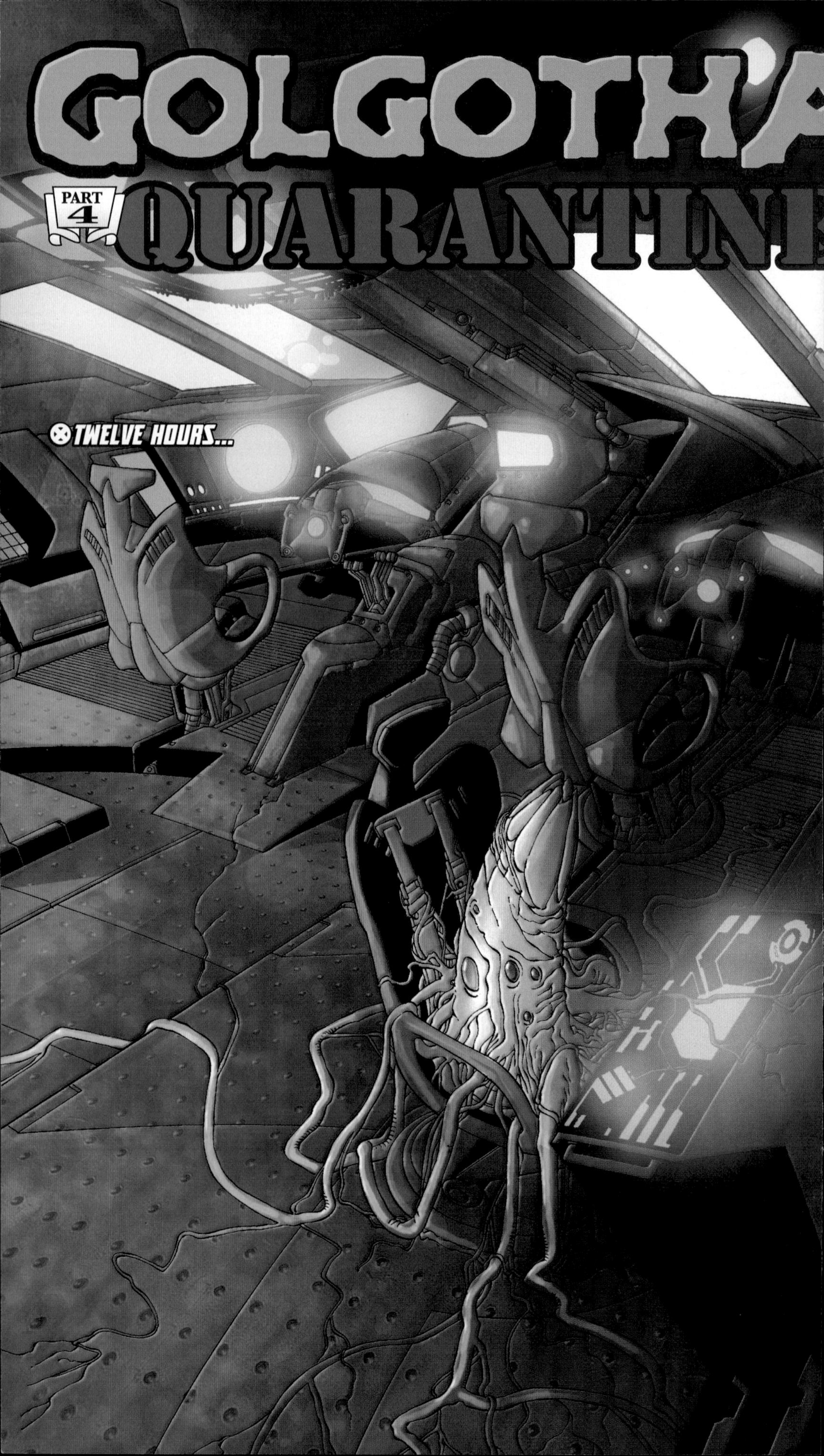
GOLGOTHA
PART 4
QUARANTINE
TWELVE HOURS...

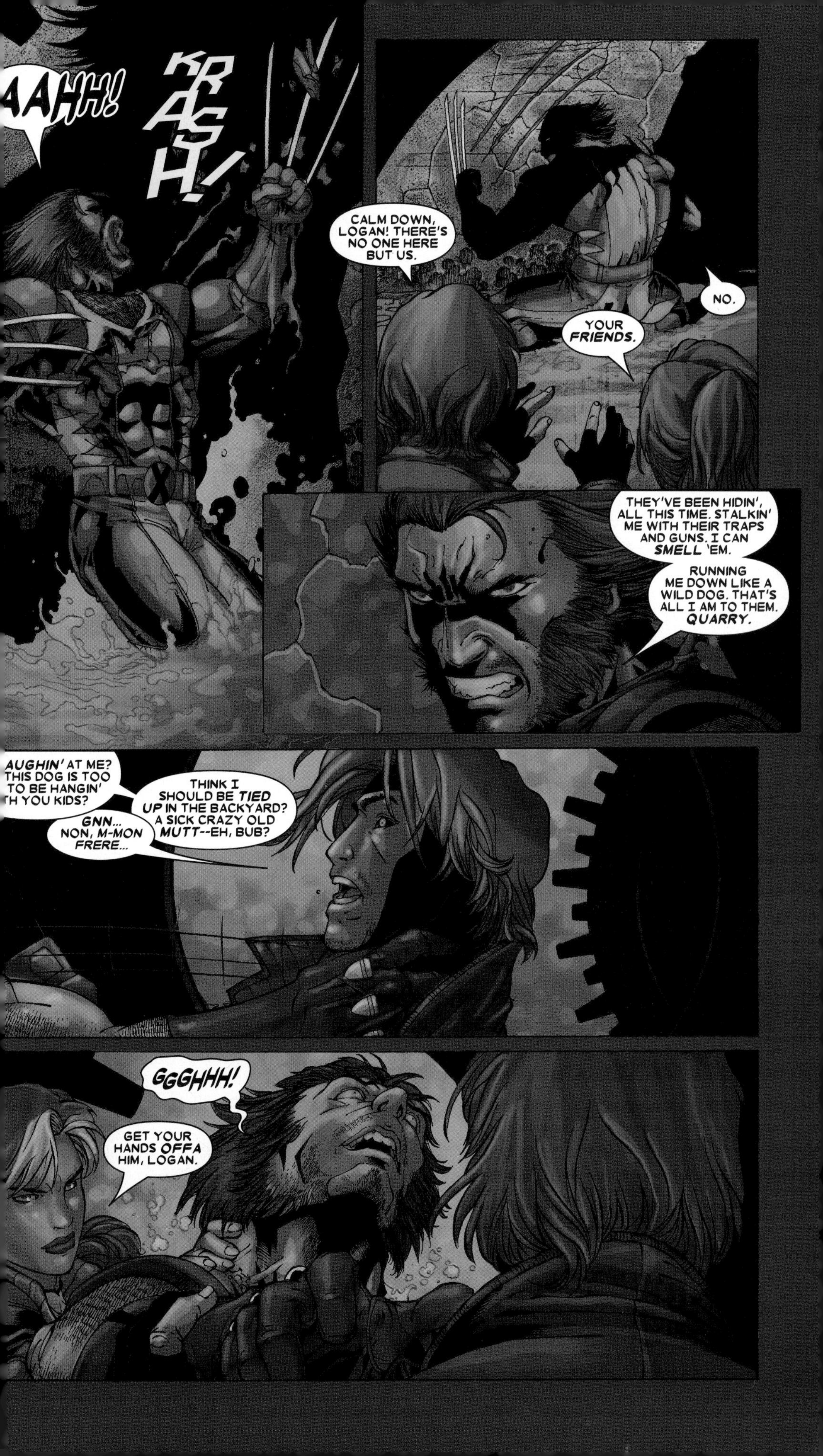
AAHHH!
KRASH!
CALM DOWN, LOGAN! THERE'S NO ONE HERE BUT US.
NO.
YOUR FRIENDS.
THEY'VE BEEN HIDIN', ALL THIS TIME. STALKIN' ME WITH THEIR TRAPS AND GUNS. I CAN SMELL 'EM.
RUNNING ME DOWN LIKE A WILD DOG. THAT'S ALL I AM TO THEM. QUARRY.
AUGHIN' AT ME? THIS DOG IS TOO TO BE HANGIN' TH YOU KIDS?
THINK I SHOULD BE TIED UP IN THE BACKYARD? A SICK CRAZY OLD MUTT--EH, BUB?
GNN... NON, M-MON FRERE...
GGGHHH!
GET YOUR HANDS OFFA HIM, LOGAN.

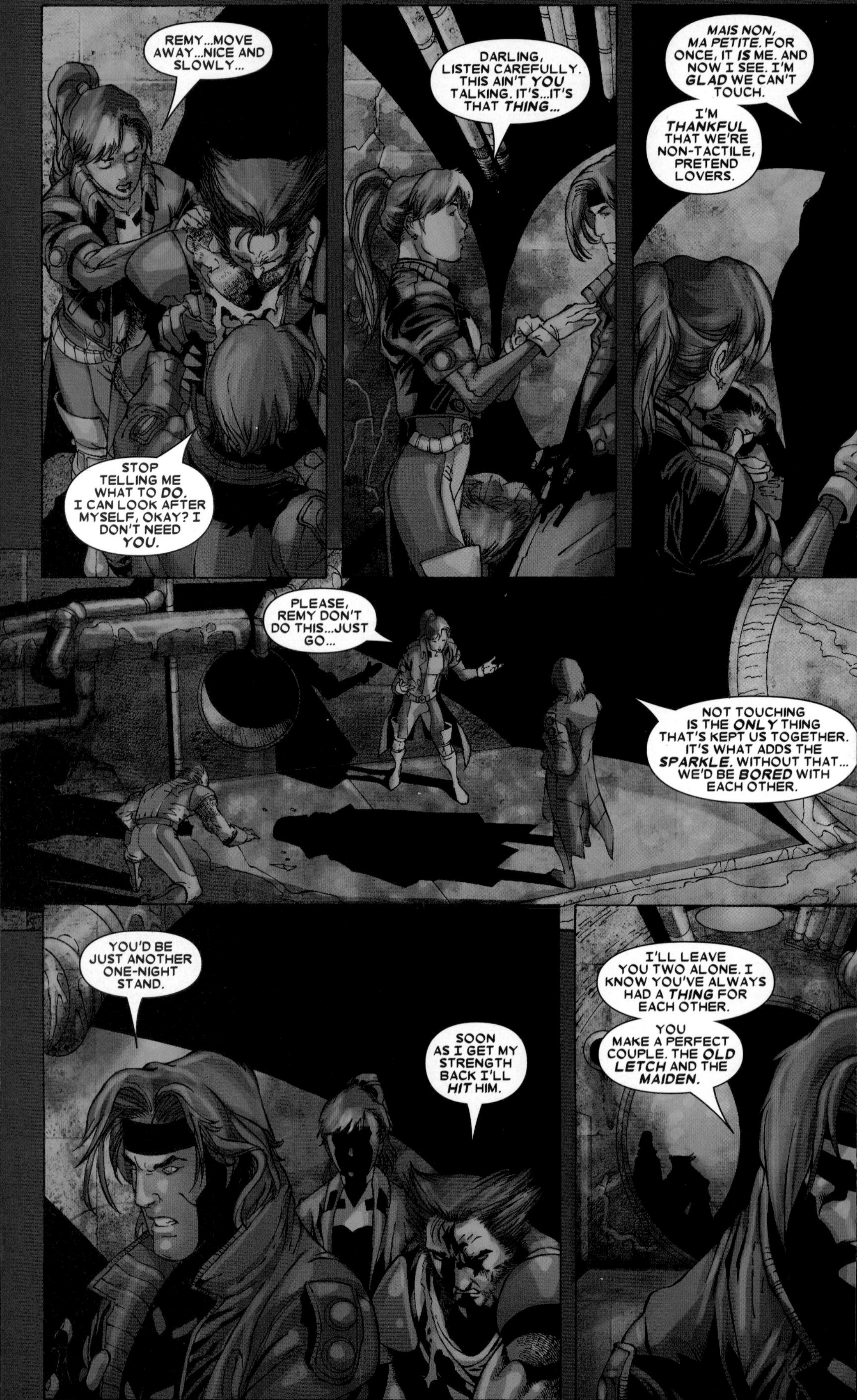
REMY...MOVE AWAY...NICE AND SLOWLY...
STOP TELLING ME WHAT TO DO. I CAN LOOK AFTER MYSELF, OKAY? I DON'T NEED YOU.
DARLING, LISTEN CAREFULLY. THIS AIN'T YOU TALKING. IT'S...IT'S THAT THING...
MAIS NON, MA PETITE. FOR ONCE, IT IS ME. AND NOW I SEE. I'M GLAD WE CAN'T TOUCH.
I'M THANKFUL THAT WE'RE NON-TACTILE, PRETEND LOVERS.
PLEASE, REMY DON'T DO THIS...JUST GO...
NOT TOUCHING IS THE ONLY THING THAT'S KEPT US TOGETHER. IT'S WHAT ADDS THE SPARKLE. WITHOUT THAT... WE'D BE BORED WITH EACH OTHER.
YOU'D BE JUST ANOTHER ONE-NIGHT STAND.
SOON AS I GET MY STRENGTH BACK I'LL HIT HIM.
I'LL LEAVE YOU TWO ALONE. I KNOW YOU'VE ALWAYS HAD A THING FOR EACH OTHER.
YOU MAKE A PERFECT COUPLE. THE OLD LETCH AND THE MAIDEN.

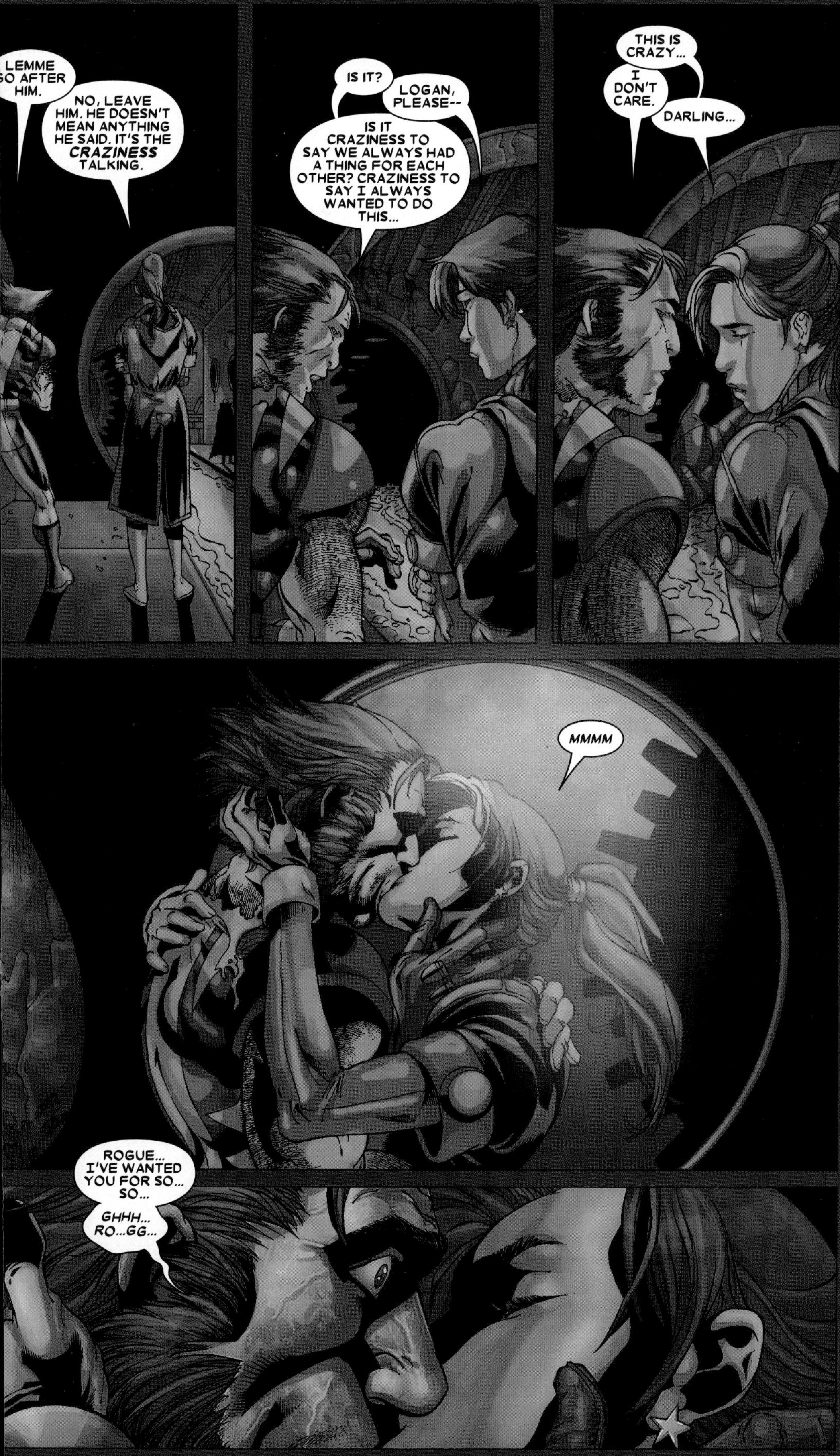

LEMME GO AFTER HIM.
NO, LEAVE HIM. HE DOESN'T MEAN ANYTHING HE SAID. IT'S THE *CRAZINESS* TALKING.
IS IT?
LOGAN, PLEASE--
IS IT CRAZINESS TO SAY WE ALWAYS HAD A THING FOR EACH OTHER? CRAZINESS TO SAY I ALWAYS WANTED TO DO THIS...
THIS IS CRAZY...
I DON'T CARE.
DARLING...
MMMM
ROGUE... I'VE WANTED YOU FOR SO... SO...
GHHH... RO...GG...

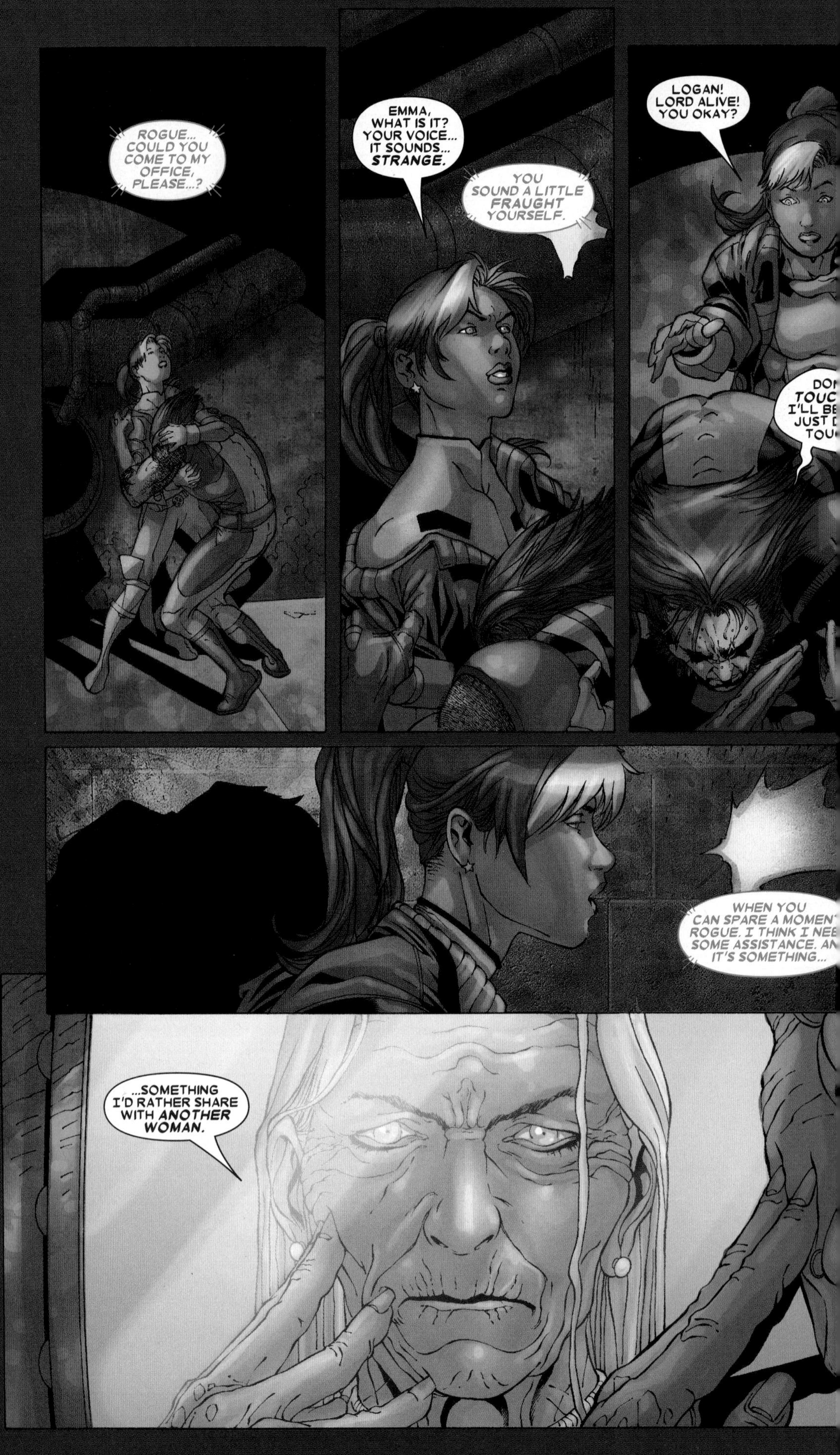
ROGUE... COULD YOU COME TO MY OFFICE, PLEASE...?
EMMA, WHAT IS IT? YOUR VOICE... IT SOUNDS... STRANGE.
YOU SOUND A LITTLE FRAUGHT YOURSELF.
LOGAN! LORD ALIVE! YOU OKAY?
WHEN YOU CAN SPARE A MOMENT ROGUE. I THINK I NEE SOME ASSISTANCE. AN IT'S SOMETHING...
...SOMETHING I'D RATHER SHARE WITH ANOTHER WOMAN.

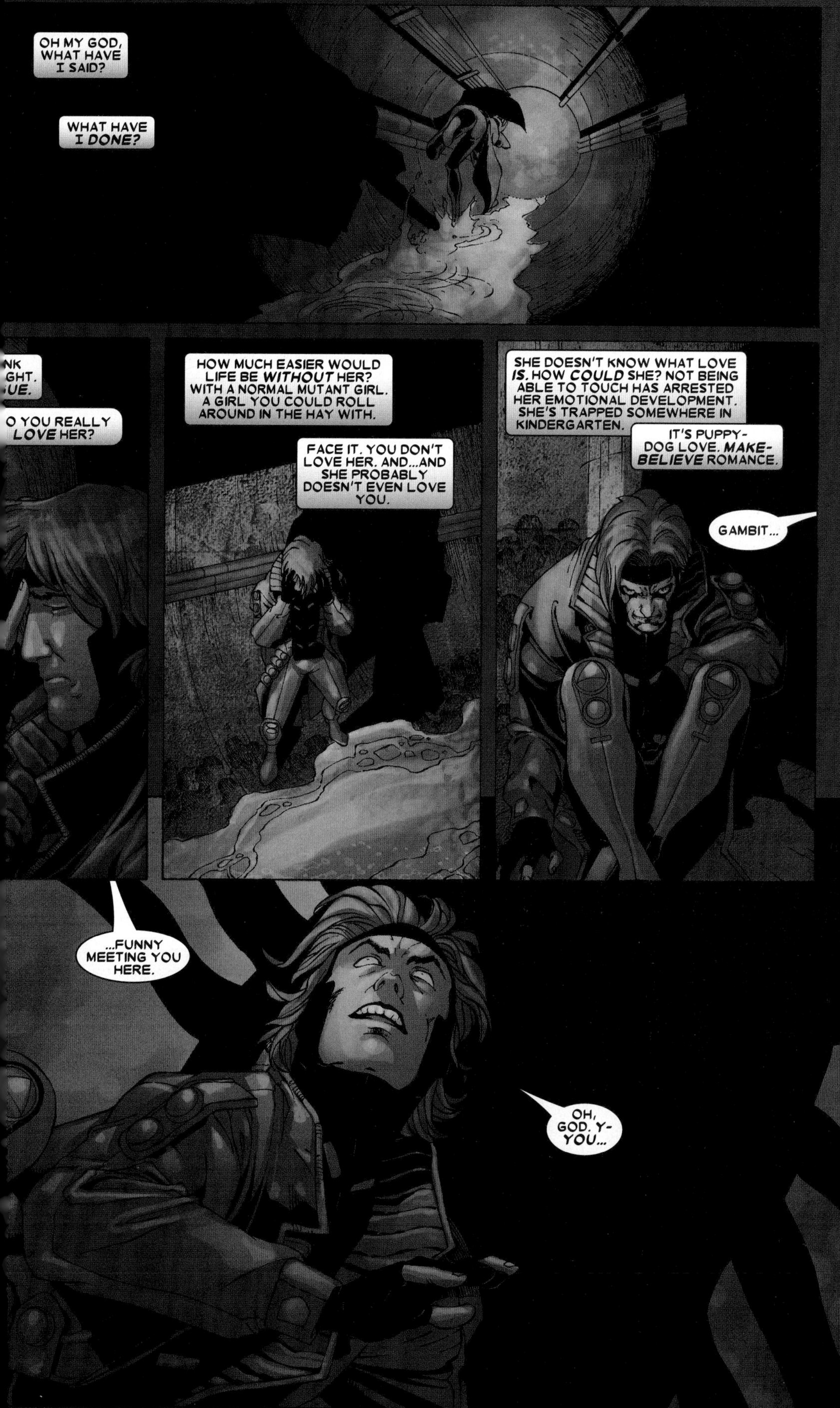

OH MY GOD, WHAT HAVE I SAID?
WHAT HAVE I DONE?
NK GHT. GUE.
O YOU REALLY LOVE HER?
HOW MUCH EASIER WOULD LIFE BE WITHOUT HER? WITH A NORMAL MUTANT GIRL. A GIRL YOU COULD ROLL AROUND IN THE HAY WITH.
FACE IT. YOU DON'T LOVE HER. AND...AND SHE PROBABLY DOESN'T EVEN LOVE YOU.
SHE DOESN'T KNOW WHAT LOVE IS. HOW COULD SHE? NOT BEING ABLE TO TOUCH HAS ARRESTED HER EMOTIONAL DEVELOPMENT. SHE'S TRAPPED SOMEWHERE IN KINDERGARTEN.
IT'S PUPPY-DOG LOVE. MAKE-BELIEVE ROMANCE.
GAMBIT...
...FUNNY MEETING YOU HERE.
OH, GOD. Y-YOU...

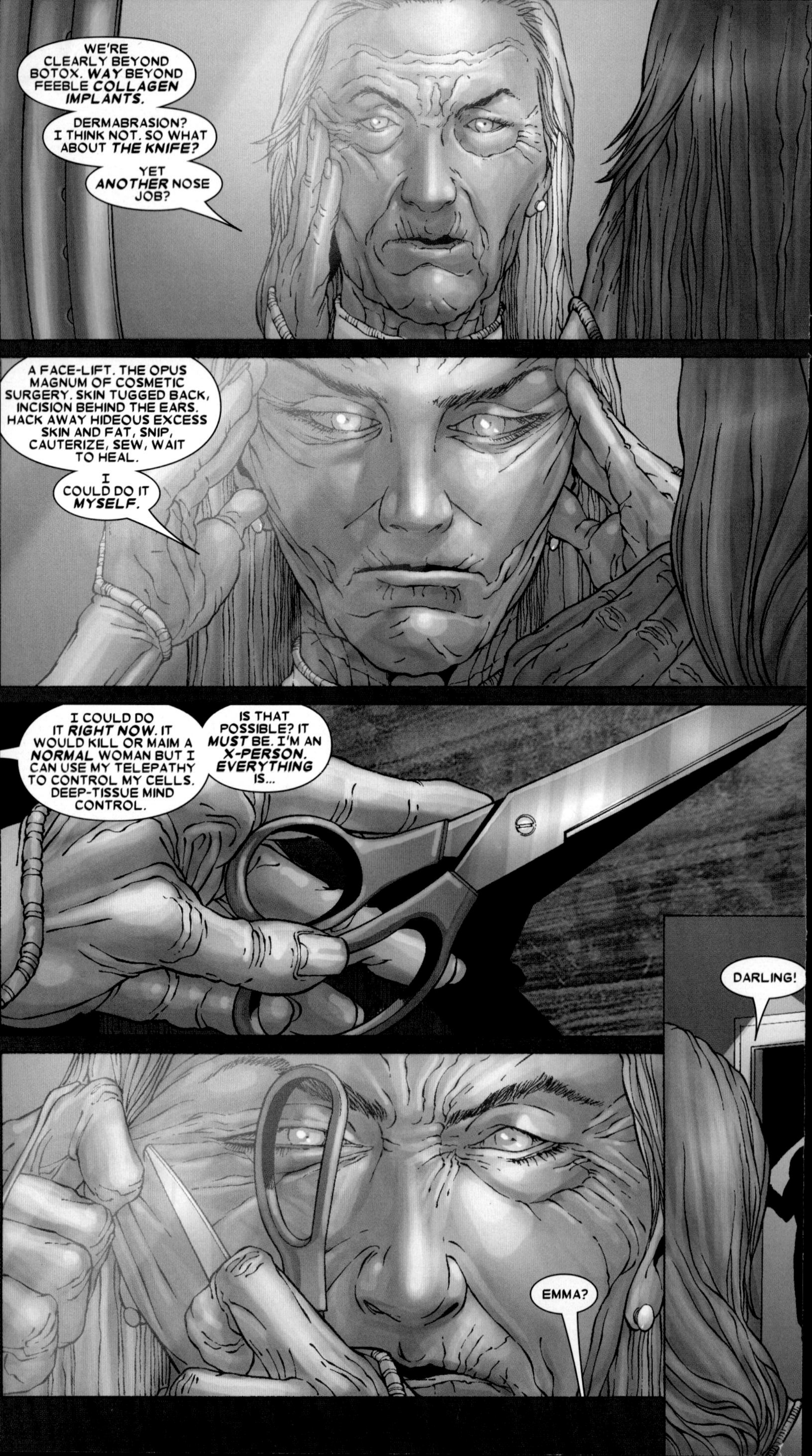
WE'RE CLEARLY BEYOND BOTOX. WAY BEYOND FEEBLE COLLAGEN IMPLANTS.
DERMABRASION? I THINK NOT. SO WHAT ABOUT THE KNIFE?
YET ANOTHER NOSE JOB?
A FACE-LIFT. THE OPUS MAGNUM OF COSMETIC SURGERY. SKIN TUGGED BACK, INCISION BEHIND THE EARS. HACK AWAY HIDEOUS EXCESS SKIN AND FAT, SNIP, CAUTERIZE, SEW, WAIT TO HEAL.
I COULD DO IT MYSELF.
I COULD DO IT RIGHT NOW. IT WOULD KILL OR MAIM A NORMAL WOMAN BUT I CAN USE MY TELEPATHY TO CONTROL MY CELLS. DEEP-TISSUE MIND CONTROL.
IS THAT POSSIBLE? IT MUST BE. I'M AN X-PERSON. EVERYTHING IS...
DARLING!
EMMA?

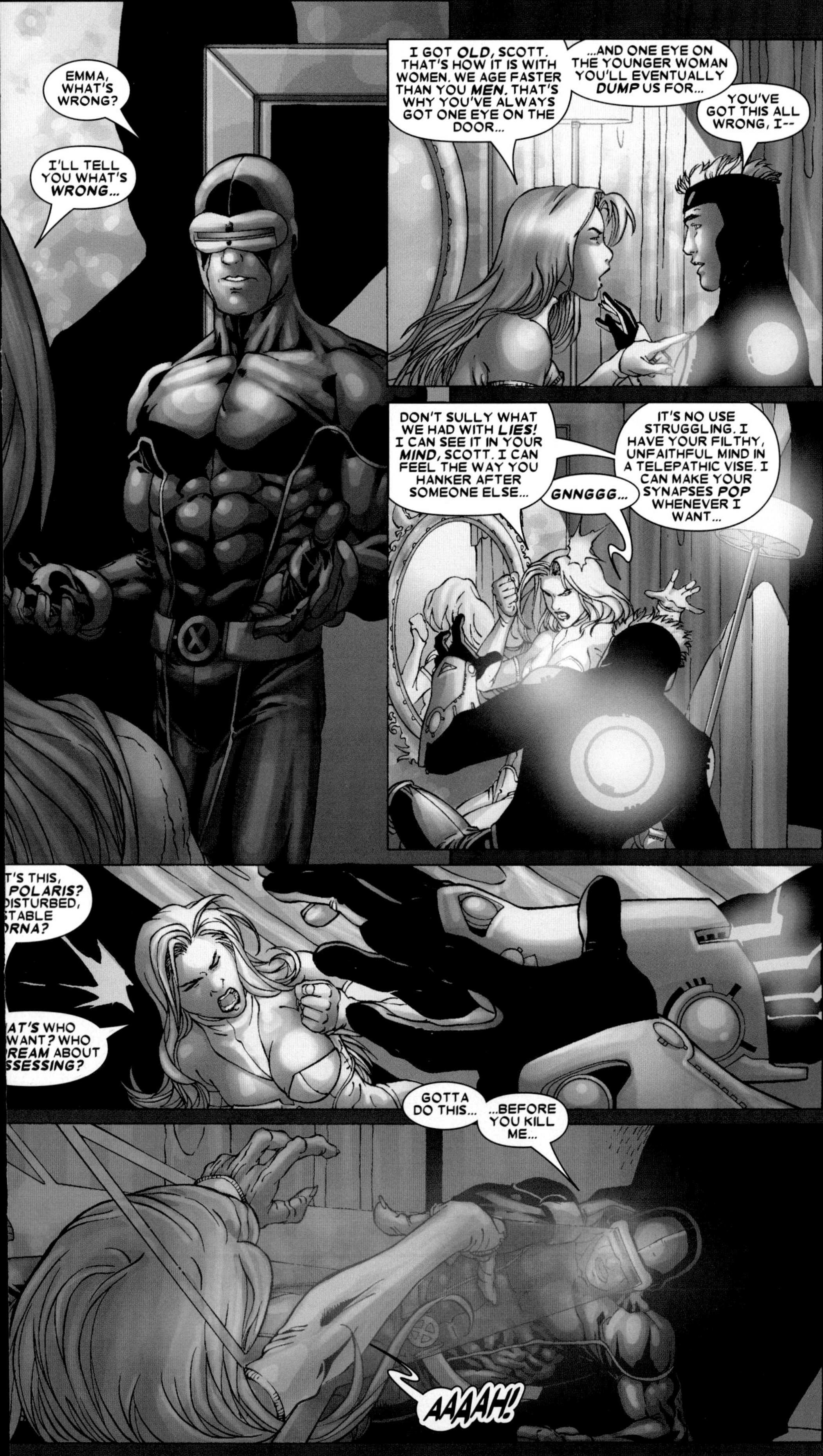
EMMA, WHAT'S WRONG?
I'LL TELL YOU WHAT'S WRONG...
I GOT OLD, SCOTT. THAT'S HOW IT IS WITH WOMEN. WE AGE FASTER THAN YOU MEN. THAT'S WHY YOU'VE ALWAYS GOT ONE EYE ON THE DOOR...
...AND ONE EYE ON THE YOUNGER WOMAN YOU'LL EVENTUALLY DUMP US FOR...
YOU'VE GOT THIS ALL WRONG, I--
DON'T SULLY WHAT WE HAD WITH LIES! I CAN SEE IT IN YOUR MIND, SCOTT. I CAN FEEL THE WAY YOU HANKER AFTER SOMEONE ELSE...
IT'S NO USE STRUGGLING. I HAVE YOUR FILTHY, UNFAITHFUL MIND IN A TELEPATHIC VISE. I CAN MAKE YOUR SYNAPSES POP WHENEVER I WANT...
GNNGGG...
T'S THIS, POLARIS? DISTURBED, STABLE RNA?
AT'S WHO WANT? WHO REAM ABOUT SSESSING?
GOTTA DO THIS...
...BEFORE YOU KILL ME...
AAAAH!

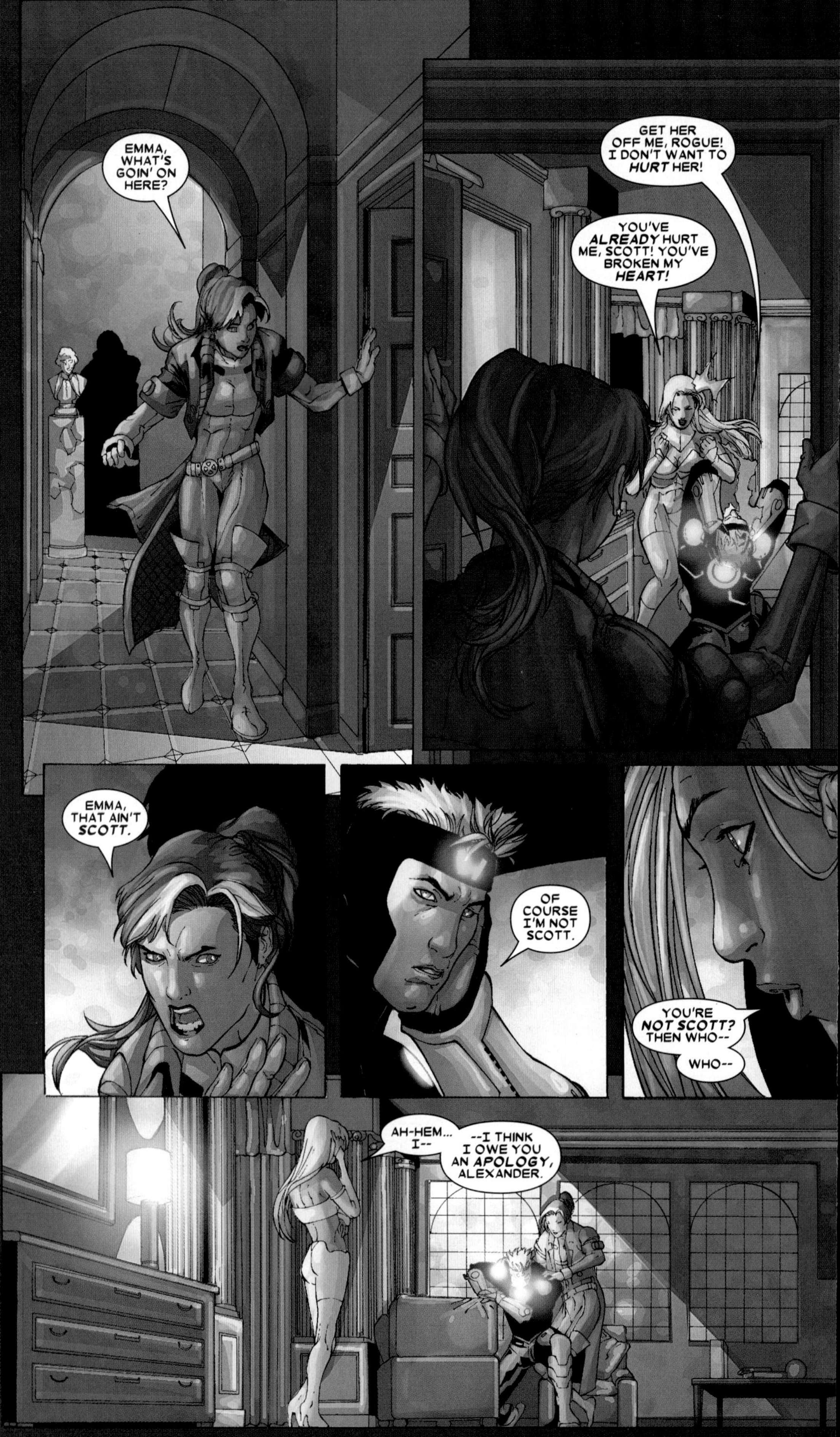
EMMA, WHAT'S GOIN' ON HERE?
GET HER OFF ME, ROGUE! I DON'T WANT TO *HURT* HER!
YOU'VE *ALREADY* HURT ME, SCOTT! YOU'VE BROKEN MY *HEART!*
EMMA, THAT AIN'T *SCOTT.*
OF COURSE I'M NOT SCOTT.
YOU'RE *NOT SCOTT?* THEN WHO--
WHO--
AH-HEM... I--
--I THINK I OWE YOU AN *APOLOGY,* ALEXANDER.

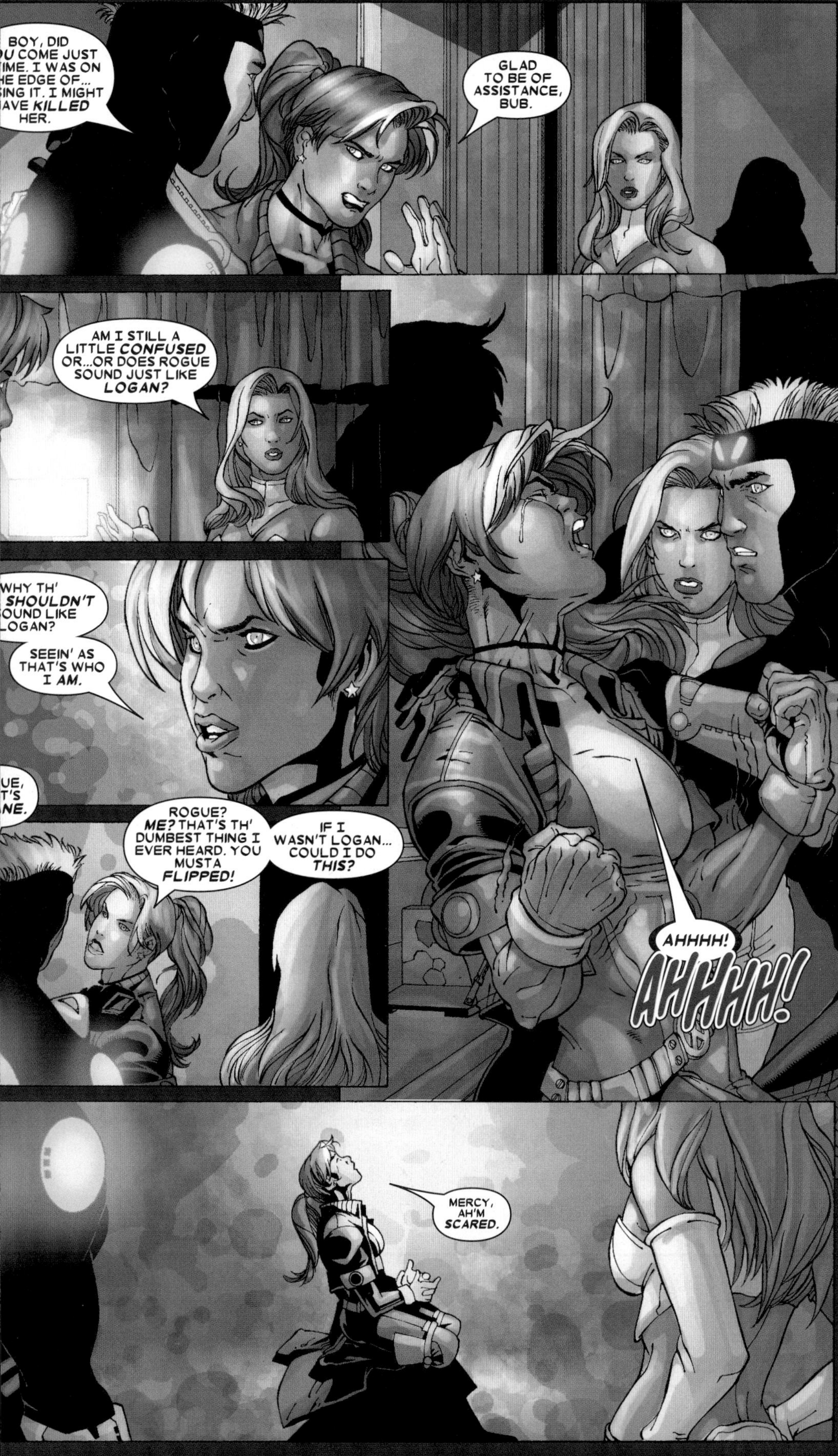
BOY, DID OU COME JUST IME. I WAS ON HE EDGE OF... SING IT. I MIGHT AVE *KILLED* HER.
GLAD TO BE OF ASSISTANCE, BUB.
AM I STILL A LITTLE *CONFUSED* OR...OR DOES ROGUE SOUND JUST LIKE *LOGAN?*
WHY TH' *SHOULDN'T* OUND LIKE LOGAN?
SEEIN' AS THAT'S WHO I *AM.*
UE, T'S NE.
ROGUE? *ME?* THAT'S TH' DUMBEST THING I EVER HEARD. YOU MUSTA *FLIPPED!*
IF I WASN'T LOGAN... COULD I DO *THIS?*
AHHHH!
AHHHH!
MERCY, AH'M *SCARED.*

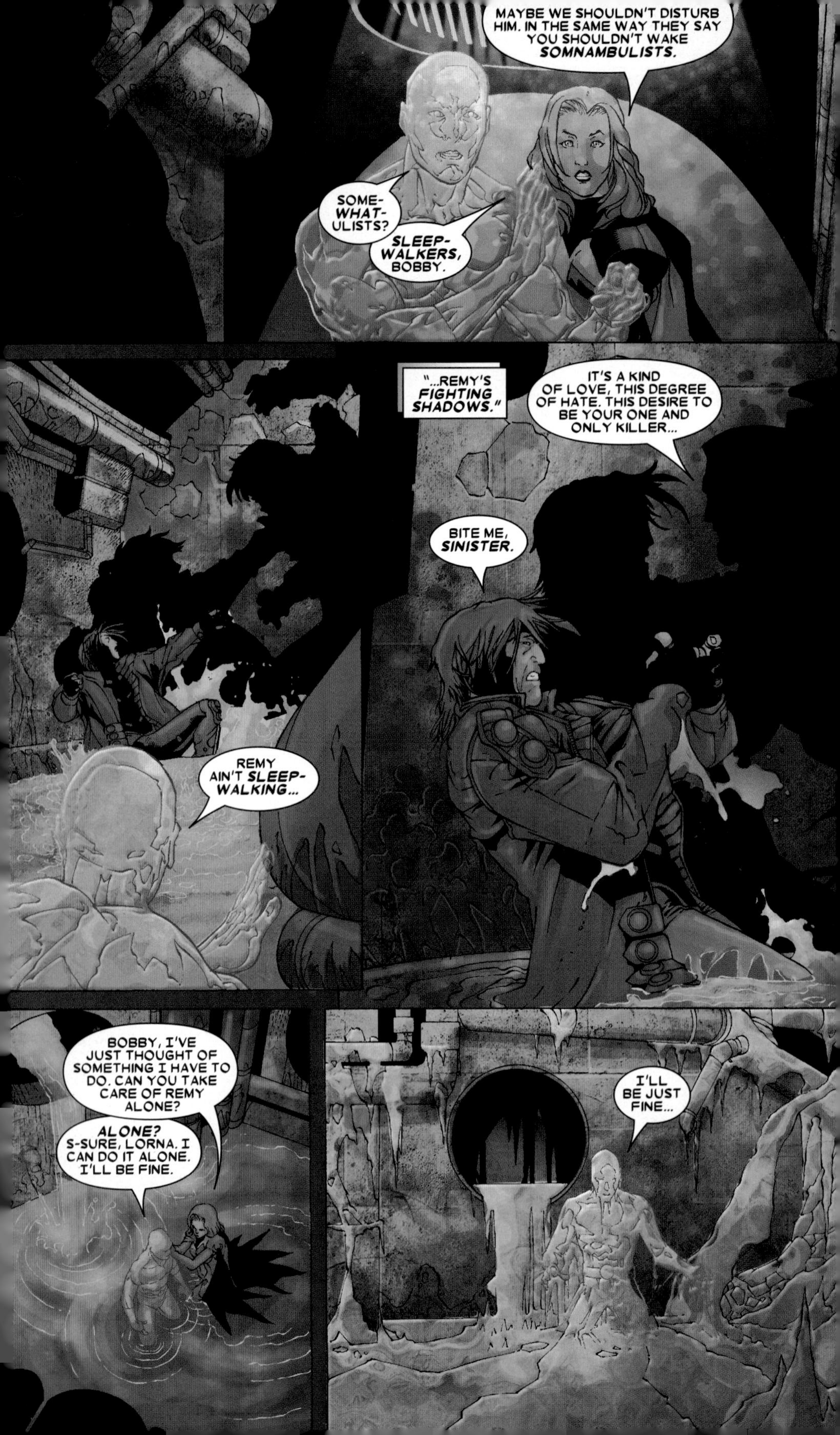
MAYBE WE SHOULDN'T DISTURB HIM. IN THE SAME WAY THEY SAY YOU SHOULDN'T WAKE SOMNAMBULISTS.
SOME-WHAT-ULISTS?
SLEEP-WALKERS, BOBBY.
"...REMY'S FIGHTING SHADOWS."
IT'S A KIND OF LOVE, THIS DEGREE OF HATE. THIS DESIRE TO BE YOUR ONE AND ONLY KILLER...
BITE ME, SINISTER.
REMY AIN'T SLEEP-WALKING...
BOBBY, I'VE JUST THOUGHT OF SOMETHING I HAVE TO DO. CAN YOU TAKE CARE OF REMY ALONE?
ALONE? S-SURE, LORNA. I CAN DO IT ALONE. I'LL BE FINE.
I'LL BE JUST FINE...

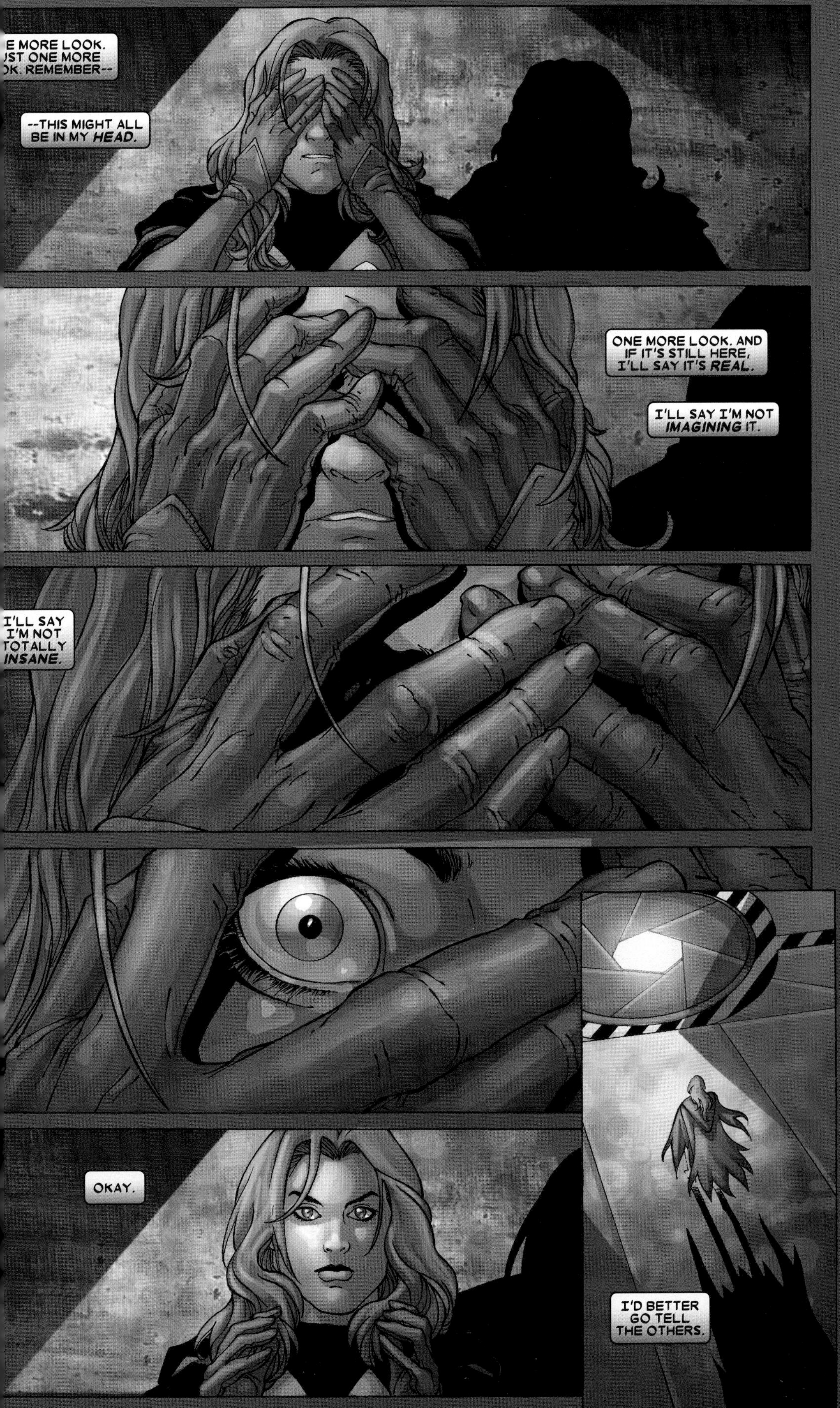

E MORE LOOK. UST ONE MORE OK. REMEMBER--
--THIS MIGHT ALL BE IN MY HEAD.
ONE MORE LOOK. AND IF IT'S STILL HERE, I'LL SAY IT'S REAL.
I'LL SAY I'M NOT IMAGINING IT.
I'LL SAY I'M NOT TOTALLY INSANE.
OKAY.
I'D BETTER GO TELL THE OTHERS.

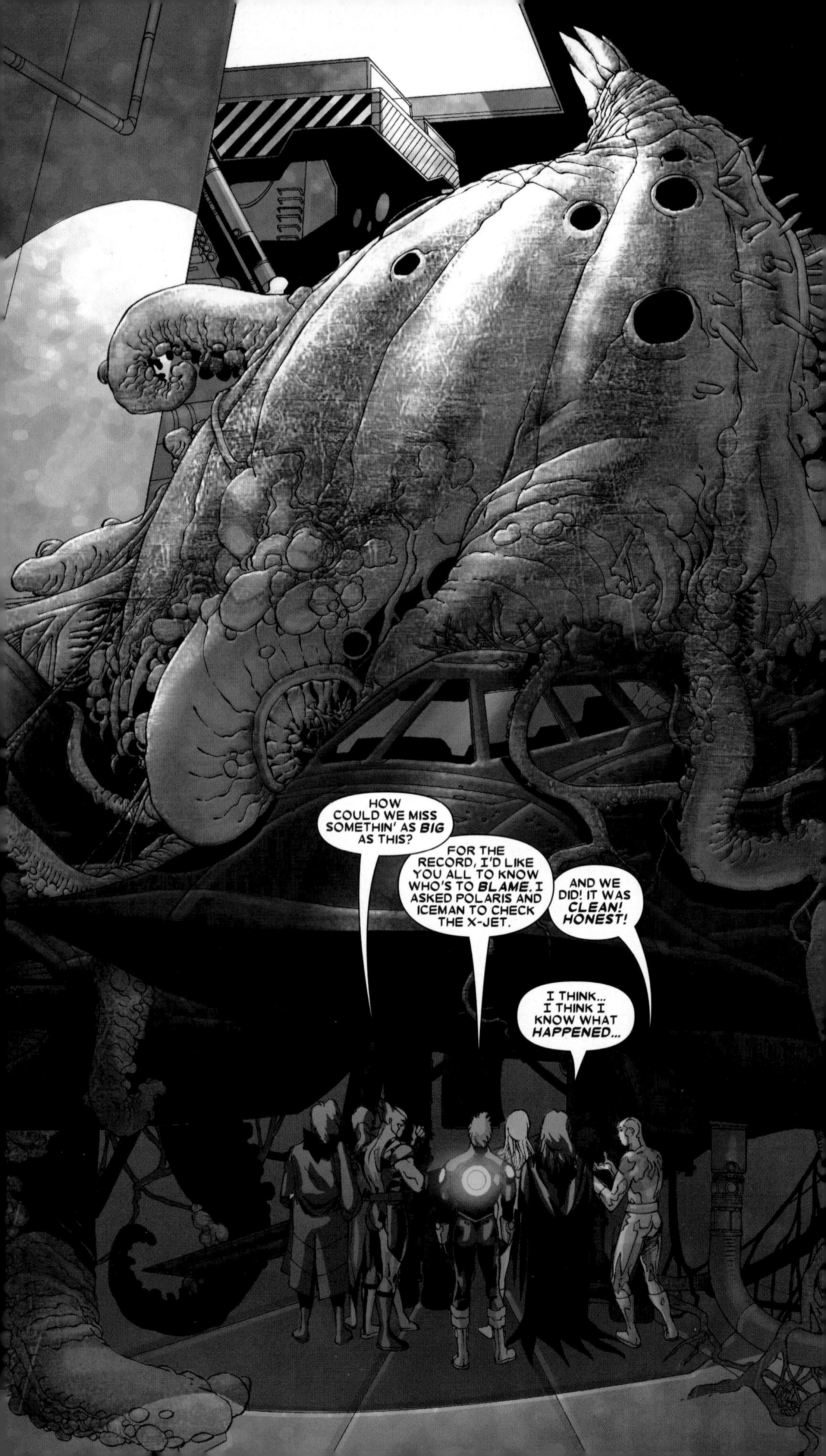
HOW COULD WE MISS SOMETHIN' AS BIG AS THIS?
FOR THE RECORD, I'D LIKE YOU ALL TO KNOW WHO'S TO BLAME. I ASKED POLARIS AND ICEMAN TO CHECK THE X-JET.
AND WE DID! IT WAS CLEAN! HONEST!
I THINK... I THINK I KNOW WHAT HAPPENED...

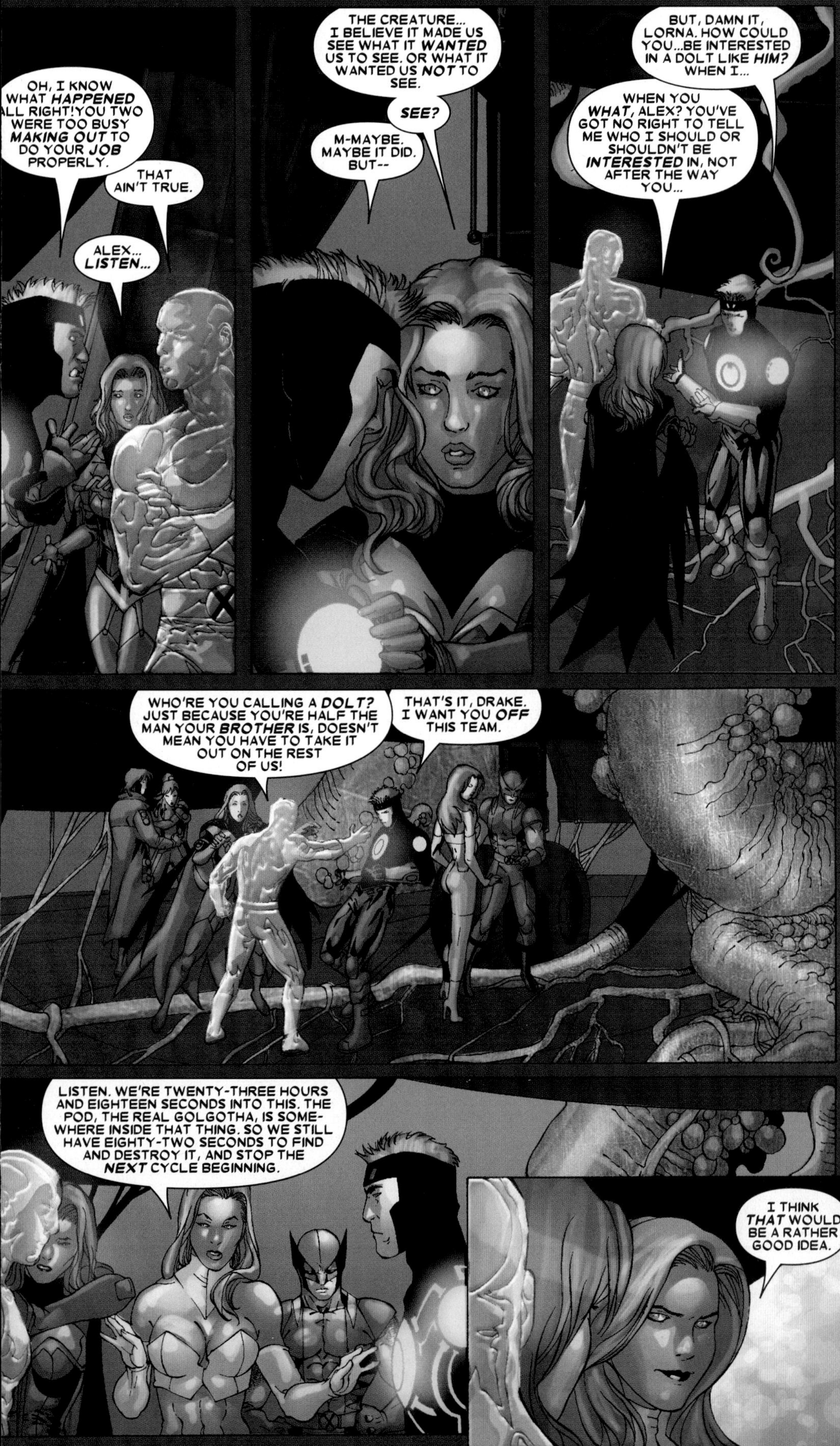

OH, I KNOW WHAT HAPPENED ALL RIGHT! YOU TWO WERE TOO BUSY MAKING OUT TO DO YOUR JOB PROPERLY.
THAT AIN'T TRUE.
ALEX... LISTEN...
THE CREATURE... I BELIEVE IT MADE US SEE WHAT IT WANTED US TO SEE. OR WHAT IT WANTED US NOT TO SEE.
SEE?
M-MAYBE. MAYBE IT DID. BUT--
BUT, DAMN IT, LORNA. HOW COULD YOU...BE INTERESTED IN A DOLT LIKE HIM? WHEN I...
WHEN YOU WHAT, ALEX? YOU'VE GOT NO RIGHT TO TELL ME WHO I SHOULD OR SHOULDN'T BE INTERESTED IN, NOT AFTER THE WAY YOU...
WHO'RE YOU CALLING A DOLT? JUST BECAUSE YOU'RE HALF THE MAN YOUR BROTHER IS, DOESN'T MEAN YOU HAVE TO TAKE IT OUT ON THE REST OF US!
THAT'S IT, DRAKE. I WANT YOU OFF THIS TEAM.
LISTEN. WE'RE TWENTY-THREE HOURS AND EIGHTEEN SECONDS INTO THIS. THE POD, THE REAL GOLGOTHA, IS SOME-WHERE INSIDE THAT THING. SO WE STILL HAVE EIGHTY-TWO SECONDS TO FIND AND DESTROY IT, AND STOP THE NEXT CYCLE BEGINNING.
I THINK THAT WOULD BE A RATHER GOOD IDEA.

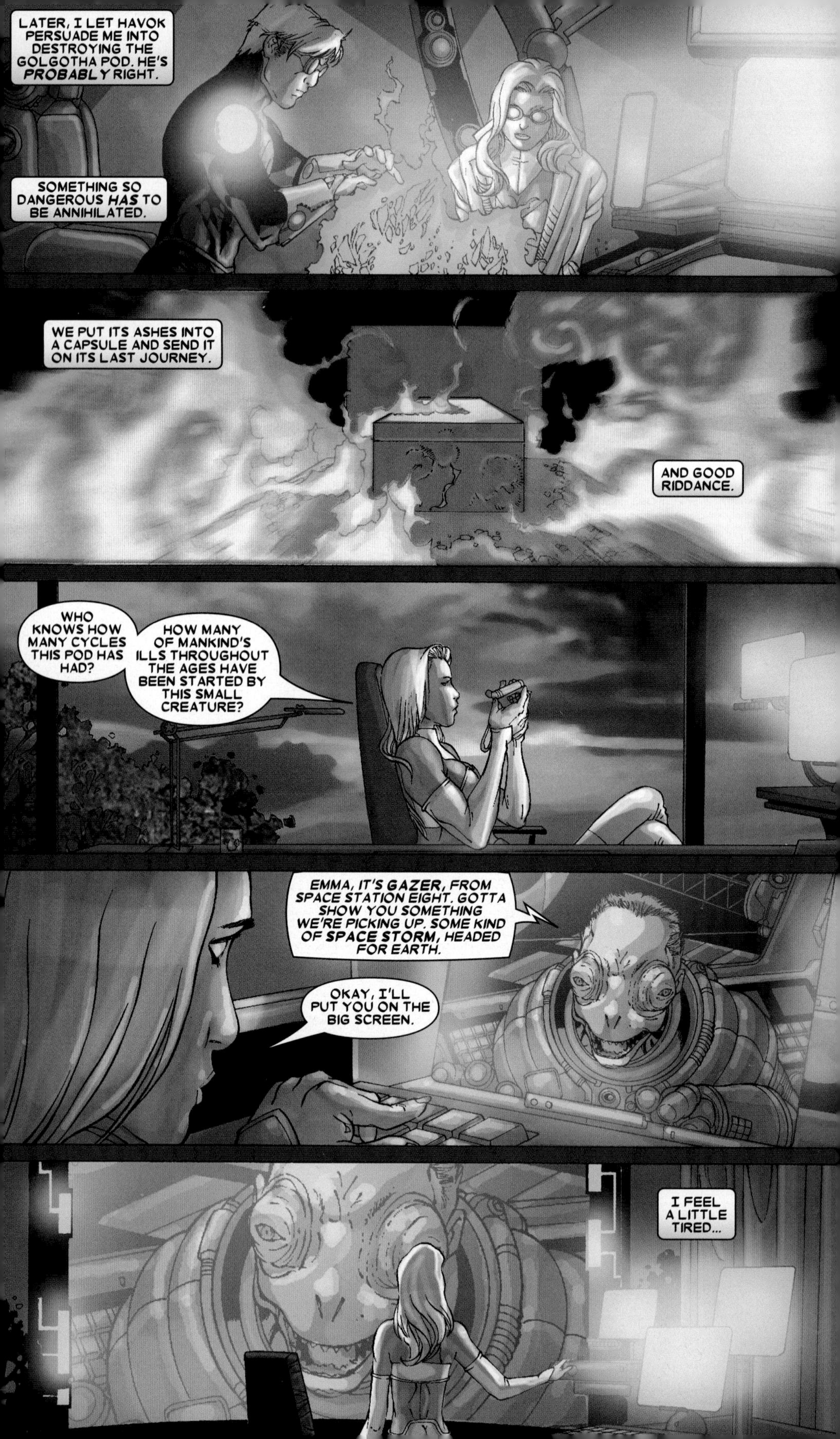
LATER, I LET HAVOK PERSUADE ME INTO DESTROYING THE GOLGOTHA POD. HE'S *PROBABLY* RIGHT.
SOMETHING SO DANGEROUS *HAS* TO BE ANNIHILATED.
WE PUT ITS ASHES INTO A CAPSULE AND SEND IT ON ITS LAST JOURNEY.
AND GOOD RIDDANCE.
WHO KNOWS HOW MANY CYCLES THIS POD HAS HAD?
HOW MANY OF MANKIND'S ILLS THROUGHOUT THE AGES HAVE BEEN STARTED BY THIS SMALL CREATURE?
EMMA, IT'S **GAZER**, FROM SPACE STATION EIGHT. GOTTA SHOW YOU SOMETHING WE'RE PICKING UP. SOME KIND OF **SPACE STORM**, HEADED FOR EARTH.
OKAY, I'LL PUT YOU ON THE BIG SCREEN.
I FEEL A LITTLE TIRED...

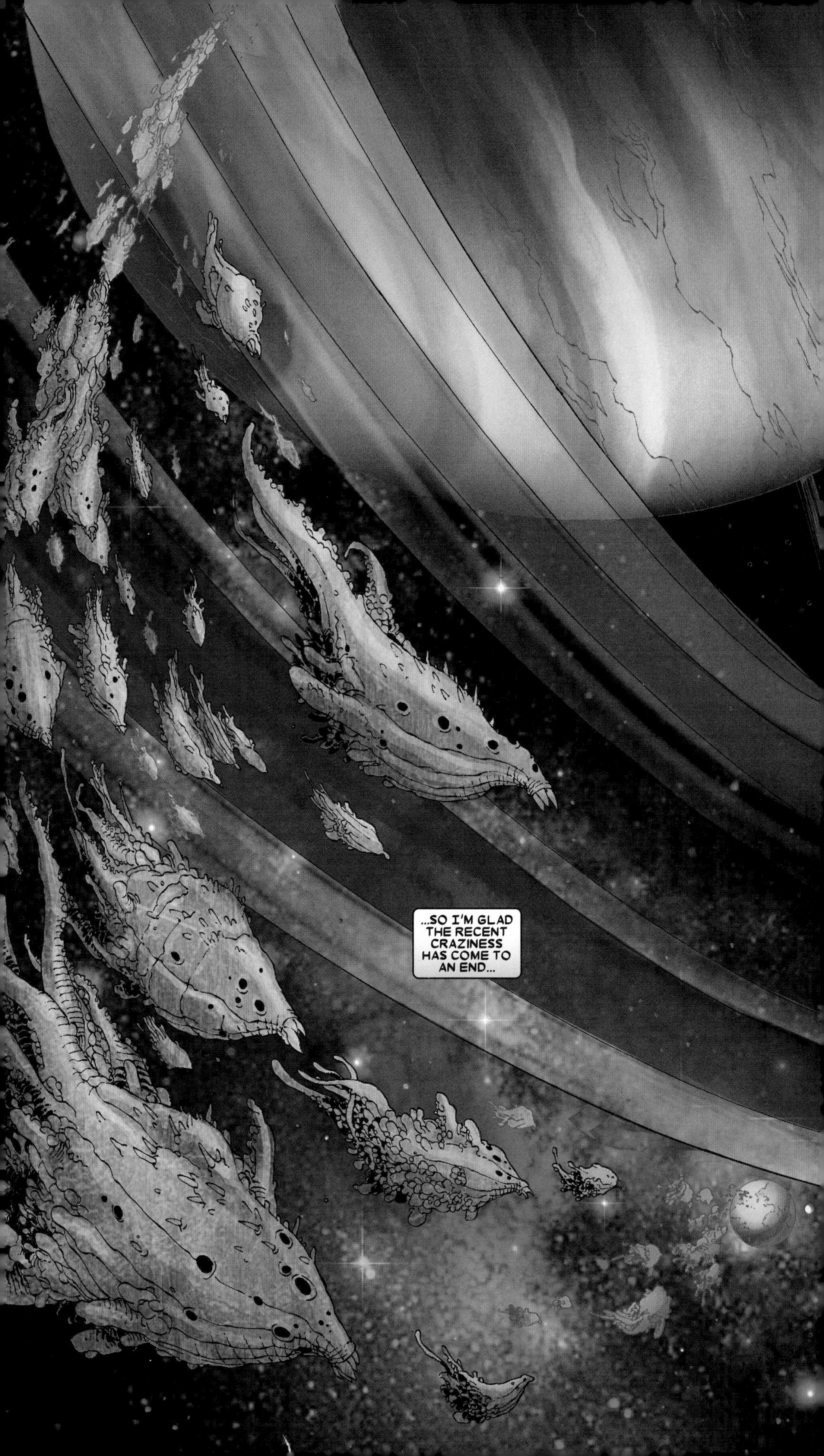
...SO I'M GLAD THE RECENT CRAZINESS HAS COME TO AN END...

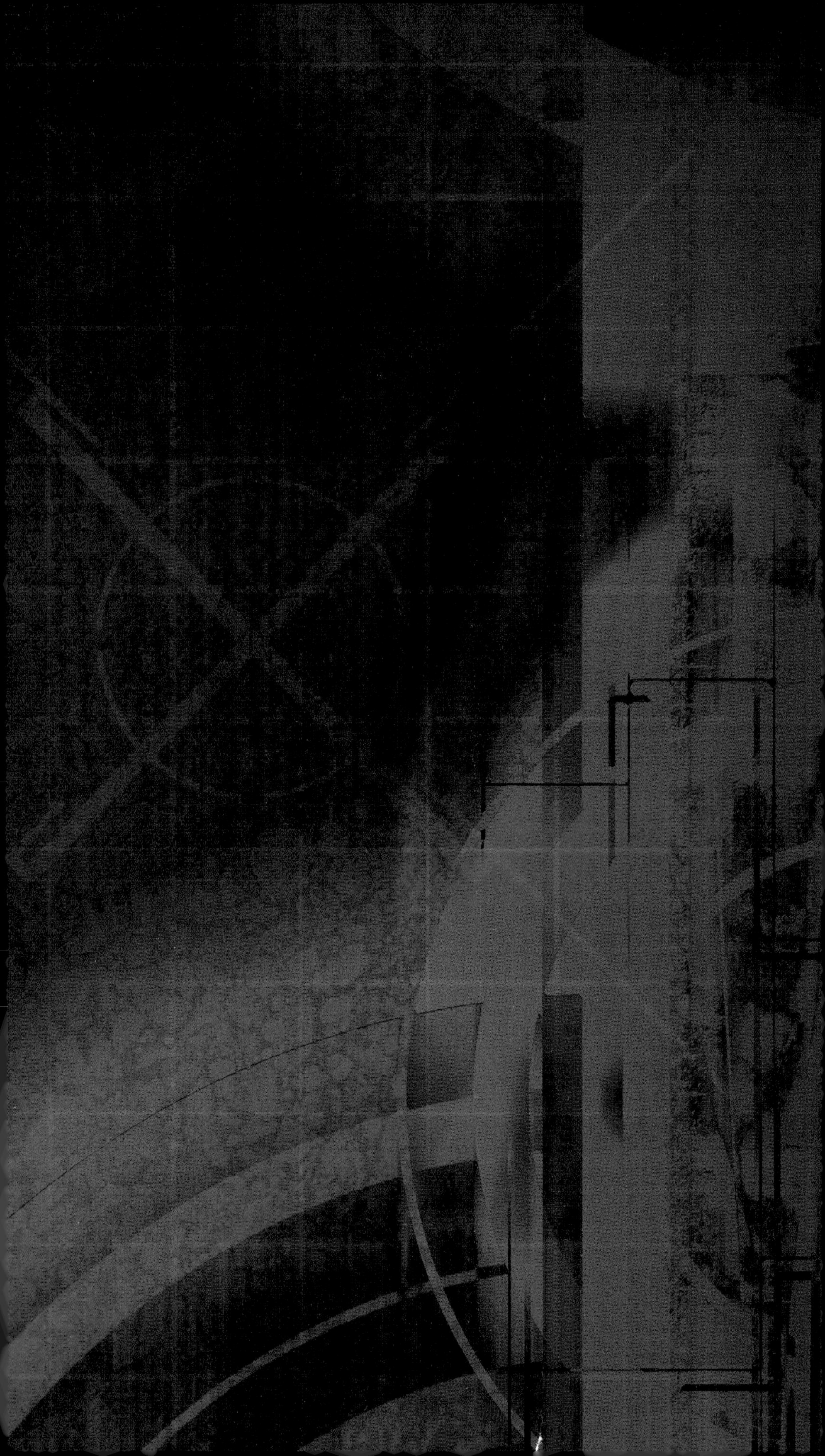

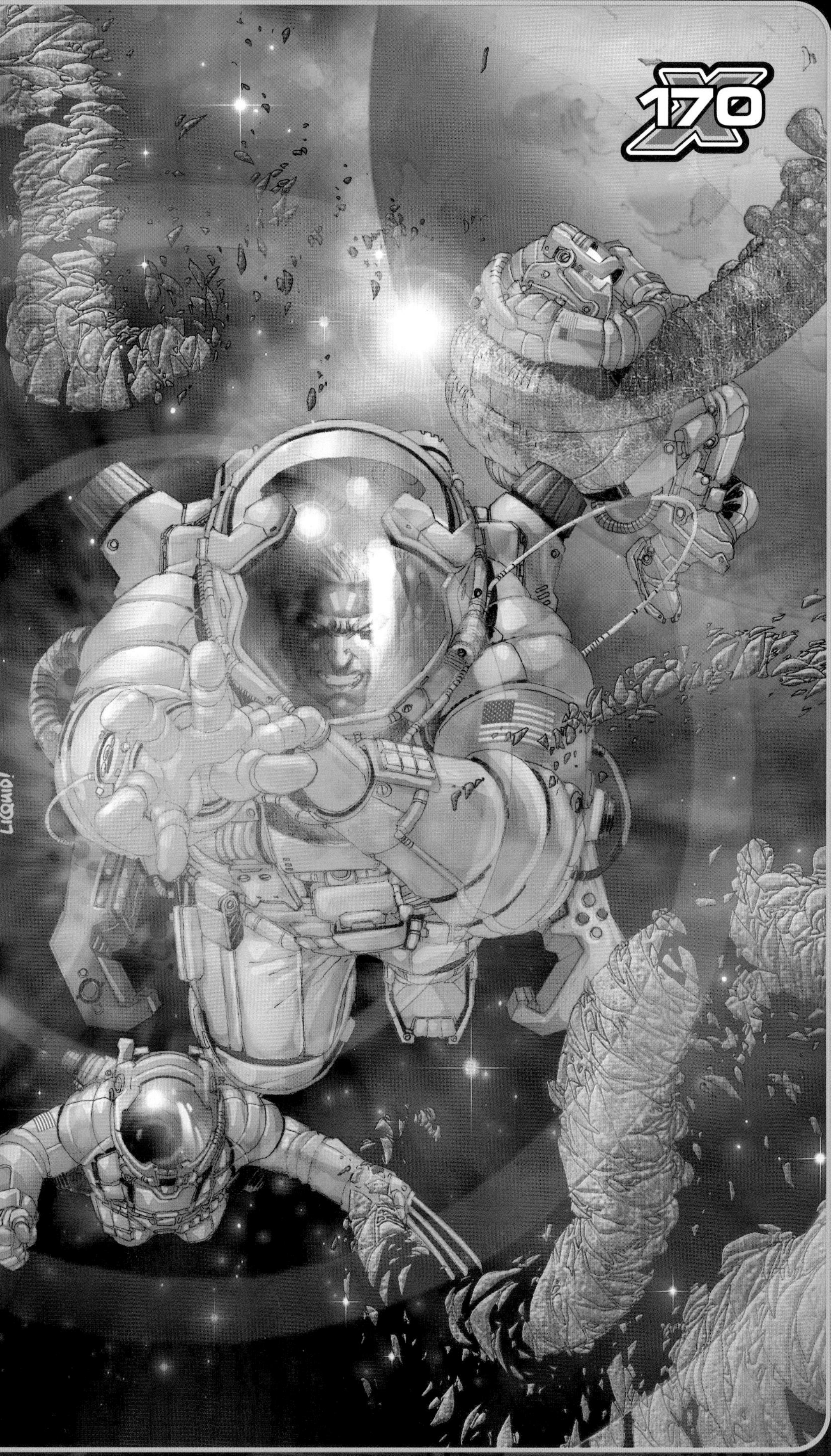
170

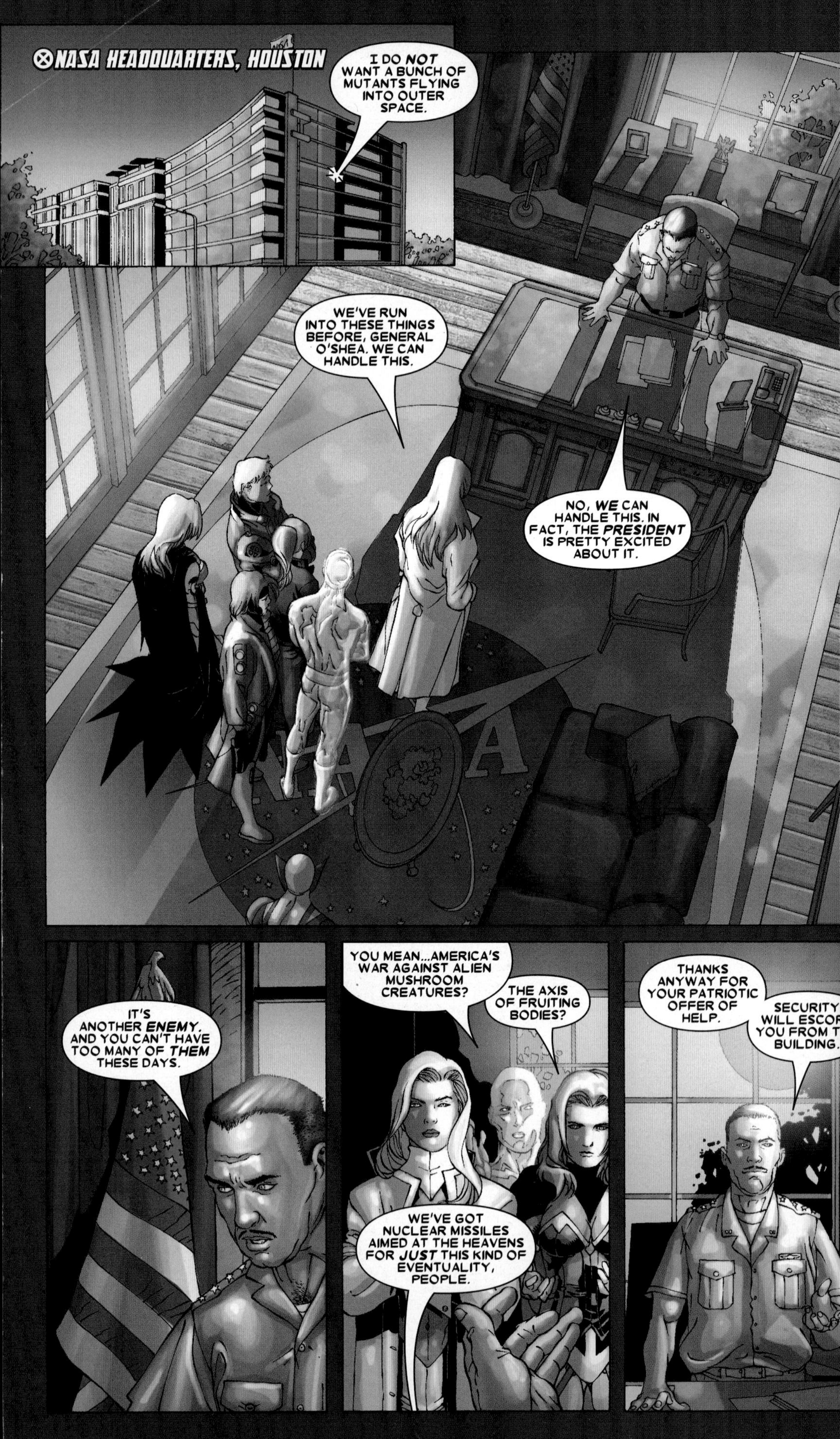
NASA HEADQUARTERS, HOUSTON
I DO NOT WANT A BUNCH OF MUTANTS FLYING INTO OUTER SPACE.
WE'VE RUN INTO THESE THINGS BEFORE, GENERAL O'SHEA. WE CAN HANDLE THIS.
NO, WE CAN HANDLE THIS. IN FACT, THE PRESIDENT IS PRETTY EXCITED ABOUT IT.
IT'S ANOTHER ENEMY. AND YOU CAN'T HAVE TOO MANY OF THEM THESE DAYS.
YOU MEAN...AMERICA'S WAR AGAINST ALIEN MUSHROOM CREATURES?
THE AXIS OF FRUITING BODIES?
WE'VE GOT NUCLEAR MISSILES AIMED AT THE HEAVENS FOR JUST THIS KIND OF EVENTUALITY, PEOPLE.
THANKS ANYWAY FOR YOUR PATRIOTIC OFFER OF HELP.
SECURITY WILL ESCOR YOU FROM T BUILDING.

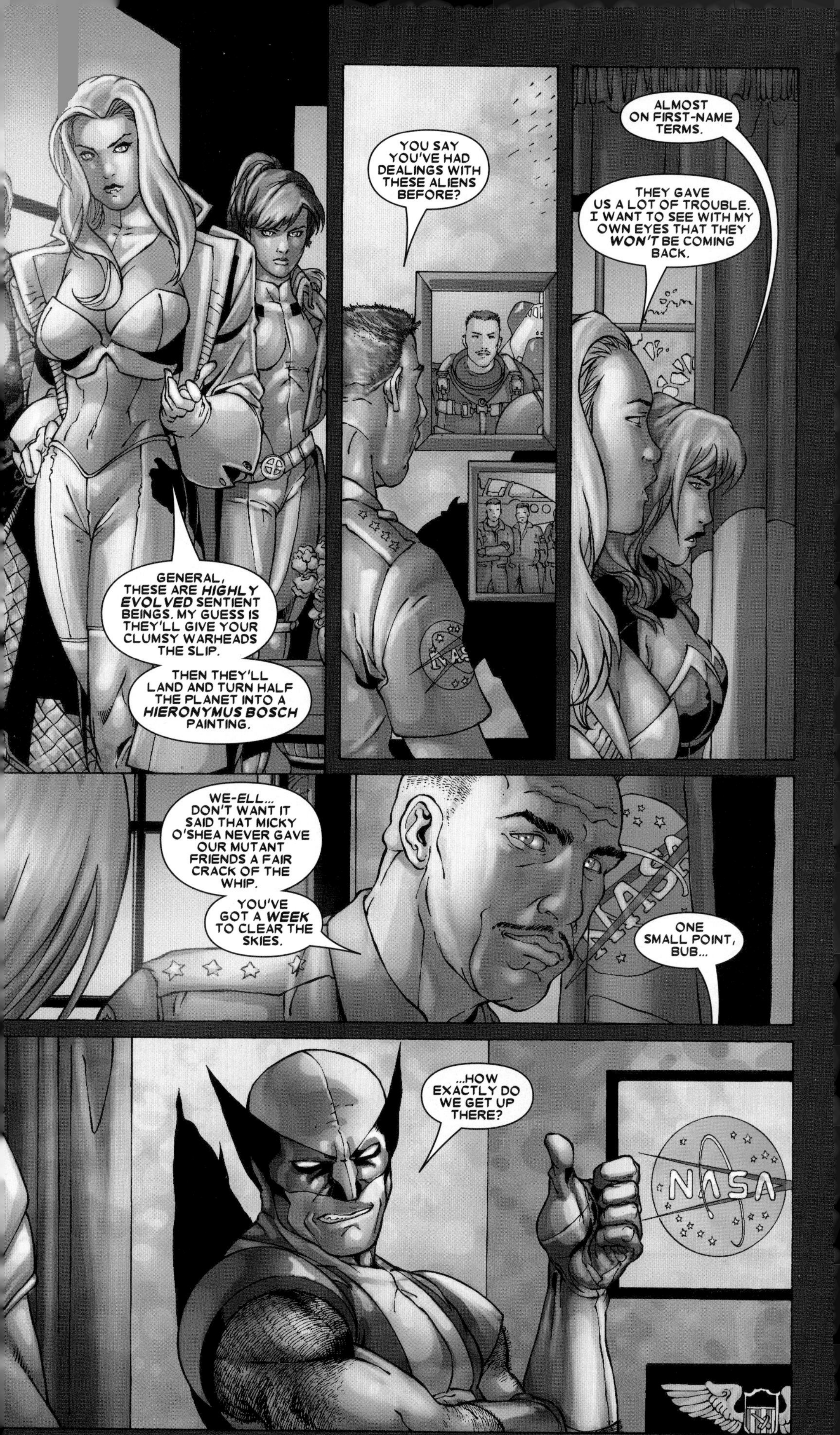
GENERAL, THESE ARE HIGHLY EVOLVED SENTIENT BEINGS. MY GUESS IS THEY'LL GIVE YOUR CLUMSY WARHEADS THE SLIP.
THEN THEY'LL LAND AND TURN HALF THE PLANET INTO A HIERONYMUS BOSCH PAINTING.
YOU SAY YOU'VE HAD DEALINGS WITH THESE ALIENS BEFORE?
ALMOST ON FIRST-NAME TERMS.
THEY GAVE US A LOT OF TROUBLE. I WANT TO SEE WITH MY OWN EYES THAT THEY WON'T BE COMING BACK.
WE-ELL... DON'T WANT IT SAID THAT MICKY O'SHEA NEVER GAVE OUR MUTANT FRIENDS A FAIR CRACK OF THE WHIP.
YOU'VE GOT A WEEK TO CLEAR THE SKIES.
ONE SMALL POINT, BUB...
...HOW EXACTLY DO WE GET UP THERE?
NASA

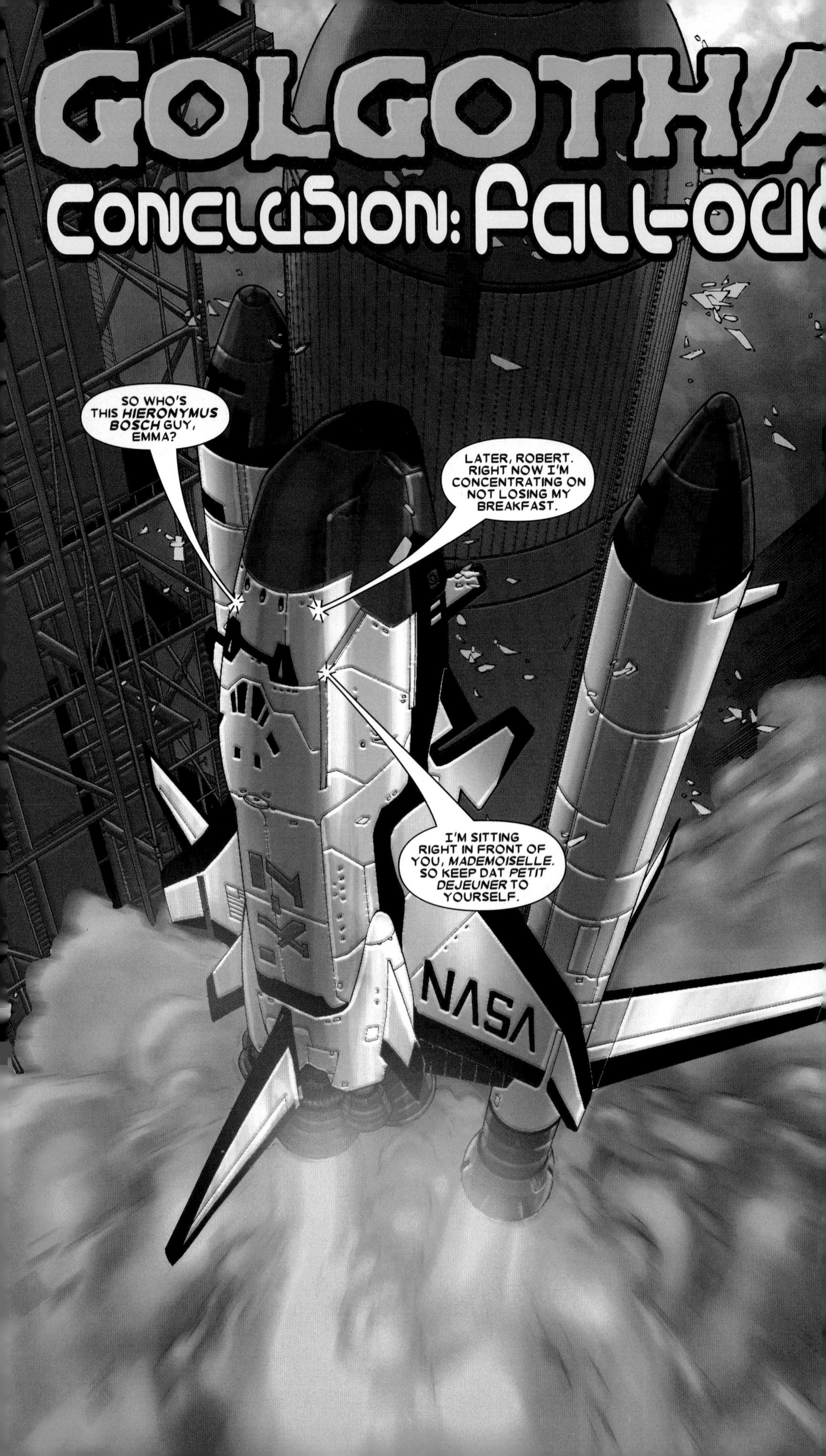
GOLGOTHA
CONCLUSION: FALLOUT
SO WHO'S THIS *HIERONYMUS BOSCH* GUY, EMMA?
LATER, ROBERT. RIGHT NOW I'M CONCENTRATING ON NOT LOSING MY BREAKFAST.
I'M SITTING RIGHT IN FRONT OF YOU, *MADEMOISELLE*. SO KEEP DAT *PETIT DEJEUNER* TO YOURSELF.
NASA

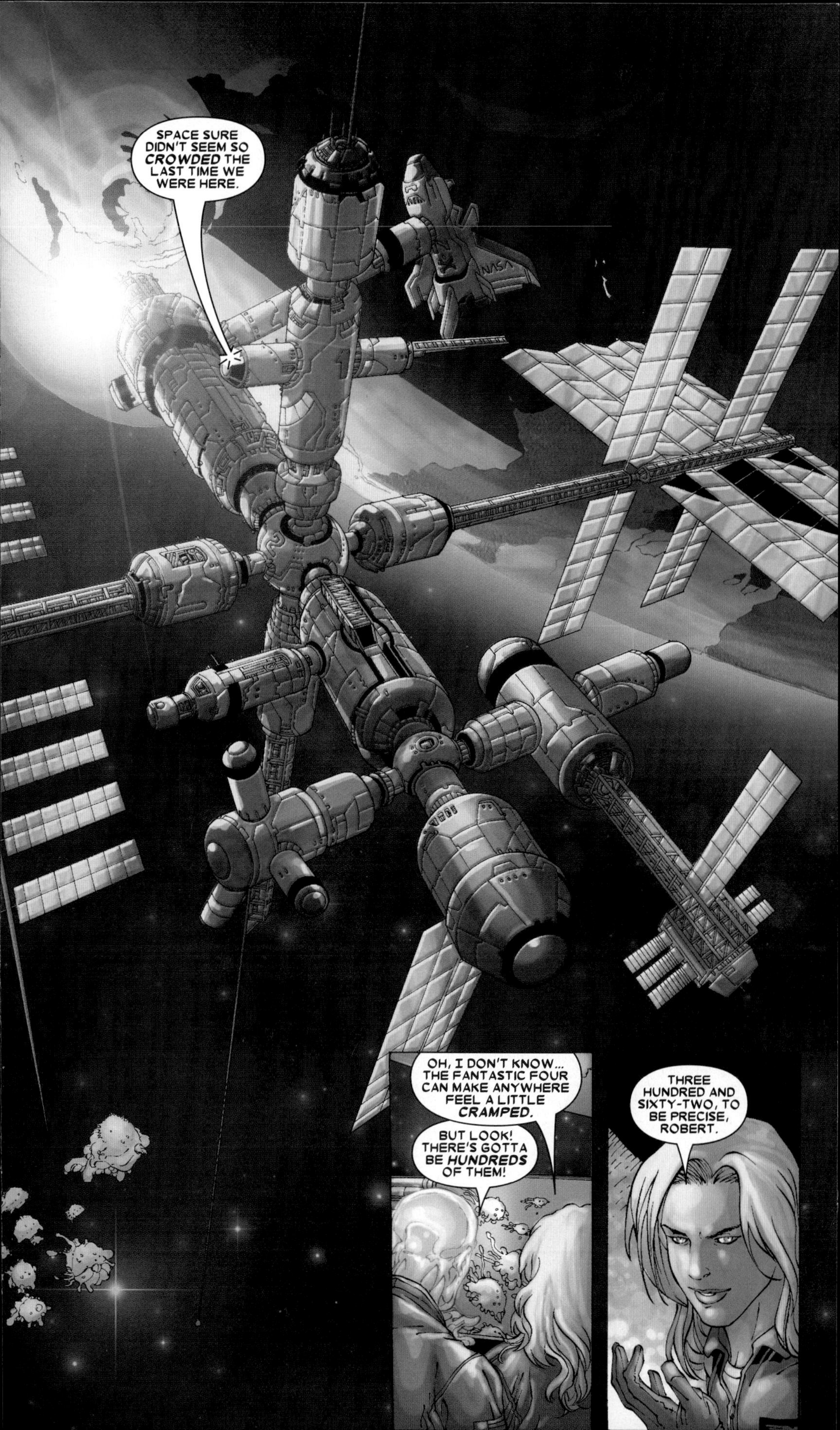
SPACE SURE DIDN'T SEEM SO CROWDED THE LAST TIME WE WERE HERE.
NASA
OH, I DON'T KNOW... THE FANTASTIC FOUR CAN MAKE ANYWHERE FEEL A LITTLE CRAMPED.
BUT LOOK! THERE'S GOTTA BE HUNDREDS OF THEM!
THREE HUNDRED AND SIXTY-TWO, TO BE PRECISE, ROBERT.

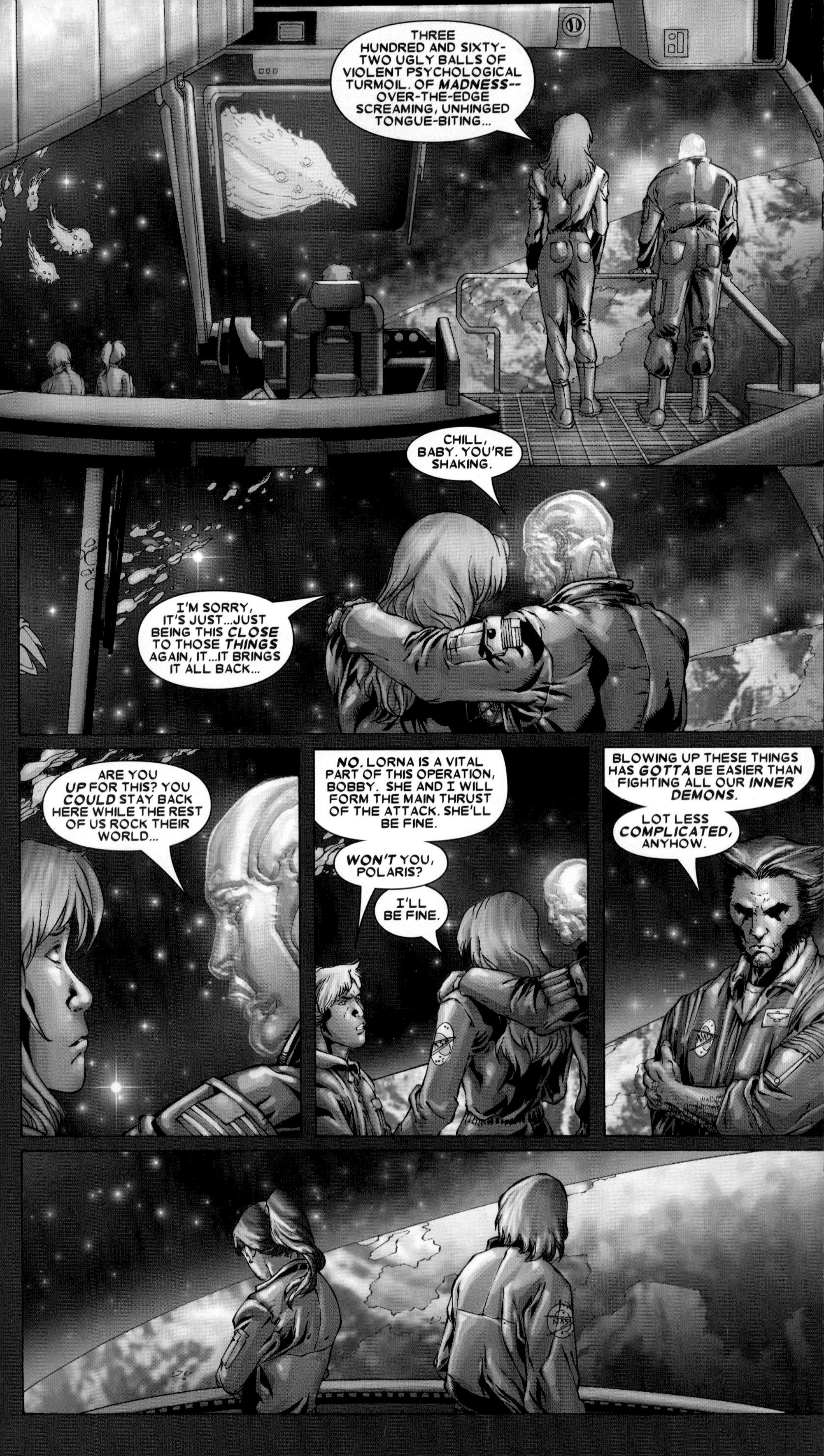
THREE HUNDRED AND SIXTY-TWO UGLY BALLS OF VIOLENT PSYCHOLOGICAL TURMOIL. OF MADNESS-- OVER-THE-EDGE SCREAMING, UNHINGED TONGUE-BITING...
CHILL, BABY. YOU'RE SHAKING.
I'M SORRY, IT'S JUST...JUST BEING THIS CLOSE TO THOSE THINGS AGAIN, IT...IT BRINGS IT ALL BACK...
ARE YOU UP FOR THIS? YOU COULD STAY BACK HERE WHILE THE REST OF US ROCK THEIR WORLD...
NO. LORNA IS A VITAL PART OF THIS OPERATION, BOBBY. SHE AND I WILL FORM THE MAIN THRUST OF THE ATTACK. SHE'LL BE FINE.
WON'T YOU, POLARIS?
I'LL BE FINE.
BLOWING UP THESE THINGS HAS GOTTA BE EASIER THAN FIGHTING ALL OUR INNER DEMONS.
LOT LESS COMPLICATED, ANYHOW.

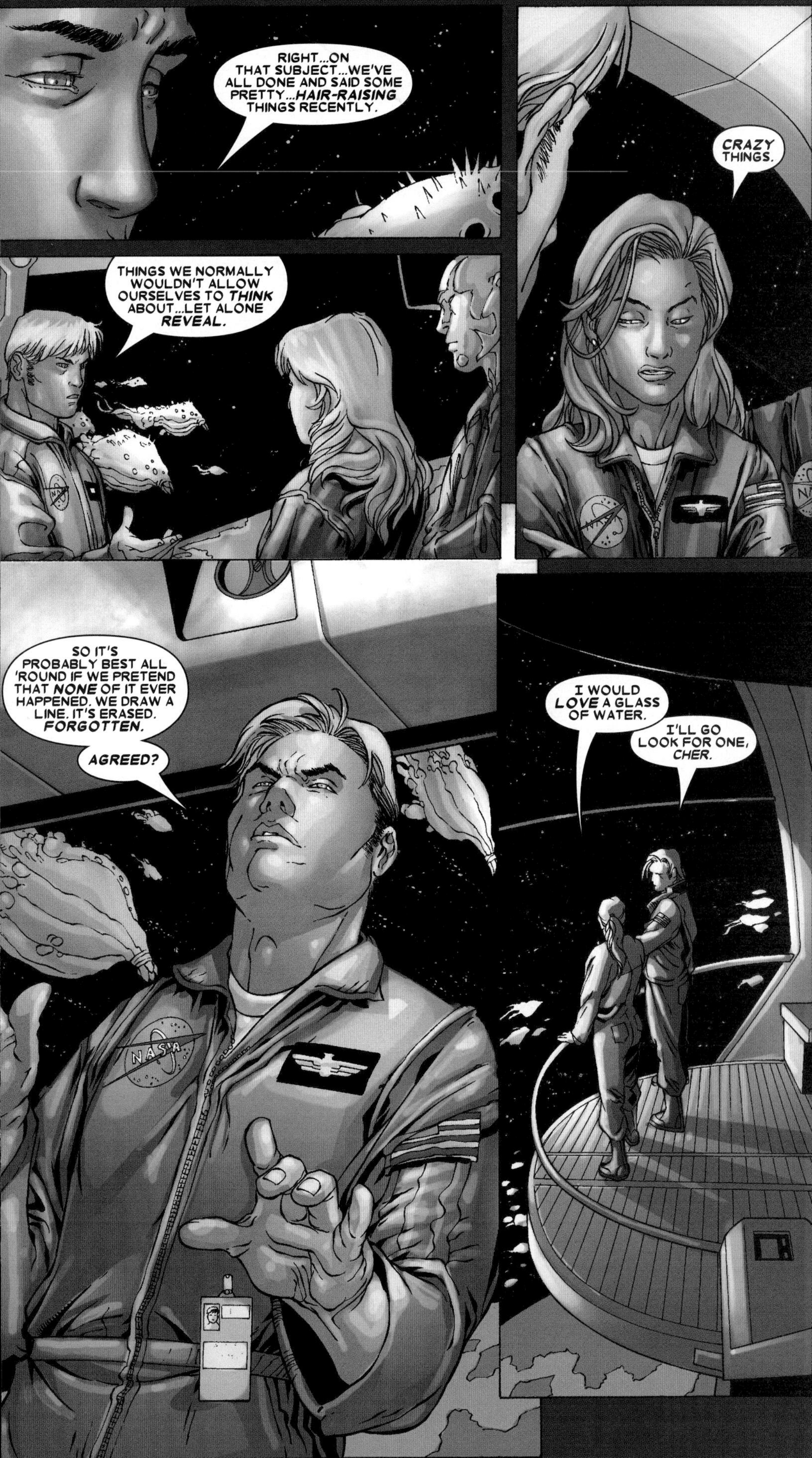
RIGHT...ON THAT SUBJECT...WE'VE ALL DONE AND SAID SOME PRETTY...HAIR-RAISING THINGS RECENTLY.
CRAZY THINGS.
THINGS WE NORMALLY WOULDN'T ALLOW OURSELVES TO THINK ABOUT...LET ALONE REVEAL.
SO IT'S PROBABLY BEST ALL 'ROUND IF WE PRETEND THAT NONE OF IT EVER HAPPENED. WE DRAW A LINE. IT'S ERASED. FORGOTTEN.
AGREED?
I WOULD LOVE A GLASS OF WATER.
I'LL GO LOOK FOR ONE, CHER.

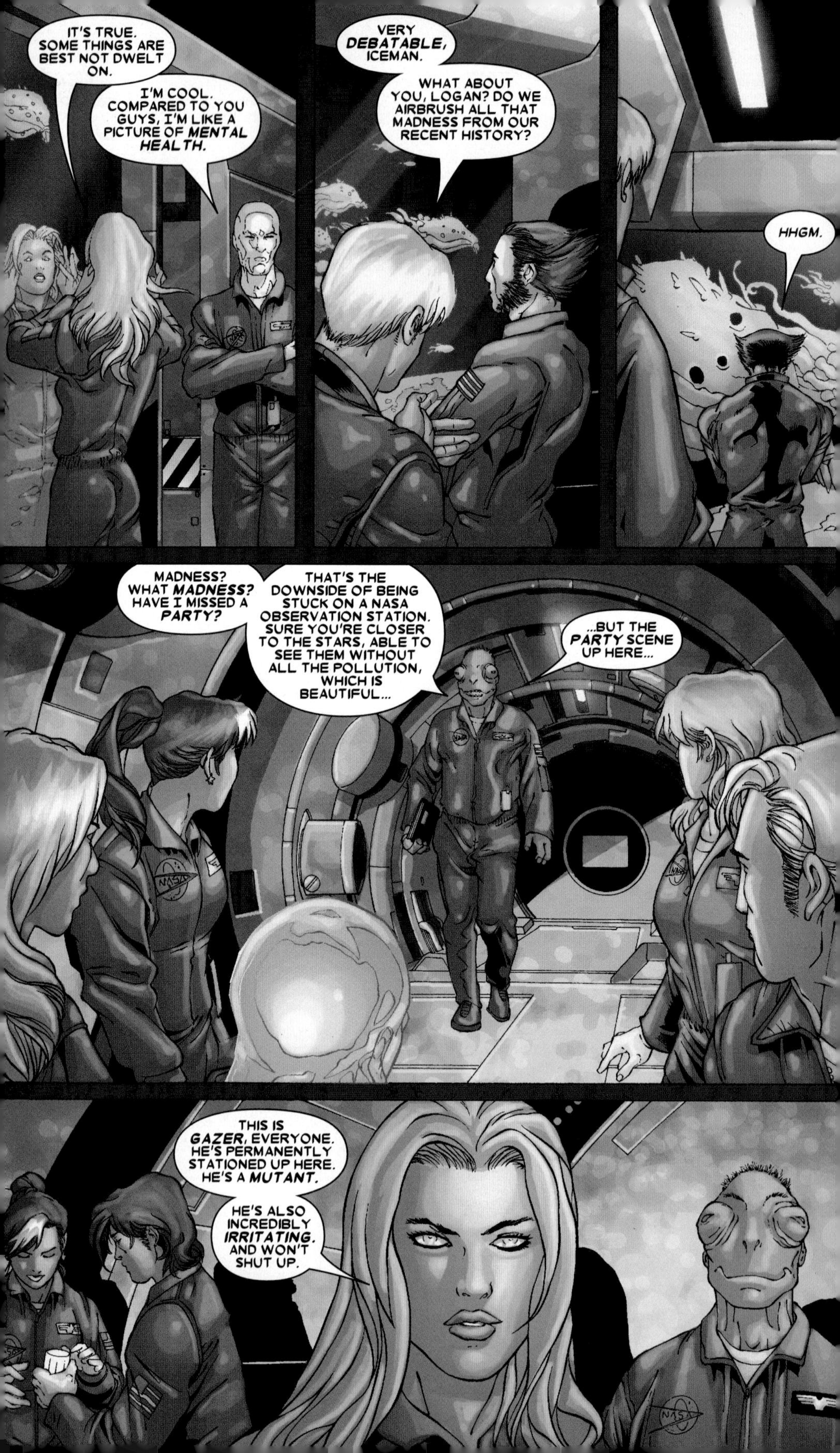
IT'S TRUE. SOME THINGS ARE BEST NOT DWELT ON.
I'M COOL. COMPARED TO YOU GUYS, I'M LIKE A PICTURE OF MENTAL HEALTH.
VERY DEBATABLE, ICEMAN.
WHAT ABOUT YOU, LOGAN? DO WE AIRBRUSH ALL THAT MADNESS FROM OUR RECENT HISTORY?
HHGM.
MADNESS? WHAT MADNESS? HAVE I MISSED A PARTY?
THAT'S THE DOWNSIDE OF BEING STUCK ON A NASA OBSERVATION STATION. SURE YOU'RE CLOSER TO THE STARS, ABLE TO SEE THEM WITHOUT ALL THE POLLUTION, WHICH IS BEAUTIFUL...
...BUT THE PARTY SCENE UP HERE...
THIS IS GAZER, EVERYONE. HE'S PERMANENTLY STATIONED UP HERE. HE'S A MUTANT.
HE'S ALSO INCREDIBLY IRRITATING. AND WON'T SHUT UP.

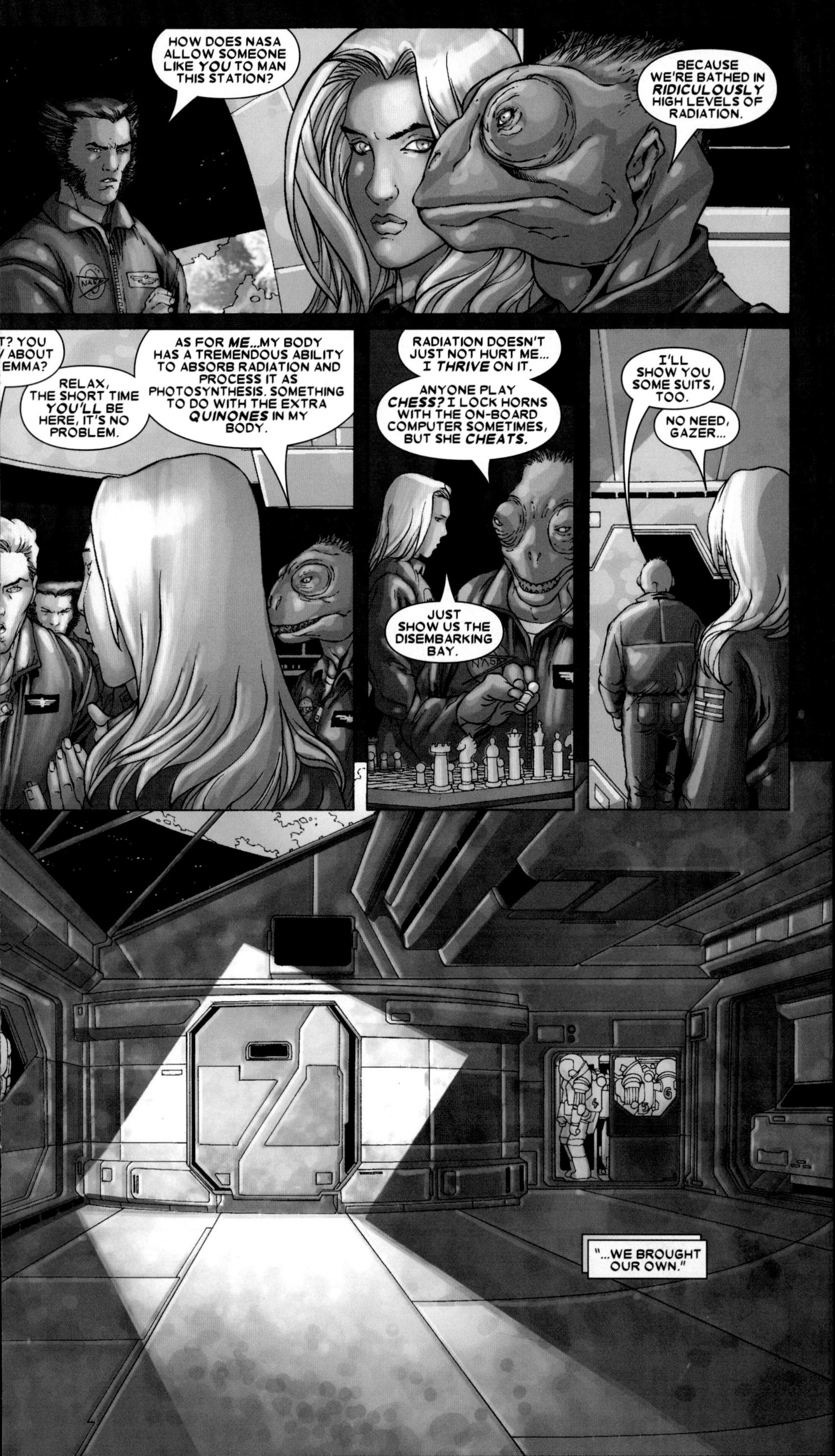

HOW DOES NASA ALLOW SOMEONE LIKE YOU TO MAN THIS STATION?
BECAUSE WE'RE BATHED IN RIDICULOUSLY HIGH LEVELS OF RADIATION.
T? YOU ABOUT EMMA?
RELAX, THE SHORT TIME YOU'LL BE HERE, IT'S NO PROBLEM.
AS FOR ME...MY BODY HAS A TREMENDOUS ABILITY TO ABSORB RADIATION AND PROCESS IT AS PHOTOSYNTHESIS. SOMETHING TO DO WITH THE EXTRA QUINONES IN MY BODY.
RADIATION DOESN'T JUST NOT HURT ME... I THRIVE ON IT.
ANYONE PLAY CHESS? I LOCK HORNS WITH THE ON-BOARD COMPUTER SOMETIMES, BUT SHE CHEATS.
JUST SHOW US THE DISEMBARKING BAY.
I'LL SHOW YOU SOME SUITS, TOO.
NO NEED, GAZER...
"...WE BROUGHT OUR OWN."

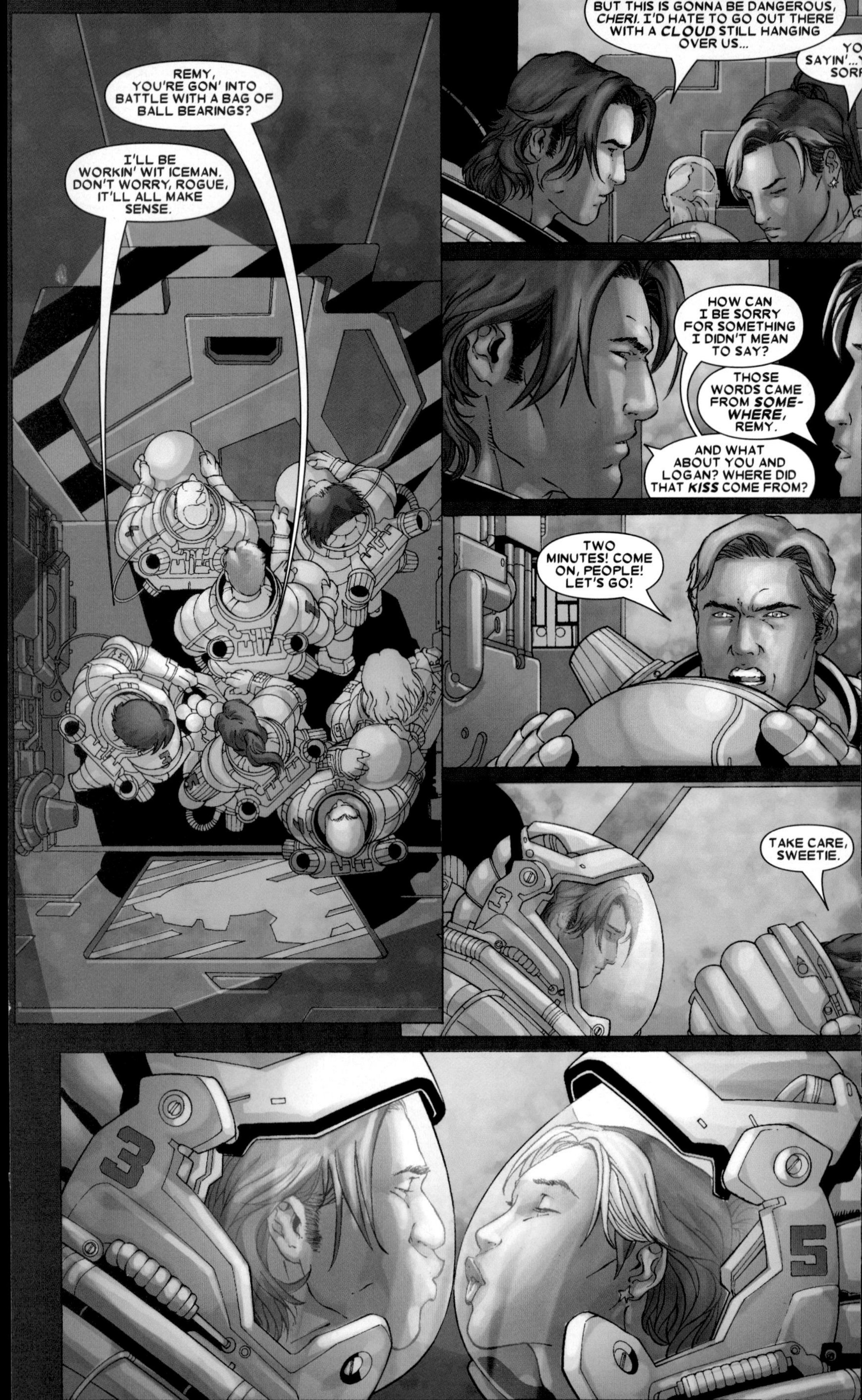
REMY, YOU'RE GON' INTO BATTLE WITH A BAG OF BALL BEARINGS?
I'LL BE WORKIN' WIT ICEMAN. DON'T WORRY, ROGUE, IT'LL ALL MAKE SENSE.
BUT THIS IS GONNA BE DANGEROUS, CHERI. I'D HATE TO GO OUT THERE WITH A CLOUD STILL HANGING OVER US...
HOW CAN I BE SORRY FOR SOMETHING I DIDN'T MEAN TO SAY?
THOSE WORDS CAME FROM SOME-WHERE, REMY.
AND WHAT ABOUT YOU AND LOGAN? WHERE DID THAT KISS COME FROM?
TWO MINUTES! COME ON, PEOPLE! LET'S GO!
TAKE CARE, SWEETIE.

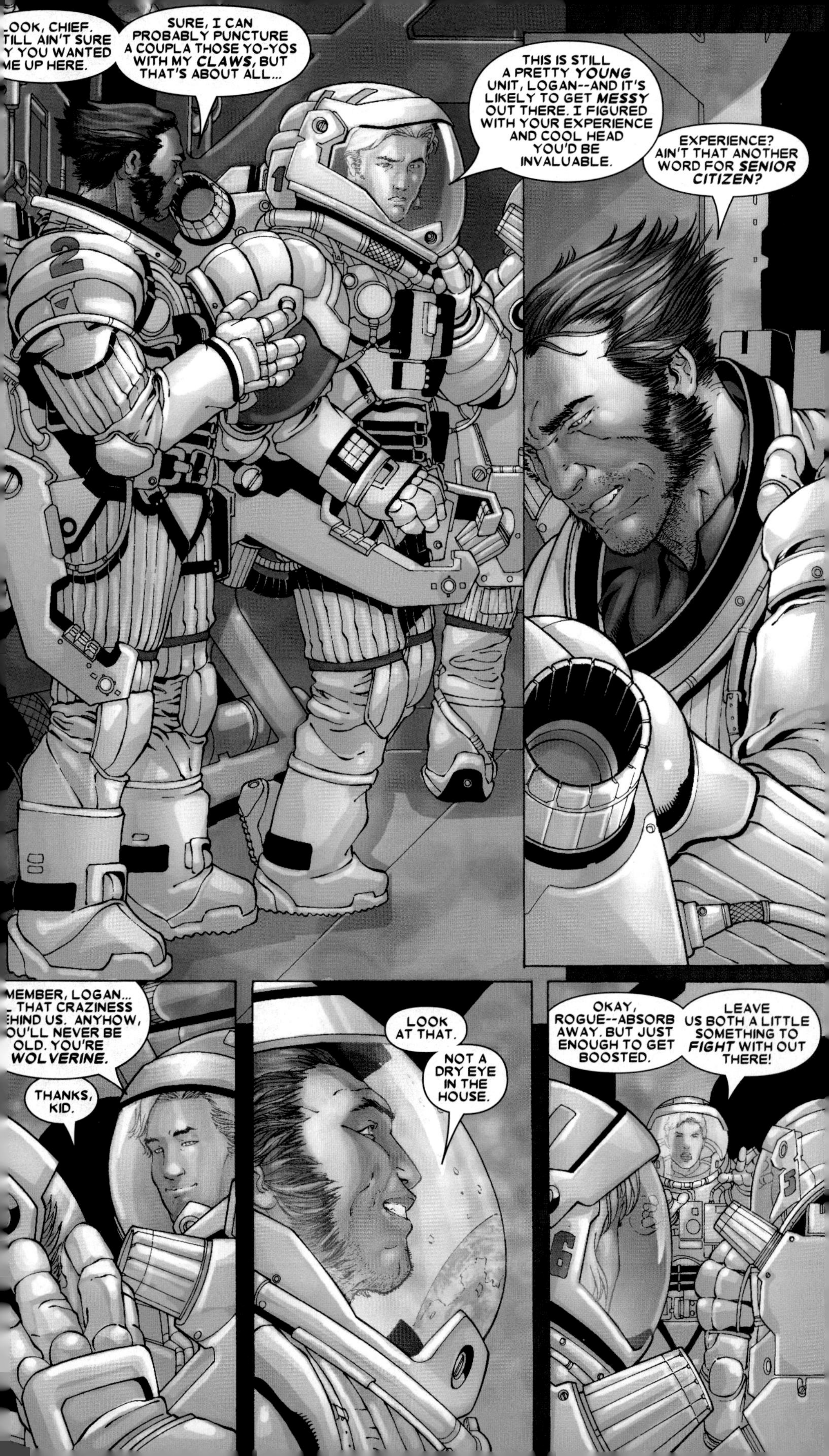
LOOK, CHIEF. STILL AIN'T SURE Y YOU WANTED ME UP HERE.
SURE, I CAN PROBABLY PUNCTURE A COUPLA THOSE YO-YOS WITH MY CLAWS, BUT THAT'S ABOUT ALL...
THIS IS STILL A PRETTY YOUNG UNIT, LOGAN--AND IT'S LIKELY TO GET MESSY OUT THERE. I FIGURED WITH YOUR EXPERIENCE AND COOL HEAD YOU'D BE INVALUABLE.
EXPERIENCE? AIN'T THAT ANOTHER WORD FOR SENIOR CITIZEN?
MEMBER, LOGAN... THAT CRAZINESS EHIND US. ANYHOW, OU'LL NEVER BE OLD. YOU'RE WOLVERINE.
THANKS, KID.
LOOK AT THAT.
NOT A DRY EYE IN THE HOUSE.
OKAY, ROGUE--ABSORB AWAY. BUT JUST ENOUGH TO GET BOOSTED.
LEAVE US BOTH A LITTLE SOMETHING TO FIGHT WITH OUT THERE!

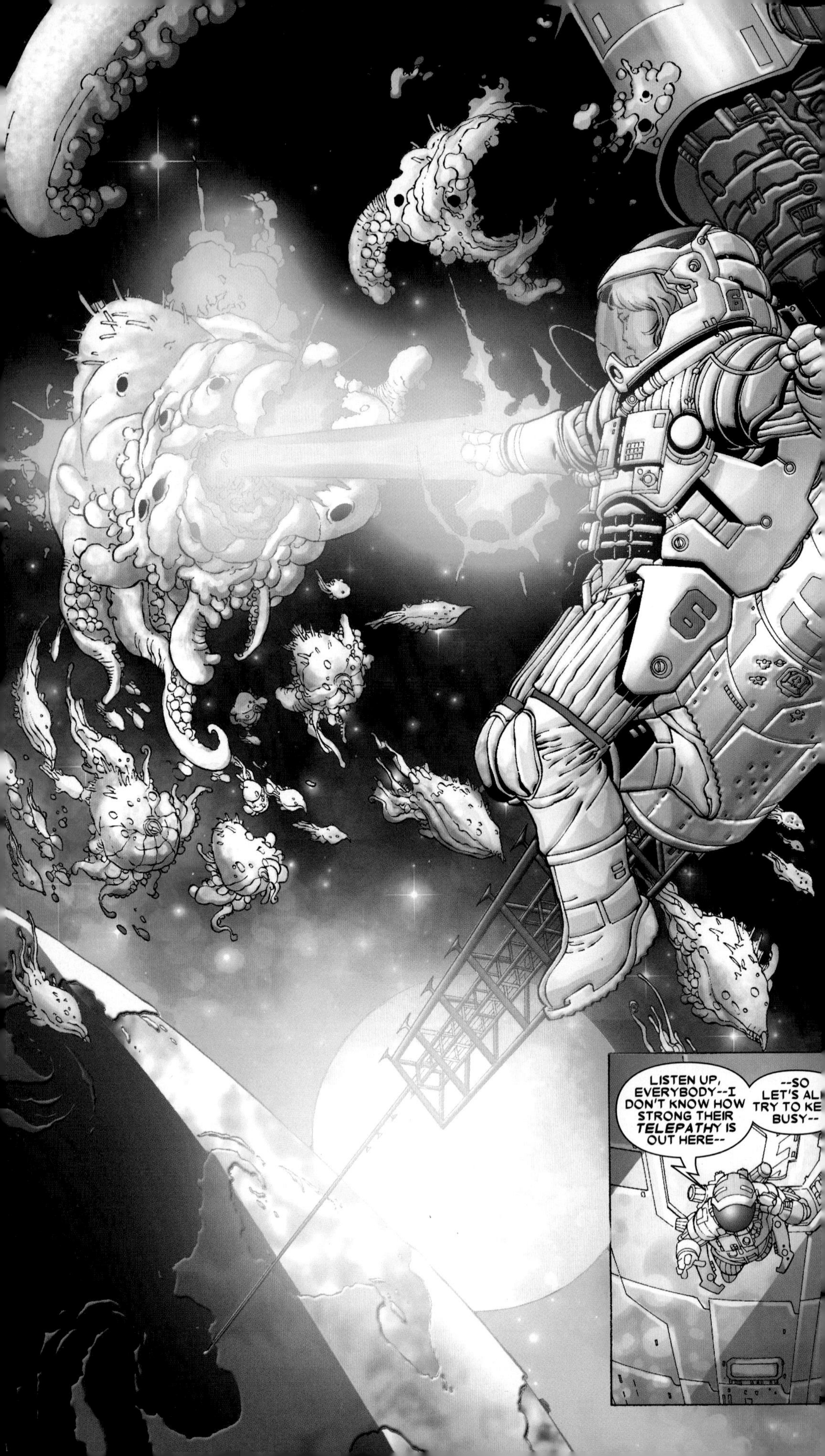
LISTEN UP, EVERYBODY--I DON'T KNOW HOW STRONG THEIR *TELEPATHY* IS OUT HERE--
--SO LET'S AL TRY TO KE BUSY--

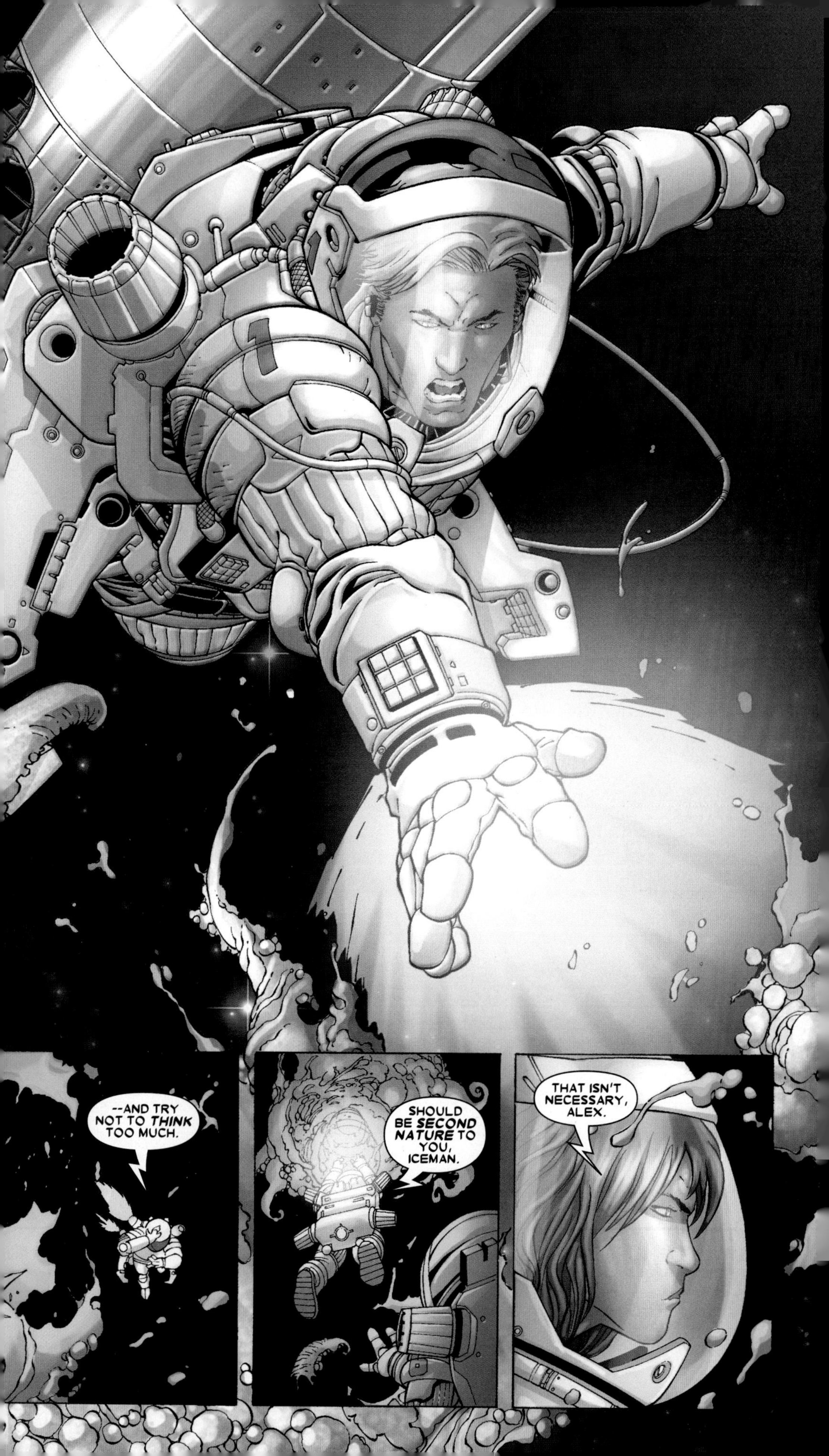
--AND TRY NOT TO THINK TOO MUCH.
SHOULD BE SECOND NATURE TO YOU, ICEMAN.
THAT ISN'T NECESSARY, ALEX.

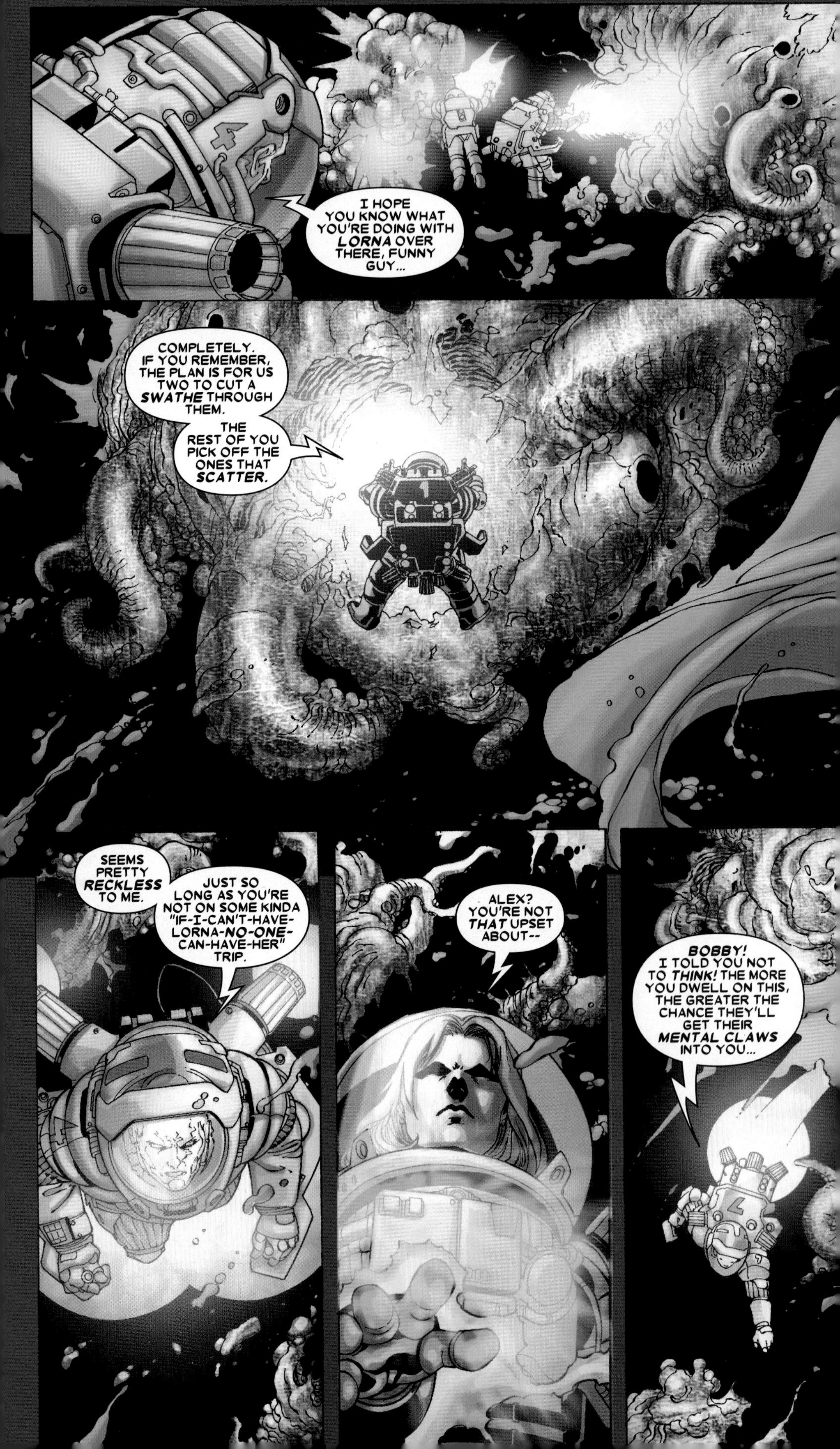
I HOPE YOU KNOW WHAT YOU'RE DOING WITH *LORNA* OVER THERE, FUNNY GUY...
COMPLETELY. IF YOU REMEMBER, THE PLAN IS FOR US TWO TO CUT A *SWATHE* THROUGH THEM.
THE REST OF YOU PICK OFF THE ONES THAT *SCATTER.*
SEEMS PRETTY *RECKLESS* TO ME.
JUST SO LONG AS YOU'RE NOT ON SOME KINDA "IF-I-CAN'T-HAVE-LORNA-*NO-ONE*-CAN-HAVE-HER" TRIP.
ALEX? YOU'RE NOT *THAT* UPSET ABOUT--
*BOBBY!* I TOLD YOU NOT TO *THINK!* THE MORE YOU DWELL ON THIS, THE GREATER THE CHANCE THEY'LL GET THEIR *MENTAL CLAWS* INTO YOU...

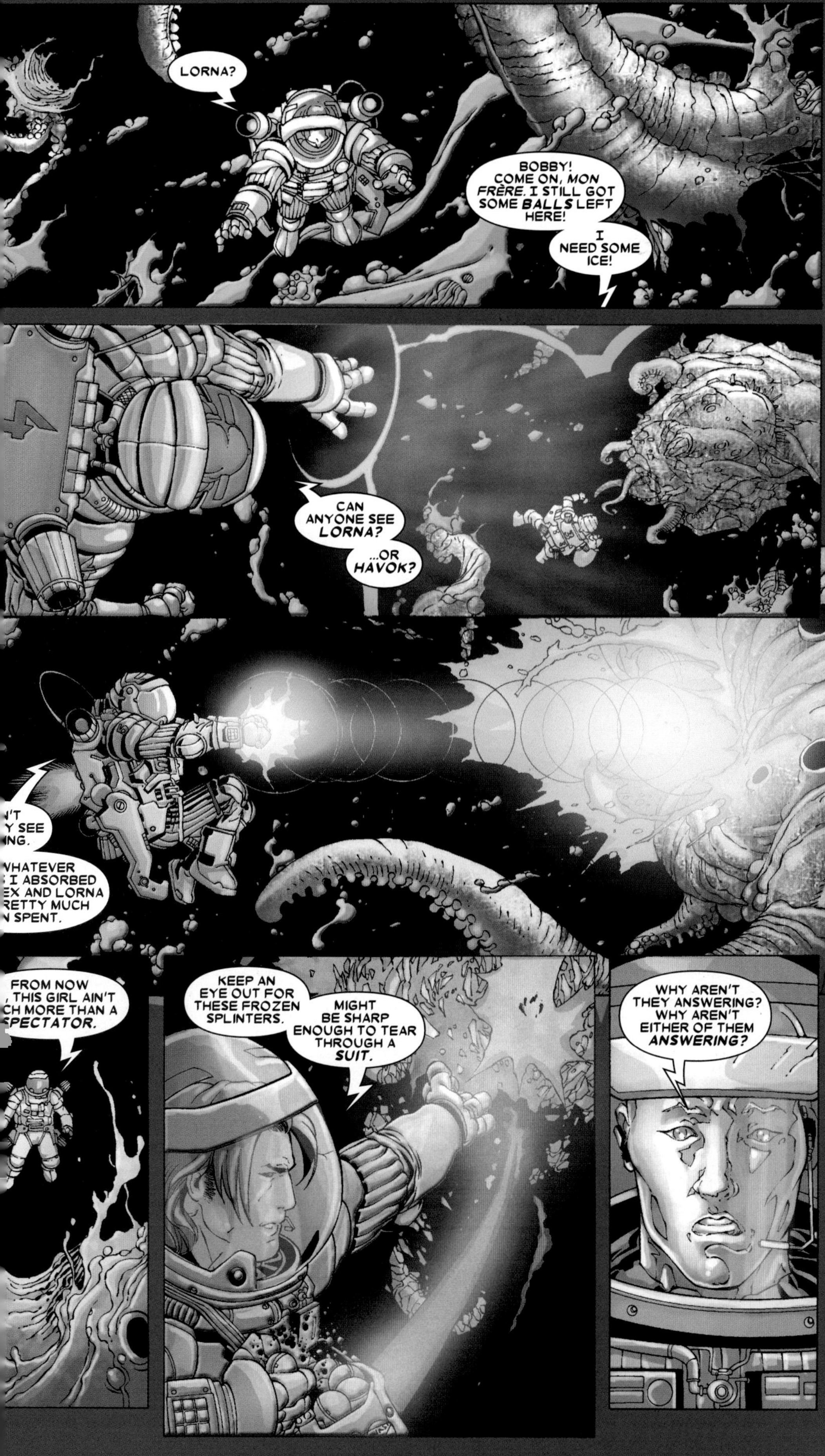
LORNA?
BOBBY! COME ON, MON FRÈRE. I STILL GOT SOME BALLS LEFT HERE!
I NEED SOME ICE!
CAN ANYONE SEE LORNA?
...OR HAVOK?
N'T Y SEE NG.
WHATEVER I ABSORBED EX AND LORNA RETTY MUCH N SPENT.
FROM NOW , THIS GIRL AIN'T CH MORE THAN A SPECTATOR.
KEEP AN EYE OUT FOR THESE FROZEN SPLINTERS.
MIGHT BE SHARP ENOUGH TO TEAR THROUGH A SUIT.
WHY AREN'T THEY ANSWERING? WHY AREN'T EITHER OF THEM ANSWERING?

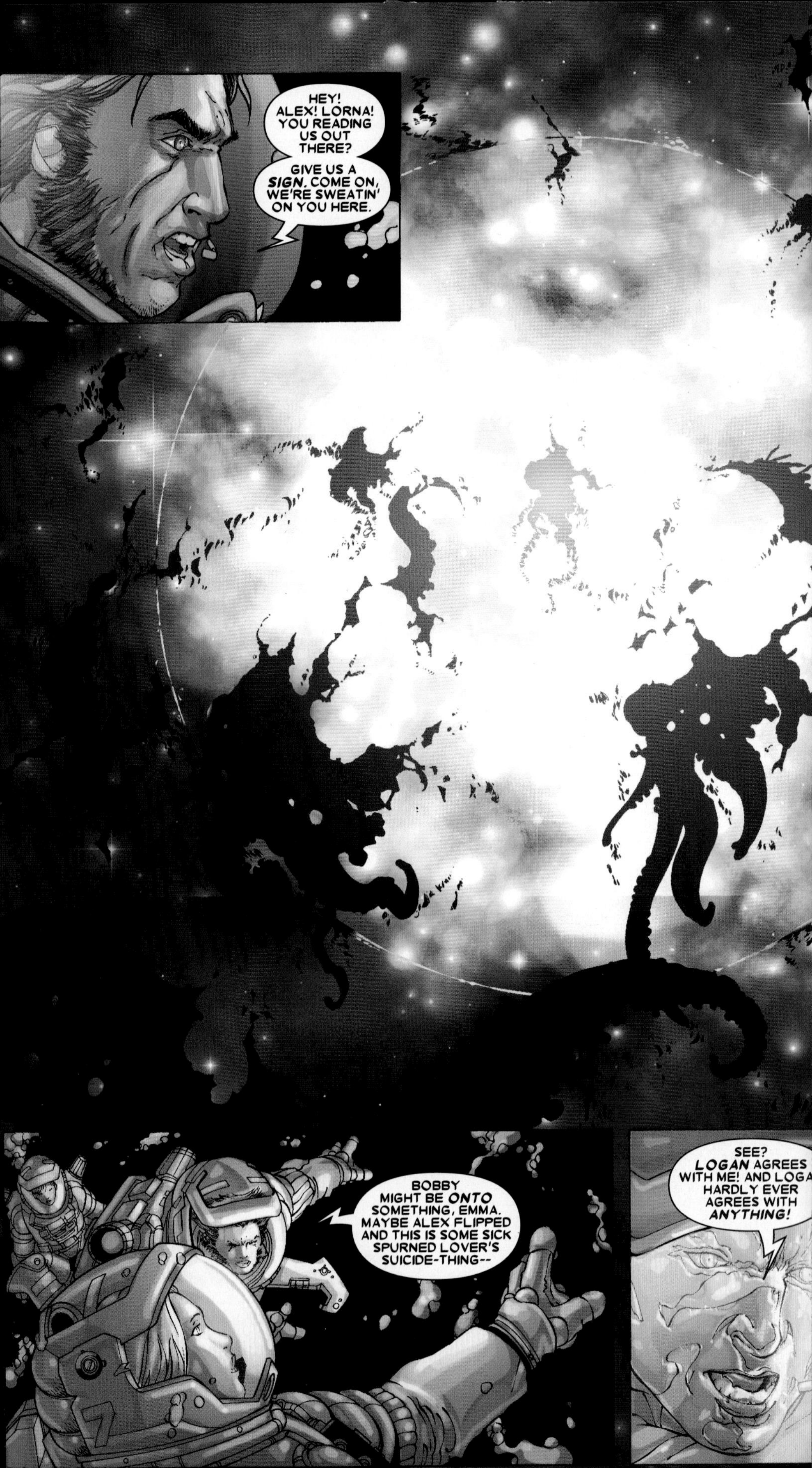

HEY! ALEX! LORNA! YOU READING US OUT THERE?
GIVE US A SIGN. COME ON, WE'RE SWEATIN' ON YOU HERE.
BOBBY MIGHT BE ONTO SOMETHING, EMMA. MAYBE ALEX FLIPPED AND THIS IS SOME SICK SPURNED LOVER'S SUICIDE-THING--
SEE? LOGAN AGREES WITH ME! AND LOGA HARDLY EVER AGREES WITH ANYTHING!

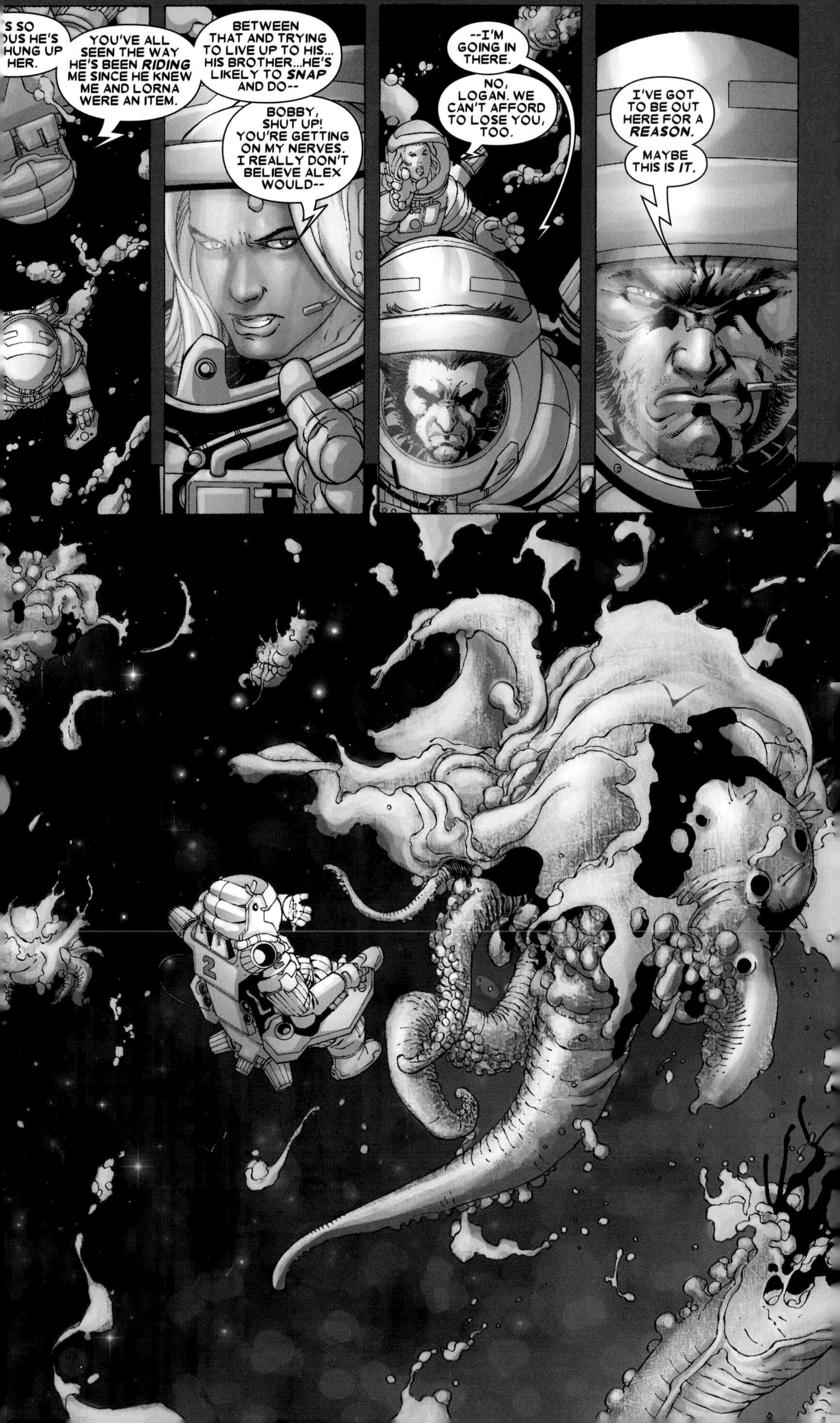

'S SO
OUS HE'S
HUNG UP
HER.
YOU'VE ALL SEEN THE WAY HE'S BEEN RIDING ME SINCE HE KNEW ME AND LORNA WERE AN ITEM.
BETWEEN THAT AND TRYING TO LIVE UP TO HIS... HIS BROTHER...HE'S LIKELY TO SNAP AND DO--
BOBBY, SHUT UP! YOU'RE GETTING ON MY NERVES. I REALLY DON'T BELIEVE ALEX WOULD--
--I'M GOING IN THERE.
NO, LOGAN. WE CAN'T AFFORD TO LOSE YOU, TOO.
I'VE GOT TO BE OUT HERE FOR A REASON.
MAYBE THIS IS IT.

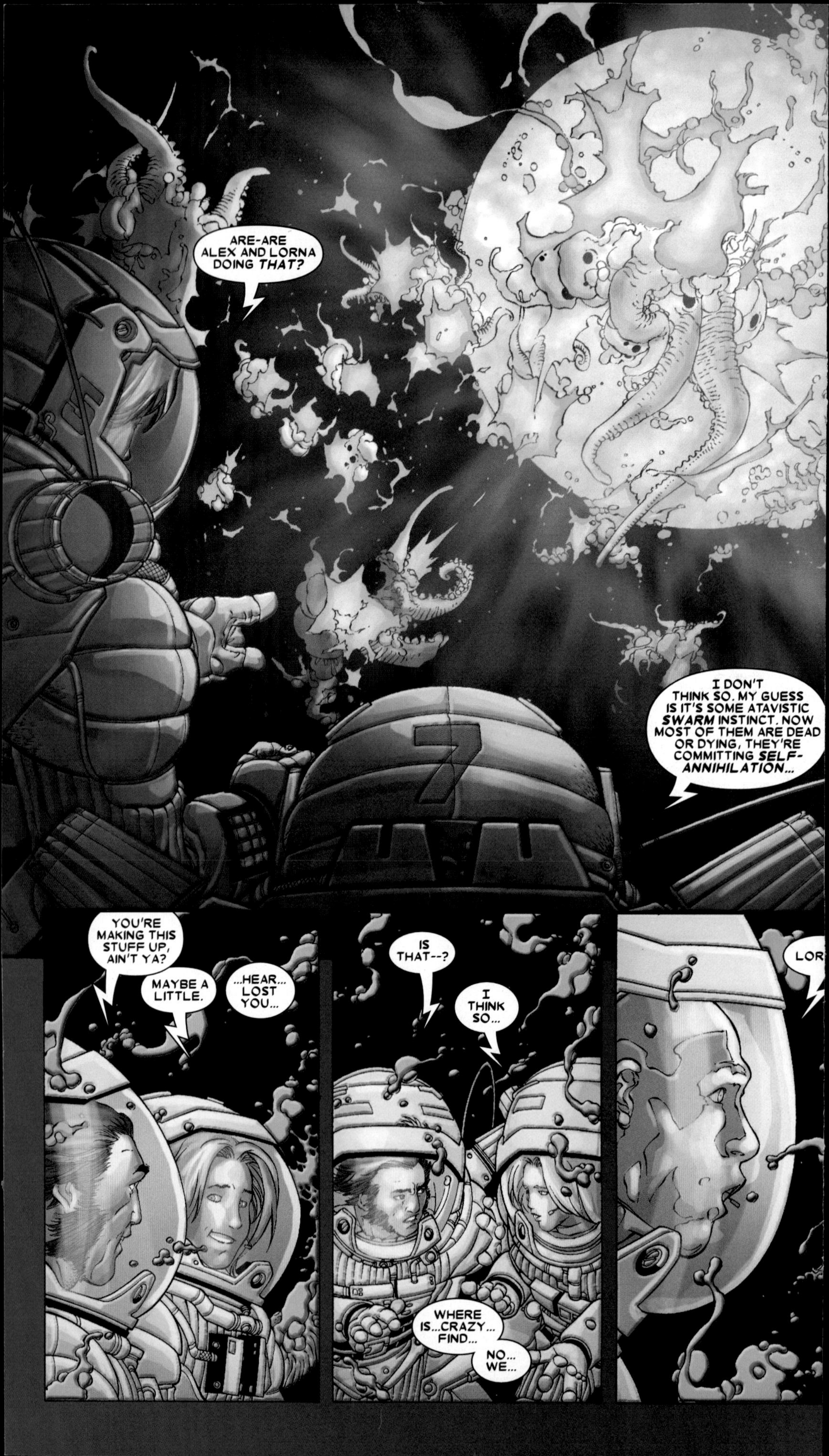
ARE-ARE ALEX AND LORNA DOING *THAT?*
I DON'T THINK SO. MY GUESS IS IT'S SOME ATAVISTIC *SWARM* INSTINCT. NOW MOST OF THEM ARE DEAD OR DYING, THEY'RE COMMITTING *SELF-ANNIHILATION*...
YOU'RE MAKING THIS STUFF UP, AIN'T YA?
MAYBE A LITTLE.
...HEAR... LOST YOU...
IS THAT--?
I THINK SO...
WHERE IS...CRAZY... FIND...
NO... WE...
LOR

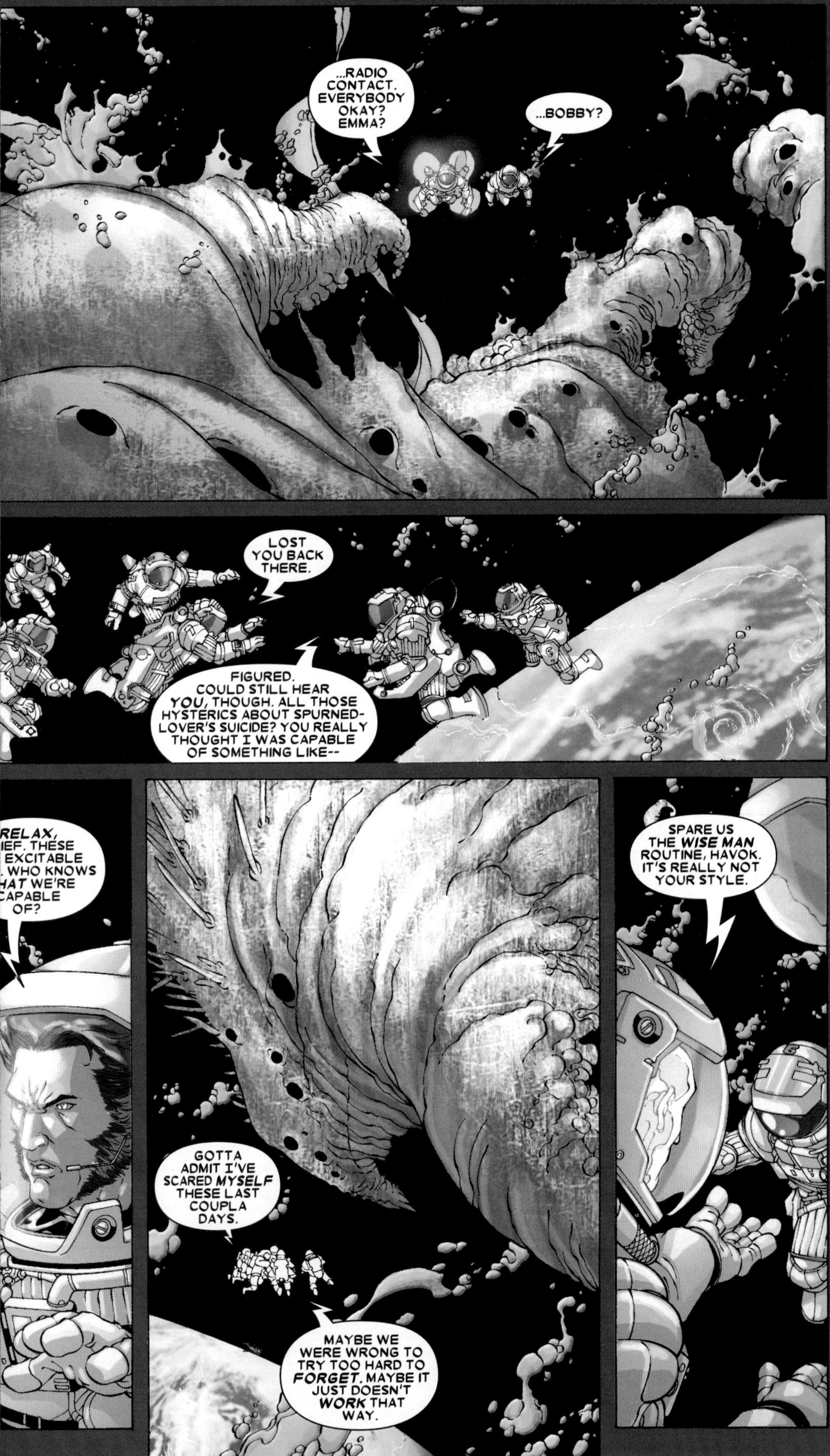

...RADIO CONTACT. EVERYBODY OKAY? EMMA?
...BOBBY?
LOST YOU BACK THERE.
FIGURED. COULD STILL HEAR YOU, THOUGH. ALL THOSE HYSTERICS ABOUT SPURNED-LOVER'S SUICIDE? YOU REALLY THOUGHT I WAS CAPABLE OF SOMETHING LIKE--
RELAX, IEF. THESE EXCITABLE . WHO KNOWS HAT WE'RE CAPABLE OF?
GOTTA ADMIT I'VE SCARED MYSELF THESE LAST COUPLA DAYS.
MAYBE WE WERE WRONG TO TRY TOO HARD TO FORGET. MAYBE IT JUST DOESN'T WORK THAT WAY.
SPARE US THE WISE MAN ROUTINE, HAVOK. IT'S REALLY NOT YOUR STYLE.

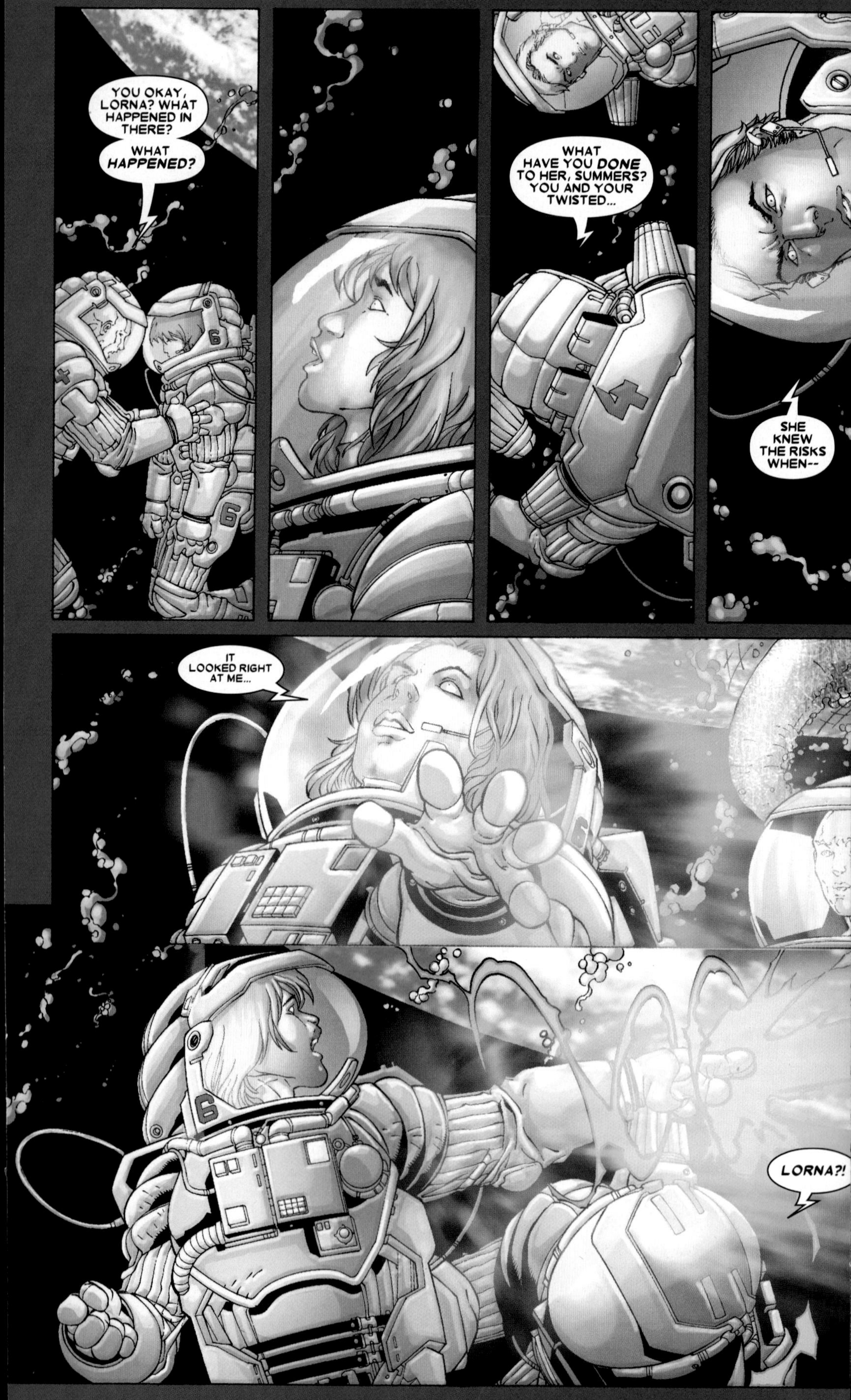
YOU OKAY, LORNA? WHAT HAPPENED IN THERE?
WHAT *HAPPENED?*
WHAT HAVE YOU *DONE* TO HER, SUMMERS? YOU AND YOUR TWISTED...
SHE KNEW THE RISKS WHEN--
IT LOOKED RIGHT AT ME...
*LORNA?!*

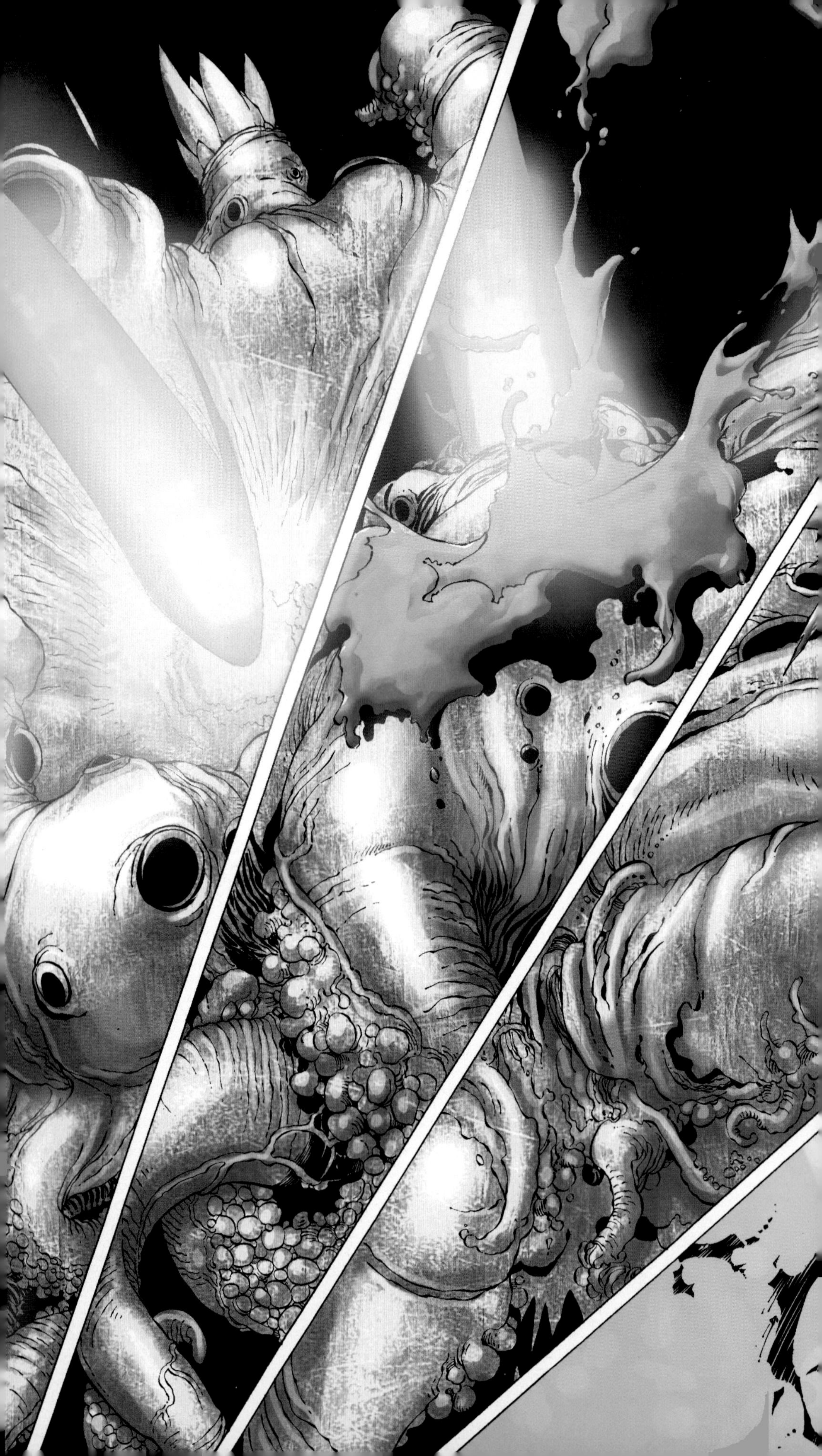

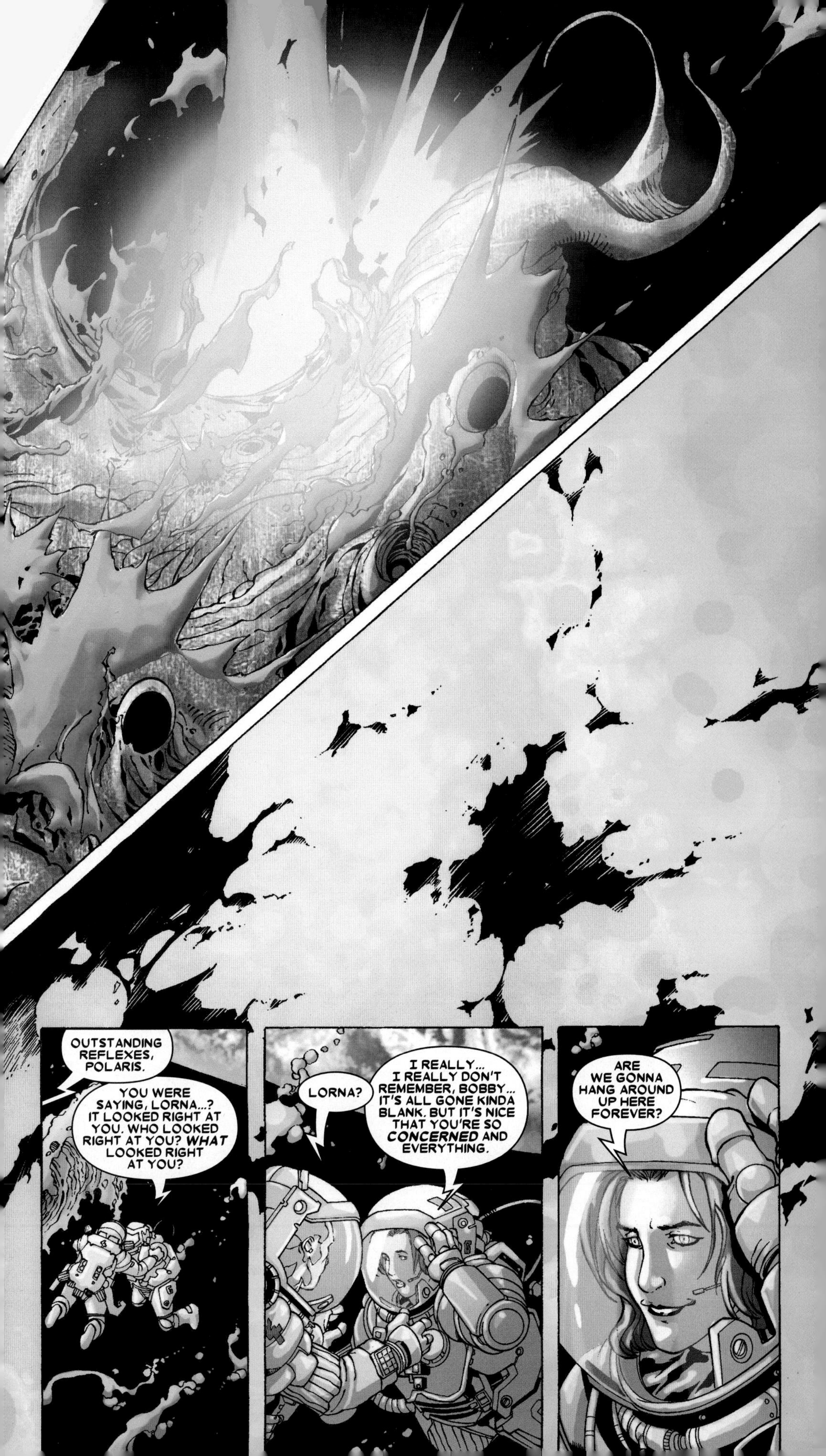
OUTSTANDING REFLEXES, POLARIS.
YOU WERE SAYING, LORNA...? IT LOOKED RIGHT AT YOU. WHO LOOKED RIGHT AT YOU? WHAT LOOKED RIGHT AT YOU?
LORNA?
I REALLY... I REALLY DON'T REMEMBER, BOBBY... IT'S ALL GONE KINDA BLANK. BUT IT'S NICE THAT YOU'RE SO CONCERNED AND EVERYTHING.
ARE WE GONNA HANG AROUND UP HERE FOREVER?

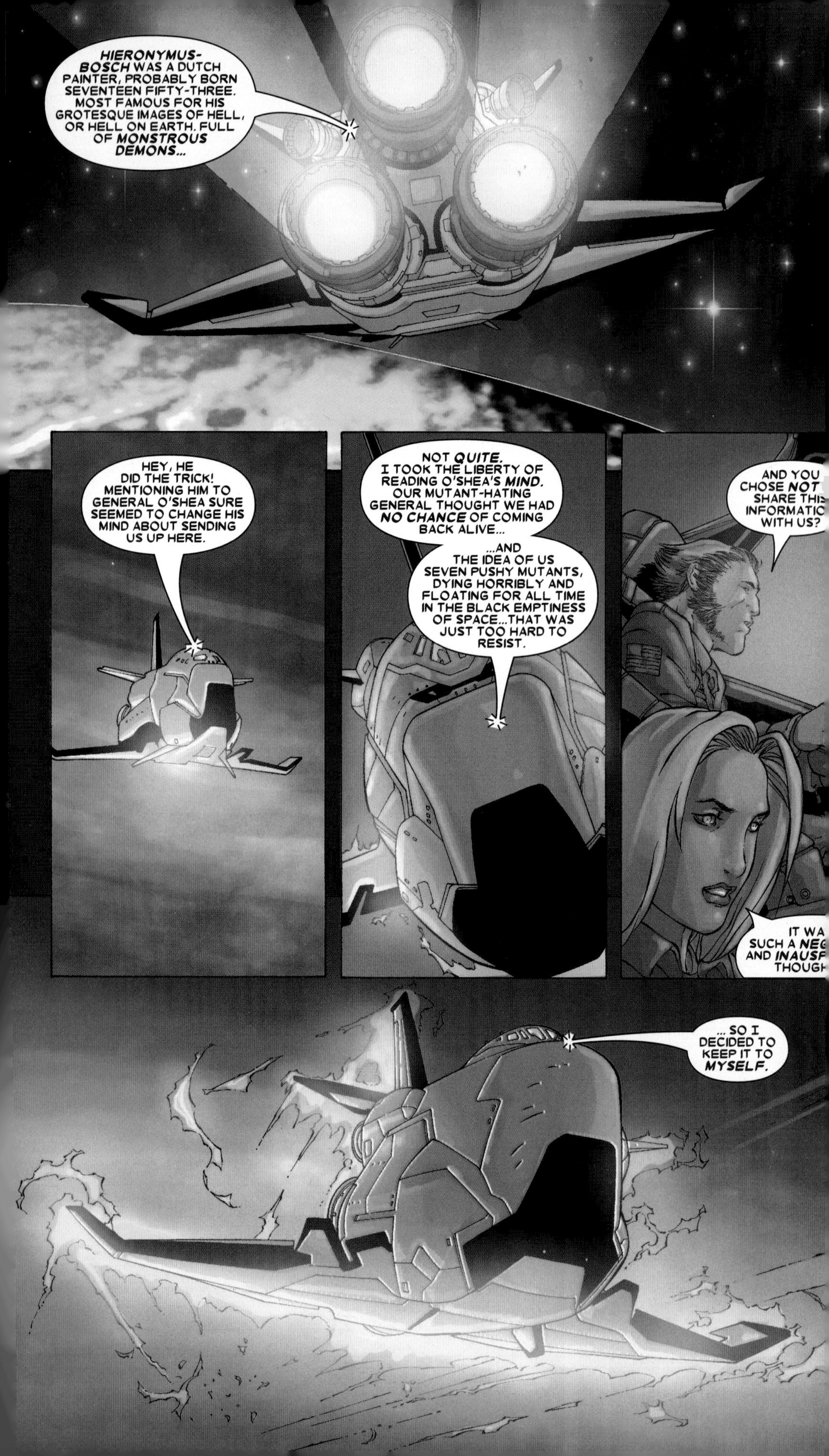
HIERONYMUS-BOSCH WAS A DUTCH PAINTER, PROBABLY BORN SEVENTEEN FIFTY-THREE. MOST FAMOUS FOR HIS GROTESQUE IMAGES OF HELL, OR HELL ON EARTH. FULL OF MONSTROUS DEMONS...
HEY, HE DID THE TRICK! MENTIONING HIM TO GENERAL O'SHEA SURE SEEMED TO CHANGE HIS MIND ABOUT SENDING US UP HERE.
NOT QUITE. I TOOK THE LIBERTY OF READING O'SHEA'S MIND. OUR MUTANT-HATING GENERAL THOUGHT WE HAD NO CHANCE OF COMING BACK ALIVE...
...AND THE IDEA OF US SEVEN PUSHY MUTANTS, DYING HORRIBLY AND FLOATING FOR ALL TIME IN THE BLACK EMPTINESS OF SPACE...THAT WAS JUST TOO HARD TO RESIST.
AND YOU CHOSE NOT SHARE THIS INFORMATIC WITH US?
IT WA SUCH A NEG AND INAUSF THOUGH
... SO I DECIDED TO KEEP IT TO MYSELF.

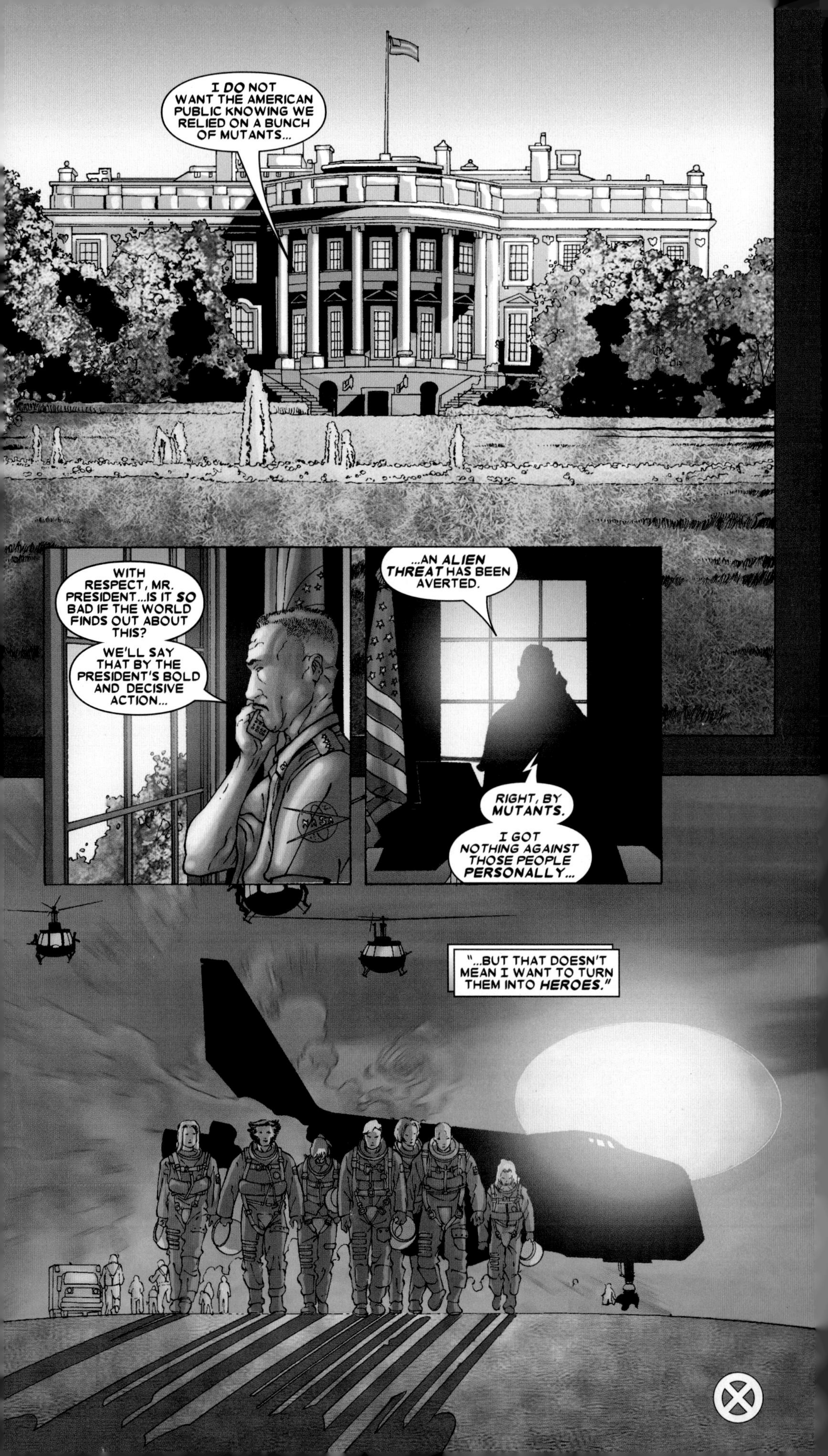
I DO NOT WANT THE AMERICAN PUBLIC KNOWING WE RELIED ON A BUNCH OF MUTANTS...
WITH RESPECT, MR. PRESIDENT...IS IT SO BAD IF THE WORLD FINDS OUT ABOUT THIS?
WE'LL SAY THAT BY THE PRESIDENT'S BOLD AND DECISIVE ACTION...
...AN ALIEN THREAT HAS BEEN AVERTED.
RIGHT, BY MUTANTS.
I GOT NOTHING AGAINST THOSE PEOPLE PERSONALLY...
"...BUT THAT DOESN'T MEAN I WANT TO TURN THEM INTO HEROES."

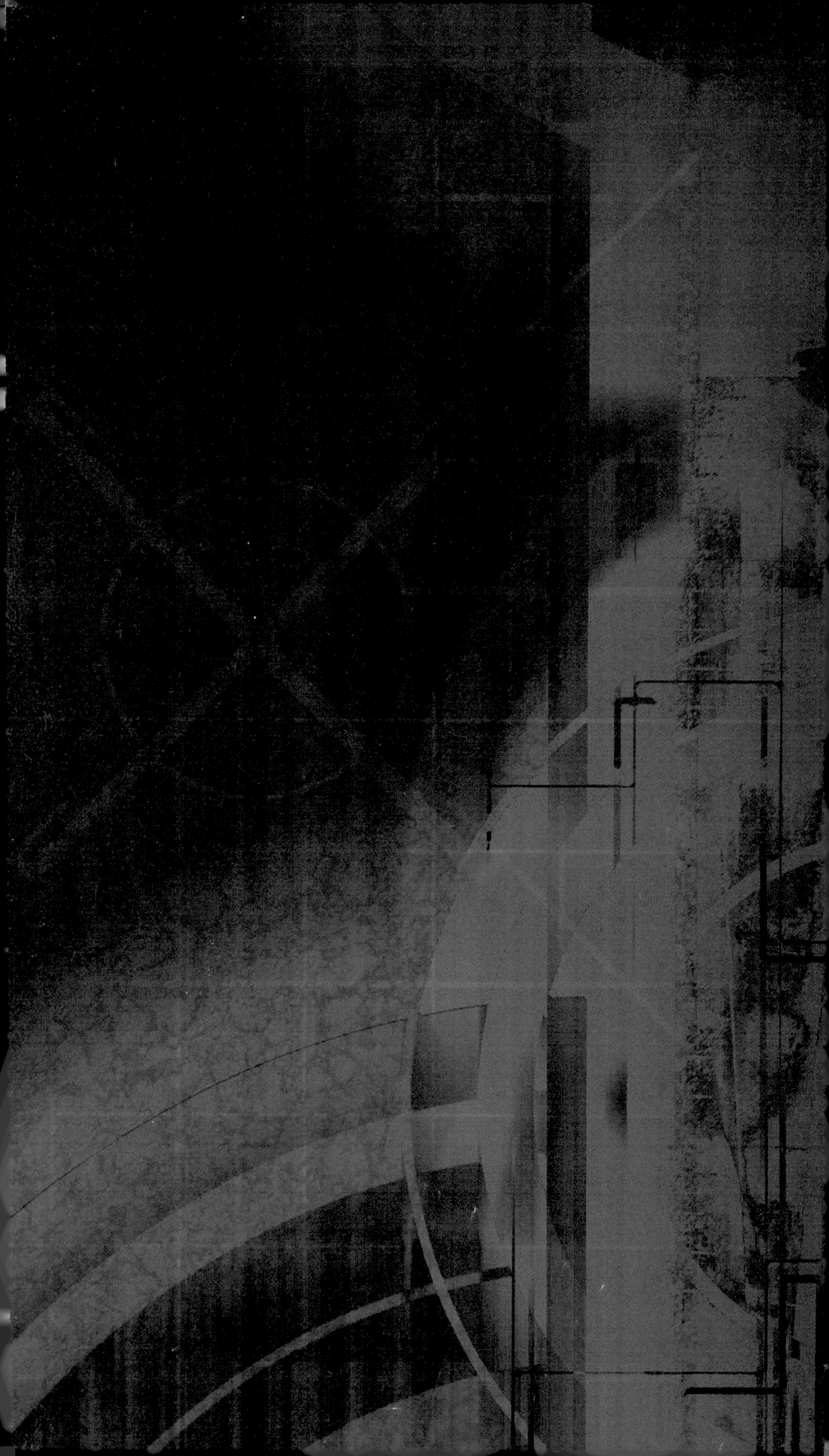